I0605504

Also by Michael G. Laramie

King William's War:
The First Contest for North America, 1689–1697

Queen Anne's War:
The Second Contest for North America, 1702–1713

King George's War and the Thirty-Year Peace:
The Third Contest for North America, 1714–1748

The Road to Ticonderoga:
The Campaign of 1758 in the Champlain Valley

Gunboats, Muskets, and Torpedoes:
Coastal North Carolina, 1861–1865

Gunboats, Muskets, and Torpedoes:
Coastal South Carolina, 1861–1865

By Wind and Iron:
Naval Campaigns in the Champlain Valley, 1665–1815

Colonial Forts of the Champlain and Hudson Valleys:
Sentinels of Wood and Stone

The European Invasion of North America:
Colonial Conflict Along the Hudson-Champlain Corridor, 1609–1760

SENTINELS *by the* SEA

COASTAL FORTIFICATIONS *of* COLONIAL NEW ENGLAND *and* NOVA SCOTIA

MICHAEL G. LARAMIE

WESTHOLME
Yardley

Westholme Publishing, LLC
904 Edgewood Road
Yardley, Pennsylvania 19067
Visit our Web site at www.westholmepublishing.com

ISBN: 978–1-59416-448-4
Also available as an eBook.

Printed in the United States of America

To my nephew Jake

CONTENTS

INTRODUCTION

Seventeenth- and eighteenth-century warfare centered on sieges, not seeking out and destroying the enemy's army. True, battles did occur, but more in the defense or relief of a fortress than the foremen-tioned objective. The reason was simple. A captured fortress or town was a bargaining piece in the inevitable peace treaty between the warring monarchs. This approach was even more prevalent when viewing the colonial conflicts in North America. Given the vast distances involved, the lack of manpower, and limited logistical resources, the war in North America became one of position, or a war of forts. This work looks at a network of coastal forts that stood in opposition to one another during the French and Indian Wars (1689–1763), those of northern New England, French Acadia (Nova Scotia), and the fortress of Louisbourg on Cape Breton Island.

Accessible by sea and located only five to six hundred miles from one another, the peril and opportunity presented to both sides by this arrangement would draw the Pro-French Wabanaki Confederacy into the regional struggle, along with the occasional intervention of France and Britain. In regard to this last point, it should be noted that intervention on the part of both Britain and France militarily was far more limited in the first three French and Indian Wars than the last one, which led to the fall of New France. Just as importantly, this regional conflict would technically come to an end at the conclusion of King George's War only to have to be repeated because of the terms of the Treaty of Aix-la-Chappelle in 1748.

Within this narrative are some of the oldest fortifications in North America, many originating in the seventeenth century. These forts and those that come later fall into several categories. Some are simple wooden palisade structures, mounting a small cannon or two if they were lucky. These frontier-style fortifications were employed in situations where cannons were unlikely to be brought against the stronghold. Thus, these forts were more a haven against raiders and a source of patrols to protect or control the local area. Even the garrison houses in the towns and villages of New England can be thought of as blockhouses, or small wooden forts, and it was not uncommon for a smaller coastal town to have nothing more than a palisade structure or an earth redoubt with a cannon or two to protect its harbor.

Other more prominent forts along the coastline took on a different form. As coastal fortifications guarding a major port or the outlet of a navigable river, they faced different design criteria than the inland forts of North America. Most, such as Castle William, were designed to bring batteries of heavy cannons to bear against an enemy fleet or a flotilla of privateers looking to force entry into the harbor. In return, these strongholds would have to be capable of withstanding fire from the heavy guns of the enemy fleet in order to carry through with their mission, and as strategic assets, they had to be built in a fashion so as to minimize maintenance and garrison costs.

These criteria led to two types of approaches to fortifications. For populace locations along the coasts of Massachusetts, Connecticut, and Rhode Island, earth redoubts containing batteries of heavy cannons often sufficed. Typically only manned during times of conflict they were relatively cheap to construct or repair, and given the population density of these locations, it all but ruled out anything but a raid by the enemy. Even if a French fleet, for instance, could land 2,500 men at Newport, within an hour they would face 1,000 men. A day later they would face four times that number and a few days later twice that as the local New England militias converged on the scene. Although an actual invasion seemed remote, this did not mean that an attacker could not suddenly descend upon a major coastal town, burn it, and put back out to sea before an effective force could be assembled to deal with the threat. In fact, we shall see how just such a threat came very close to becoming a reality.

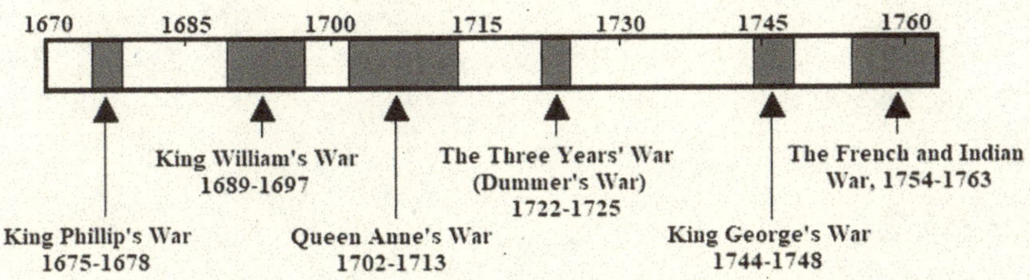

Ports like Boston and Portsmouth were protected by more traditional earth forts faced with stone, or just stone structures mounting dozens of heavy cannons. It should be pointed out that the stone was not for defensive purposes. In fact, it often proved perilous, as whirling stone shards from cannon ball strikes proved every bit as deadly as the ricocheting iron shot. Here an earth fort was better in the sense that the thick dirt wall absorbed the impact of the round shot, but without a weather-resistant stone covering, such a fort was not only doomed to rapid decay but the maintenance costs to hold this process at bay would soon lead to its abandonment. While other locations did not have the necessary funds or resources to follow this approach it was not uncommon to see forts with a section, such as a tower, built in stone and the rest of the work fashioned out of wooden palisades or earthwork. In any case, these smaller forts, plagued by a lack of funding, were in a constant state of disrepair.

Facing the ravages of the elements, neglect, and a near constant threat of war, many of these fortifications would be tested, captured, destroyed, or abandoned during this bygone era. Others, such as Castle William, would stand defiant for almost seventy-five years before being demolished when the British withdrew from Boston in the spring of 1776. Still others would be involved in the American Revolution, and a few later rebuilt and renamed. Most, however, were left to fall into ruin and are now just shadows of an age when France and Britain vied for control of North America.

Hopefully, this shines a light on their role in this long contest.

One

THE FIRST FORTS

On December 20, 1686, the new governor of the Dominion of New England, Sir Edmund Andros, arrived at Boston. Immediately upon his arrival Andros was sworn in, and as per his orders, he began to assemble representatives from the different New England colonies who would serve as his executive council. The governor's announced powers did not sit well with the colonial assemblies, and Andros did little to belay these fears, which would ultimately lead to a confrontation between the two parties.

After a quick survey of Boston, Andros shook his head at the defenses of this important colonial port. The key to the harbor's defenses was Castle Island. The main channel into the harbor passed between Governor's and Bird Islands to the north and Castle Island to the south, making a fort armed with heavy cannons at this latter location ideally suited to dispute the passage. What Andros found when he visited this key location was an "inconsiderable" four-bastioned structure, "the walls about ten feet high and out of repair." The barracks for the garrison were located up against the curtain walls, their roofs acting as the ramparts for the stronghold's cannons. In Andros's opinion the fort was simply too small to support a garrison and a battery of cannons large enough to bar the passage to enemy vessels. What was worse was that, beyond the questionable works on Castle Island, there was little else. On the northern shore of the town there was a

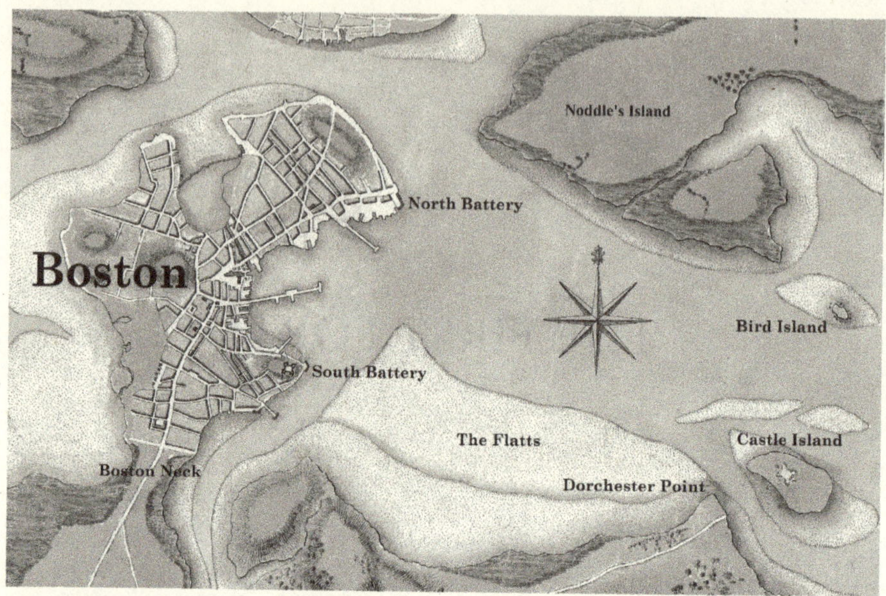

The defenses of Boston, c. 1705. This sketch shows the fort on Castle Island which dominates the main ship channel into and out of the harbor after its reconstruction by Colonel Wolfgang Romer in the early 1700s. The Hill Fort raised by Edmund Andros can be seen west of the south battery. These last two fortifications in conjunction with the north battery and the guns on Castle Island would place any enemy looking to enter the harbor in a crossfire. (*Author*)

wood and earth battery holding half a dozen cannons while, to the south, at the base of Fort Hill, he found a stone battery called the South Fort, mounting a dozen cannons in two tiers. He had discovered eighty iron cannons on Castle Island and about the town. Most could not be fired, as their wooden carriages were in disrepair, and only half of these were large enough to be effectively employed in the harbor's defense. Not that it mattered, as there was almost no powder, established magazines, storehouses, or anything resembling a fortification other than the crumbling works on Castle Island.[1]

To partially address these issues, the governor ordered the works on Castle Island repaired and a palisade fort raised on a hill along the southern portion of the waterfront. Soon called the Hill Fort, the wooden and earth structure was constructed over the course of the summer and fall of 1687. The hilltop was leveled, and the dirt from this and the ditch was used to construct the earth bastions, which would also act as powder magazines. For the moment the curtain walls were wooden palisades, but although the fort was ready to ac-

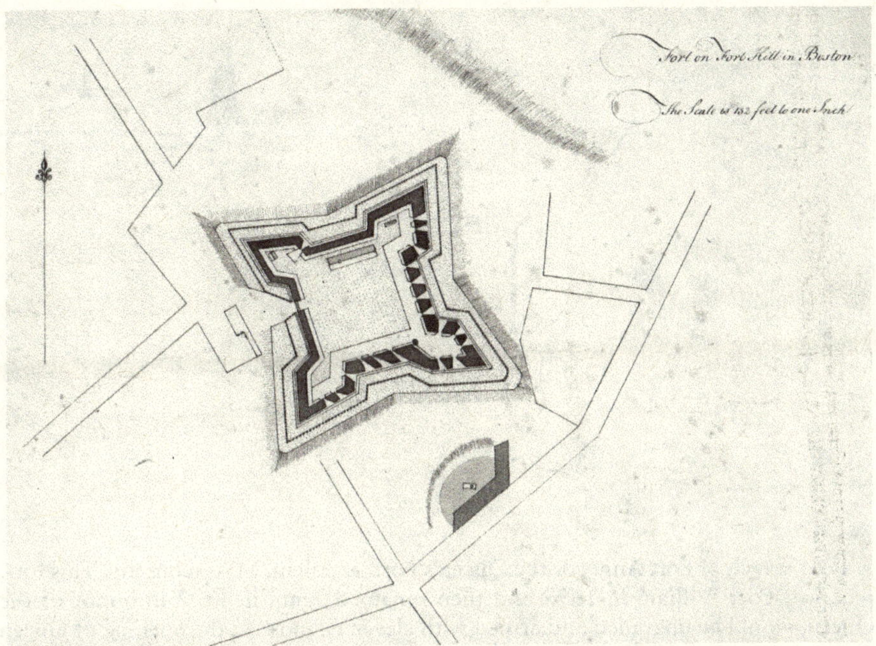

The Hill Fort at Boston c. 1700. (*Norman B. Leventhal Map Collection, Boston Public Library*)

cept a garrison by late November, a lack of heavy cannons, powder, and ammunition hampered the effectiveness of the structure. Andros had also worked at expanding the works on Castle Island by placing a new battery nearby.

These were not the only issues before the governor. The nearby towns of Plymouth and Yarmouth to the south, as well as Salem, Marblehead, Gloucester, and Ipswich to the north, required some level of defensive preparation as rumors of an upcoming war with France began to arrive. Of these, only Salem and Marblehead had already erected some form of defensive works large enough to protect their harbors. At Salem, a fort armed with small cannons had been located on Winter Island since 1643. Eleven years later, the town voted funds for a new structure to be located at the southeast point of Winter Island. With the First Anglo-Dutch War (1652–1654) as a background, the town "Ordered that the fort upon Winter Island shall be finished with all speed." While desirable, this did not actually translate into reality, as two years later the heavy cannons had still not been

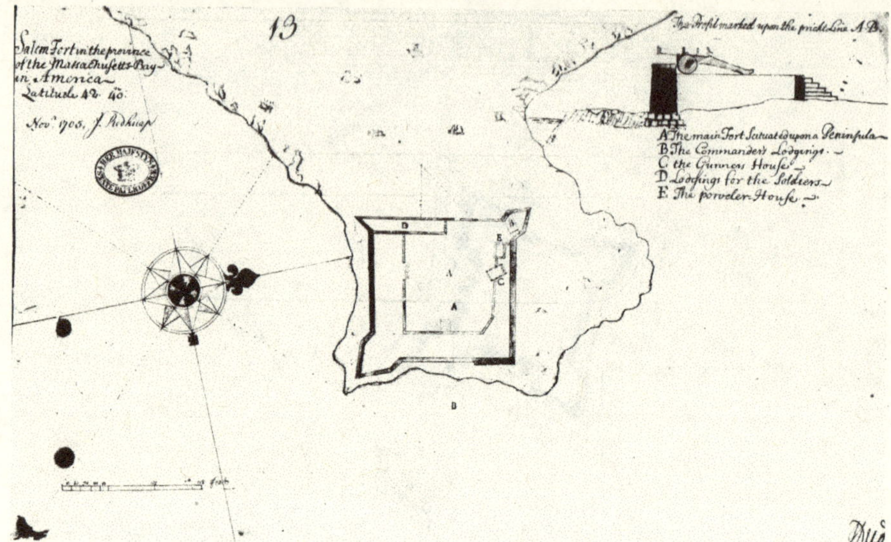

A 1705 sketch of Fort Anne, or the Queen's Fort, at Salem, Massachusetts. This fort, renamed Fort William in 1699 and then renamed again in 1702 in honor of the Queen, would be upgraded and armed with eleven cannons at the opening of Queen Anne's War. (*The Crown Collection of Photographs of American Maps, III, plate 188*)

mounted. The second (1665–1667) and third Anglo-Dutch conflicts (1672–1674) brought incremental improvements, such as a road to carry supplies to the fort, but by 1682 the structure had fallen into such disrepair that £500 was voted to tear down the old structure and raise a new one.[2]

The resulting stone and earth structure was roughly a square some 150 feet to a side. The stronghold had two different-sized bastions at its northeast and southeast corners. The earth ramparts for the cannons covered the three waterside walls with the garrison's quarters and the powder magazine located near the landside wall. At the moment only a handful of heavy cannons were mounted, but should the situation require it, more guns could be placed in the structure. Nearby, Marblehead had also erected an earth and stone redoubt in 1667. This structure was enclosed in the rear by a wooden palisade and a stone blockhouse. Like the works at Salem, the fort, located at the northern entrance of the harbor, was in constant need of repair after being lashed by wind and wave. It was sporadically upgraded over the intervening years such that, by Andros's tenure, it mounted three great guns and was garrisoned by a dozen men.

Andros urged these communities to consider their defenses, while at the same time realizing it would be nearly impossible to make all the towns and seaports along the colony's coast invulnerable to raiders. Efforts would continue, but at the moment, the governor doubted that any New England port could repel a concerted French or Spanish naval attack. This included one of the better-defended locations, Portsmouth, New Hampshire. Located near the confluence of the Piscataqua River and the Gulf of Maine, the town was important not only for its fishing, whaling, and maritime activities but because the Royal Navy drew masts for its vessels from the woods of southern New Hampshire. This timber was transported down the Piscataqua River and assembled at Portsmouth. Seasonal mast-fleets were then organized, and, escorted by Royal Navy warships, carried this important cargo back to Britain.

To protect the town and harbor, a fort was erected on the northeast point of Newcastle Island (Great Island). The jutting peninsula chosen placed the structure a little over three hundred yards from the main channel, a point-blank shot for heavy cannons. Considerations for a fort on this point were first raised in 1631, but nothing more than a small palisade work was constructed at the location. As with the other New England coastal communities, news of the Second Anglo-Dutch War brought about an effort to raise a battery of cannons at this location. A small earth fort was erected in 1665 and armed with eleven cannons, but by 1682 the neglected structure needed to be replaced. The fort was "well enough situated, but too weak at present to be sufficient defense," the government of New Hampshire informed the Lords of Trade in London. "The guns, eleven in all, are too small, none bigger than a sacker [6-pounder]." As for the defense of Portsmouth itself, the colony reported that there were five cannons in the town, all privately purchased.[3]

While the assemblies and coastal defenses of New England would prove troublesome, in the spring of 1688, Andros faced a more pressing issue. The problem centered on growing friction between the settlements in Maine, which was part of Massachusetts at the time, and the nearby pro-French Wabanaki Confederacy. The latter, often referred to in colonial records as the Eastern Indians, consisted of the Western and Eastern Abenaki, the Mi'kmaq (Micmac), the Passamaquoddy, and the Maliseet. This confederacy was sympathetic to Phillip's cause in the Native uprising led by the latter, although they had their own concerns regarding New England expansion into their territories. Aided by the French, in 1675 they attacked the Maine frontier, burning English settlements between Casco and the Saco River and raiding others as far south as Wells. The following year was a repeat of the first, eventually reaching the point that the Maine frontier settlements were abandoned.

When Andros heard rumors of a possible rupture with the Wabanaki he responded by reinforcing the frontier, but suspecting that the French were behind the current intrigues, he focused his attention on the Baron Jean-Vincent de St. Castin, a French ensign stationed at Pentagoet (Castine, Maine). The young baron, who spoke fluent Abenaki, had met with New France's Governor Louis de Buade, the Count Frontenac, in 1674, at which point the governor directed him to convince the Wabanaki and settlers throughout Acadia to take up the French cause. Castin took to the task, but he would not return to Fort Pentagoet and the nearby Penobscot village until 1676. The Franco-Dutch War (1672–1678), combined with the Third Anglo-Dutch conflict (1672–1674), had led to the recapture of New York by the Dutch, who then used this location as a launching pad to attack French Acadia. In 1674, Fort Pentagoet was briefly captured by the Dutch, who demolished the fort with its own cannons upon departing. Fortunately for Castin, his small trading post and the village were unharmed during the brief conquest. Over the next few years Castin would become an adopted Wabanaki and marry the daughter of a Penobscot chieftain.

Andros rightly suspected that Castin had encouraged and even participated in the Wabanaki raids during King Phillip's War (1675–1678) and was behind the current disturbances. Thus, when the governor discovered that Castin was away, he foolishly raided the baron's trading post and "plundered Castin's house and fort; leaving only the ornaments of his chapel to console him for the loss of his arms and goods." Andros framed the action as a search for contraband goods tied to illegal trade between the colonies, but at its heart he was clearly looking to punish Castin for what he saw as French involvement in his current border problems.[4]

At this stage it only took one event to ignite the Maine frontier, which a Saco magistrate, Benjamin Blackman, provided when he seized and imprisoned sixteen Natives under the pretense that they had been involved in killing cattle. The act brought an immediate response in the form of a raid on New Dartmouth (Newcastle, Maine) in which several English families were carried off. The Wabanaki in-

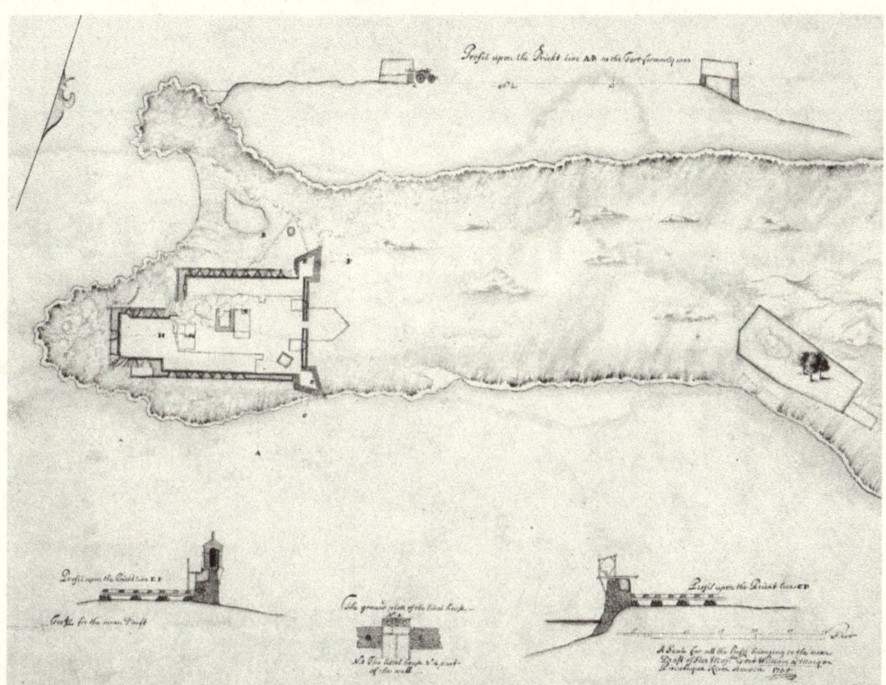

The fort on Newcastle Island, renamed Fort William and Mary with the ascension of William and Mary to the throne of England. The traces outside of the structure were the recommended changes to the stronghold. (*Norman B. Leventhal Map Collection, Boston Public Library*)

formed their prisoners that the raid was in retaliation for Blackman's actions and the attack on Castin's post. The baron was enraged at what had transpired and promised his Native allies all the French powder and ball they needed. After this, it took very little on his part to push them toward retaliation. Attempts were made to hold peace talks and exchange prisoners, but the Wabanaki were silent. "By their discourse and all their actions they Shew that they Intend War with us, & we Question not but that there is a Strong Combination with them and the French against us, and are afraid that the Captives are Carryed to the French & Indians at Penobscutt," the garrison commander of Falmouth informed Andros.[5]

While Andros may have proven a questionable politician, the former Royalist officer during the English Civil War quickly understood the perils of another Anglo-Wabanaki conflict on the Maine frontier. Most of the settlements were protected by local palisade forts. Here the best that could be done was to increase vigilance by sending de-

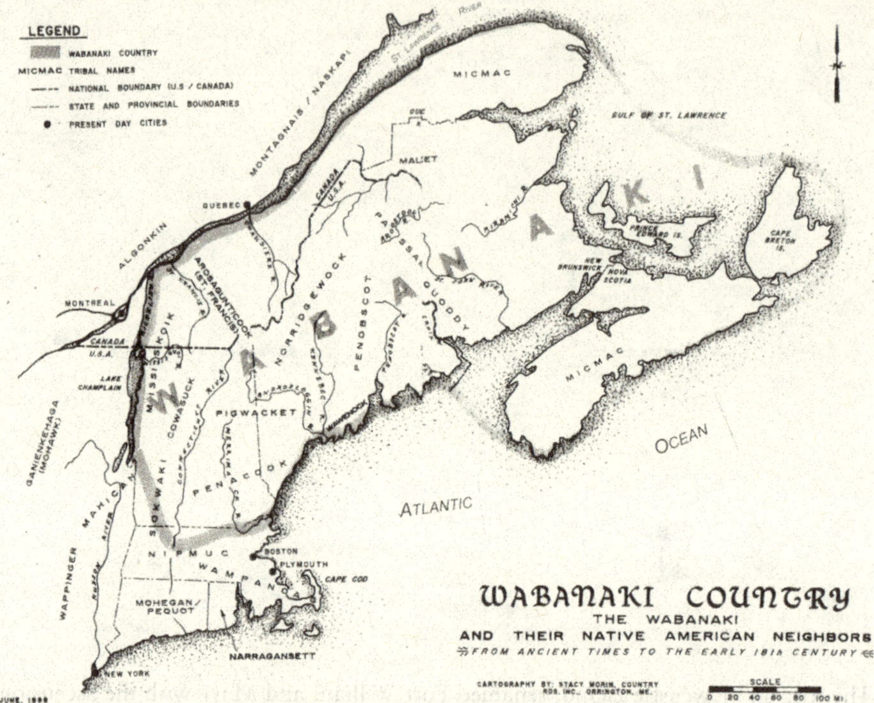

The Wabanaki Confederacy and nearby nations. In this map the Eastern Abenaki have been represented by the Penobscot and the Norridgewock (Kennebec) who are but two of eleven tribes that make up the Eastern Abenaki. Likewise, several of the fourteen Western Abenaki tribes, the Penacook being the most prominent of these, are shown covering western Maine, New Hampshire, Vermont, and parts of modern-day Quebec. This pro-French confederacy would fight alongside their allies until the British conquest of Canada in 1760. (*Stacy Morin*)

tachments to these posts. While the capture of a palisade post was possible without cannon, which the Wabanaki would not possess, most were taken by surprise. If this could be prevented, a well-manned and well-supplied wooden fort stood a very good chance of surviving a short siege. There were also few strongpoints along the coast. The first of these was Fort Saco near the mouth of the Saco River. Positioned on a bluff near the shore, this oddly shaped wood and stone stronghold guarded nearby Winter Harbor. Garrisoned by eighty to ninety men, a number of whom were routinely detached to man the smaller forts at Wells and Arundel, the fort boasted over half a dozen cannons and a pair of impressive stone towers that anchored the structure. These features, however, proved an illusion. Unable to

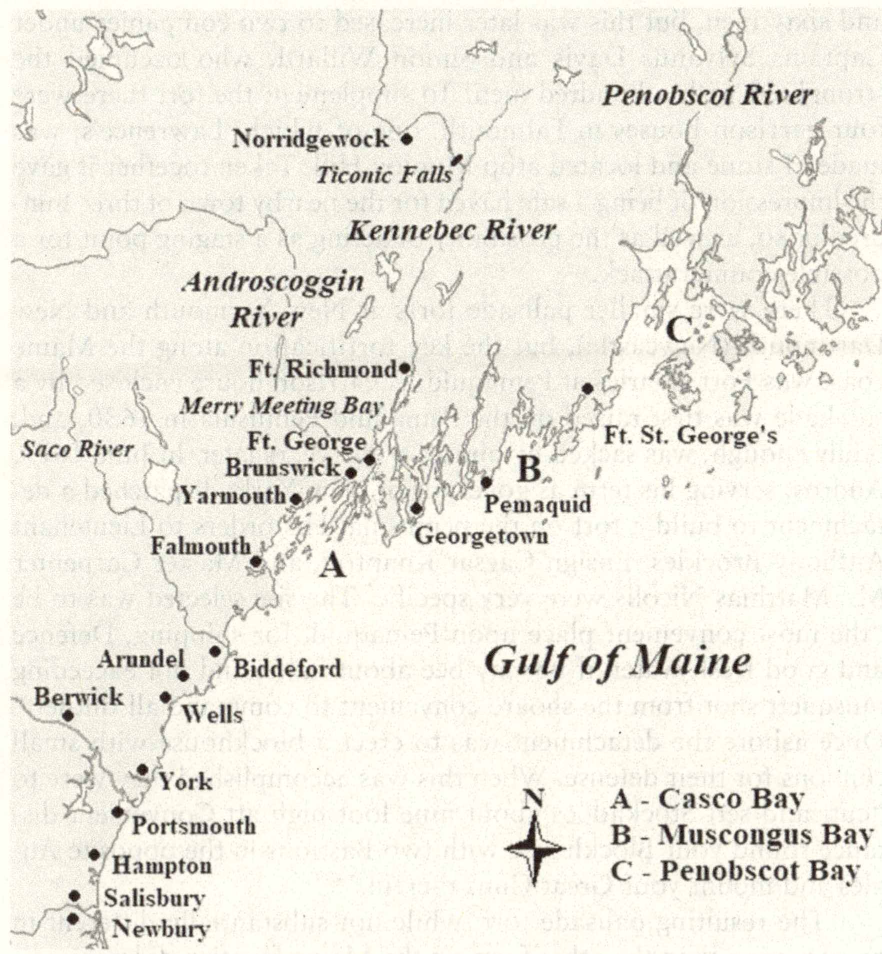

A map of the Maine and New Hampshire coast, c. 1748. (*Author*)

locate lime, the mortar for the stone towers was made with clay and sand, resulting in both quickly deteriorating to the point that it was questionable whether or not a cannon could be fired from either without causing major structural damage.

Farther up the coast, at the western edge of Casco Bay, was Fort Loyal at Falmouth (Portland). Located on a rocky bluff overlooking the harbor and the outlet of the Casco River, the fort was a square wooden palisade with two bastions located at opposite corners. Loopholes were cut in the walls for musketry, and eight cannons were mounted along its circumference. The garrison consisted of a captain and sixty men, but this was later increased to two companies under Captains Sylvanus Davis and Simon Willard, who occupied the stronghold with a hundred men. To supplement the fort there were four garrison houses in Falmouth, one of which, Lawrence's, was made of stone and located atop Munjoy Hill. Taken together it gave the impression of being a safe haven for the nearby town of three hundred or so, as well as the possibility of acting as a staging point for a possible counterattack.

There were smaller palisade forts at New Yarmouth and New Dartmouth (Newcastle), but the key fortification along the Maine coast was Fort Charles at Pemaquid. A garrison house enclosed by a stockade was first raised on the Pemaquid Peninsula in 1630, and, oddly enough, was sacked by pirates a few years later. In June 1677, Andros, serving his term as governor of New York, dispatched a detachment to build a fort on the peninsula. His orders to Lieutenant Anthony Brockles, Ensign Caesar Knapton, and Master Carpenter Mr. Matthias Nicolls were very specific. The site selected was to be "the most convenient place upon Pemaquid, for shipping, Defence and good fresh water, if itt may bee about halfe, and not exceeding musquett shot from the shoare convenient to command all thither." Once ashore the detachment was to erect a blockhouse with small cannons for their defense. When this was accomplished they were to "cutt and sett Stockadoes about nine loot high att Convenient distance round your Blockhouse with two Bastions in the opposite Angles and mount your Great Guns therein."[6]

The resulting palisade fort, while not substantially different in construction than the other forts on the Maine frontier, did possess a garrison of three companies, a little over 150 men, and was easily reinforced by sea from Portsmouth or Boston, as Andros demonstrated by dispatching seven hundred troops to repair the stronghold and overawe the Wabanaki during the summer of 1688. Further attempts were made to hold peace talks, but nothing materialized, and as the remainder of the fall and winter passed in a guarded peace Andros became convinced that the defensive measures he had erected would hold.[7]

Two

KING WILLIAM'S WAR

When news of King William's and Queen Mary's ascension to the throne of England reached the Bay Colony, the leadership and citizenry used the opportunity to not only demonstrate their allegiance and support for the new sovereigns but to rid themselves of Andros at the same time. Being a Catholic and close friend of the deposed James II, Andros and a number of his officers were arrested in April 1689 and imprisoned in Boston. While the effects of the Glorious Revolution on New England are beyond the scope of this work, one immediate consequence coming from it was a destabilization of the Maine frontier. Many of the officers appointed by Andros to command the forts in the region were arrested by their men who, loyal to the colony's actions, then foolishly abandoned their posts either in whole or in part.

To make matters worse, the action coincided with a Wabanaki attack on the Maine frontier. The confederacy's first target was Saco Falls and the nearby farms. While small raids continued for the next several months a more important target, Dover, New Hampshire, came to the forefront on the evening of June 27, 1689. Partly through deception, the assault laid waste to much of the town before the raiders disappeared with their captives. A month later the French and the Wabanaki launched a far more ambitious plan. Word had reached them of the withdrawal of English garrisons along the frontier, and as such, they targeted Fort Charles at Pemaquid.

Led by Castin and Jesuit Father Peter Thury, who had recently built a mission at Penobscot, some three hundred Wabanaki took to their canoes. Following the coast, the war party set ashore at New Harbor along Pemaquid Neck. The dozen or so homes in this area were deserted. The next day, August 2, scouts brought in several English prisoners. Under the threat of death, one of these men, John Starkey, informed Castin and Thury that half of the garrison of Fort Charles had gone to Pemaquid Falls to help gather the harvest and that the men of the nearby village were out in their fields as well. Armed with this intelligence Castin laid out a plan. Half of the raiders would attack Fort Charles and the nearby town, while the rest proceeded to Pemaquid Falls to ambush any reinforcement that might come to the aid of the fort. The plan may have been one of the best executed during all of King William's War.

Castin led the forces against the town and the fort. Creeping as close as possible without being seen, they suddenly burst upon the open ground. Although the townsfolk were caught by complete surprise, Fort Charles was not. The fort's commander, Lieutenant James Weems, ordered his garrison to fire on the advancing Wabanaki but to little avail. The attackers were simply too fast and too determined. The town was quickly cut off from the fort, and its inhabitants either seized or killed. Despite Weems's use of the fort's cannons, the Wabanaki secured several stone houses near the fort. From here they poured a fusillade upon the stronghold's defenders. The attackers were also quick to discern a large rock not far from one of the fort's walls. A detachment secured the boulder and began to pour fire down on the fort from this location.[1]

It was a nearly impossible situation for Weems. His garrison of fourteen men was too small to effectively man the cannons along the walls and deal with a possible threat to different parts of the fort's perimeter. Within the first few hours of the siege several of his troops had been killed or wounded, making the defense of the structure even more difficult. Around sunset a barrel of gunpowder "was accidentally exploded by the firing of a cannon." The flash temporarily blinded the fort's commandant but did not deter him. As the sun went down the fear was that the enemy would scale the fort's walls that evening. To prevent this, Weems ordered his men to occasionally throw a grenade over the wall to discourage anyone from storming the fortifications.

The random thump of an exploding grenade and sporadic firefights took place over the course of the night until, at daylight, the Wabanaki resumed their barrage in earnest. For Weems the situation was coming to a head. Over half his garrison had been killed or wounded, and he was being attacked along two fronts. "Towards eleven o'clock," he later wrote of his decision, "there being no Christian within a hundred miles of the fort, relief being hopeless, and the surviving men worn out with fatigue, the Lieutenant on their solicitations and those of the women and children, agreed to negotiate for surrender on condition of life."[2]

Weems, the garrison, and the civilians within the fort were allowed honors of war. They marched out of the stronghold with their arms and possessions and boarded a small sloop, which had been captured by the attackers. Within a few days they were in Boston telling their story.

The other element of the attack proved successful as well. Thomas Gyles, who had taken half of the fort's garrison to Pemaquid Falls, heard the cannons from the fort. Gyles told his son John that he hoped it was good news, perhaps even the arrival of the reinforcements Lieutenant Weems had requested. No sooner had the sound of the cannon faded when it was replaced by a scattered volley from the nearby woods and a rising yell from forty charging Wabanaki. With a quick surge it was over. Thomas Gyles and several others fell attempting to repel the attack, while the rest, including John Gyles, were captured and eventually carried back to Penobscot.

As the men in the fields responded to the alarm and made their way back to the fort, they rushed into ambushes set by Castin and Thury's troops. Few if any of the English reached their objective, and not long after the Wabanaki were fanning out burning down houses and farms as they went. When it was over Fort Charles lay in Wabanaki hands, some two dozen farms and homes had been destroyed, and perhaps as many as two hundred English settlers had been slain or captured, all at the cost of one slightly wounded Wabanaki. The following day Castin burned Fort Charles before he and his war party sailed back to Penobscot aboard a pair of captured English sloops.[3]

The news of Pemaquid, coupled with the raid on Dover, set off alarms throughout New England. Residents east of Falmouth abandoned their lands upon hearing the reports and congregated at Fort Loyal. The Maine frontier was in shambles. Small bands of Wabanaki probed the English settlements, looking for their next opportunity.

The new government of Massachusetts, which had in large part been responsible for the lack of a proper garrison at Fort Charles, was paralyzed. "We have much division among us," one correspondent informed the Board of Trade. "Every man is a governor." While another wrote to his friend that "We are in great confusion and without any government."[4]

Things did not improve when news of war between France and England arrived at Boston in the fall of 1689. Small raids returned with the spring thaws, but a much greater threat appeared on the Maine frontier in May 1690. In late 1689, Governor Frontenac, early in his second tour as governor of New France, had launched three raids against New York and New England. The first leveled the town of Schenectady, while the second had wrought a similar destruction upon Salmon Falls, Maine. The third raid was the most difficult of the three. Led by Lieutenant Rene Robinau de Portneuf, this detachment of fifty Frenchmen and sixty Abanaki from the St. Francois Mission had left Quebec in late January, and after negotiating its way through the frozen wilds of northern Maine, rendezvoused with Wabanaki forces raised by Castin a few dozen miles from its target, Falmouth, Maine. Portneuf was also delighted to see Joseph-François Hertel de la Fresnière, the commander of the successful Salmon Falls raid with thirty-six volunteers from the expedition. These men, together with Castin's forces and a hundred Wabanaki who had descended the Kennebec River just a few days before, placed Portneuf's numbers close to four hundred in all. With the garrison of Fort Loyal known to be weak, the prospects for success looked good.

Portneuf and his force descended the river system to Casco Bay and made camp on one of the islands while they waited for their scouts to return with news of Falmouth's defenses. The next afternoon a number of Wabanaki ambushed and killed a settler near the fort, which sent an alarm through the town. Now discovered, Portneuf moved his troops under the cover of darkness to Indian Cove, located at the tip of Falmouth Neck, where the wooded elevations of Munjoy Hill concealed his forces throughout the night. The next morning, as the French and Indian war party crept forward toward the top of Munjoy Hill, they were discovered by the watch at Lawrence's blockhouse.

Unfortunately for Fort Loyal's commander, Captain Davis, a number of his men had departed a few days before, but undaunted, the captain organized a sortie to go out and meet what Davis assumed

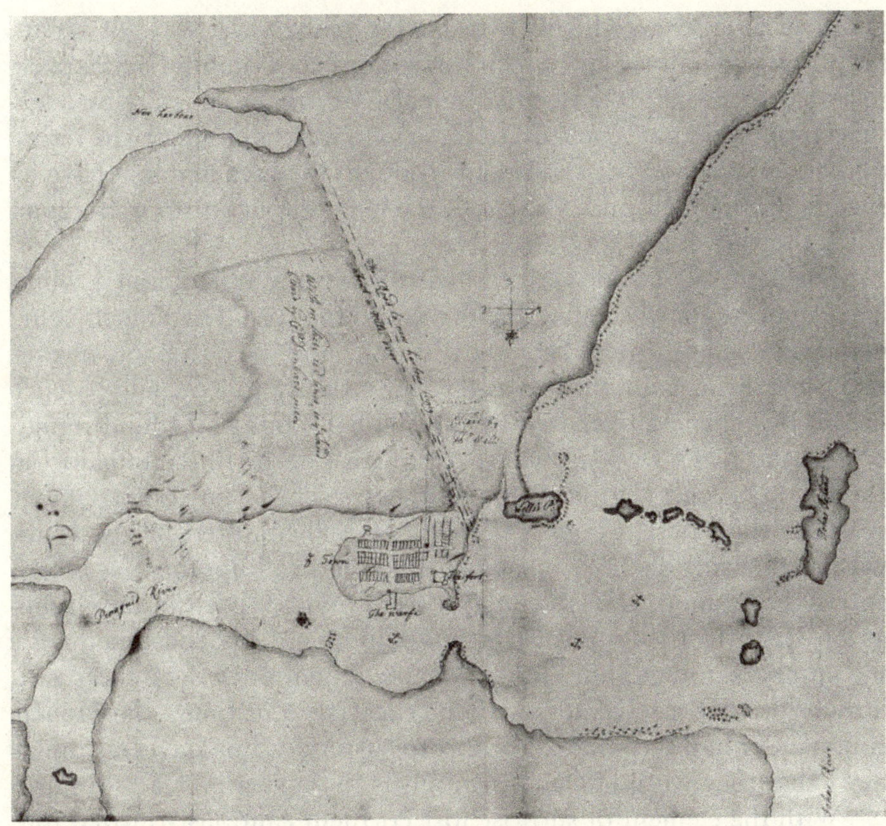

A 1730 map of Pemaquid by Thomas Wells showing the location of the fort (now Fort Frederick), the town, and anchorage at the mouth of the Pemaquid River. The dotted lines leading south from the town, end at New Harbor on the other side of the peninsula. (*Colonial Society of Massachusetts,* Transactions, *Vol. 34, 1937–1942*)

was a small raiding party. A thirty-man detachment under the command of Lieutenant Thaddeus Clark marched out of Fort Loyal around noon and in proper column formation proceeded to the foot of Munjoy Hill. From here the road was fenced in on both sides and narrowed to little more than a wagon trail as it wound its way up the hill to Lawrence's garrison house. It was a perfect trap, and Clark, true to his orders, marched straight into it. About halfway up the hill the sounds of marching and rustling equipment was shattered by the crash of musketry, first from one side of the road and then the other. The shock collapsed the English column, and as the echoes of the last shots died out a thunderous war whoop came forth before the French and their allies charged with sword and tomahawk. It was not a matter of resistance for Clark's men but escape. In a running battle back to Fort Loyal only five of the original party made it safely through the stronghold's gates, and all of these men were wounded. The retort of the fort's cannons dissuaded any thought the French might have of surprising the fort, and a pair of attackers fell victim to these guns when they advanced too far.

Portneuf moved forward to invest Lawrence's blockhouse while his advanced guard scouted the town and the fort. The French commander pulled his forces back that evening, and the occupants of garrison houses in Falmouth used the opportunity to evacuate to Fort Loyal. By morning over two hundred inhabitants had found refuge behind the fort's wooden walls. Although safe for the moment, for Davis and his charges it was not good news. The enemy looked much stronger than first thought, perhaps several hundred in all, while within the walls of the fort the captain could call upon perhaps seventy fighting men. Davis's supplies were limited, both in munitions and foodstuffs, the latter of which would be quickly consumed with the numbers now within the fort. To make matters worse, there was little hope that a relief force could reach them in time. The French commander had summoned the fort to surrender, but Davis informed him "that they would defend themselves to the death."[5]

With the element of surprise lost Portneuf cautiously moved forward the next day to invest Fort Loyal. If Davis's difficulties in defending the fort seemed daunting, so too were Portneuf's options at this point. Frontenac had directed him to avoid attacking fortifications for fear of excessive losses, but at the moment this was the only path open to him and in his estimation was a risk worth taking. The town was abandoned, and the raiders quickly occupied the houses close to the fort, sniping at its occupants while their comrades put the buildings to the torch. A black column of smoke rose from Falmouth Neck as Portneuf paused for the evening. The town was destroyed and the fort invested, but after skirmishing with its garrison during the day it was clear that it could not be taken by storm without suffering heavy casualties. As such it became a question of what to do next. It seems clear that Portneuf or one of the other partisan commanders understood the elements of siege craft. It was agreed to take advantage of a bluff some fifty paces from the fort that offered protection from cannon fire and musketry and open a trench toward the fort's waterside wall. Once at the wall they could burn the fort or use

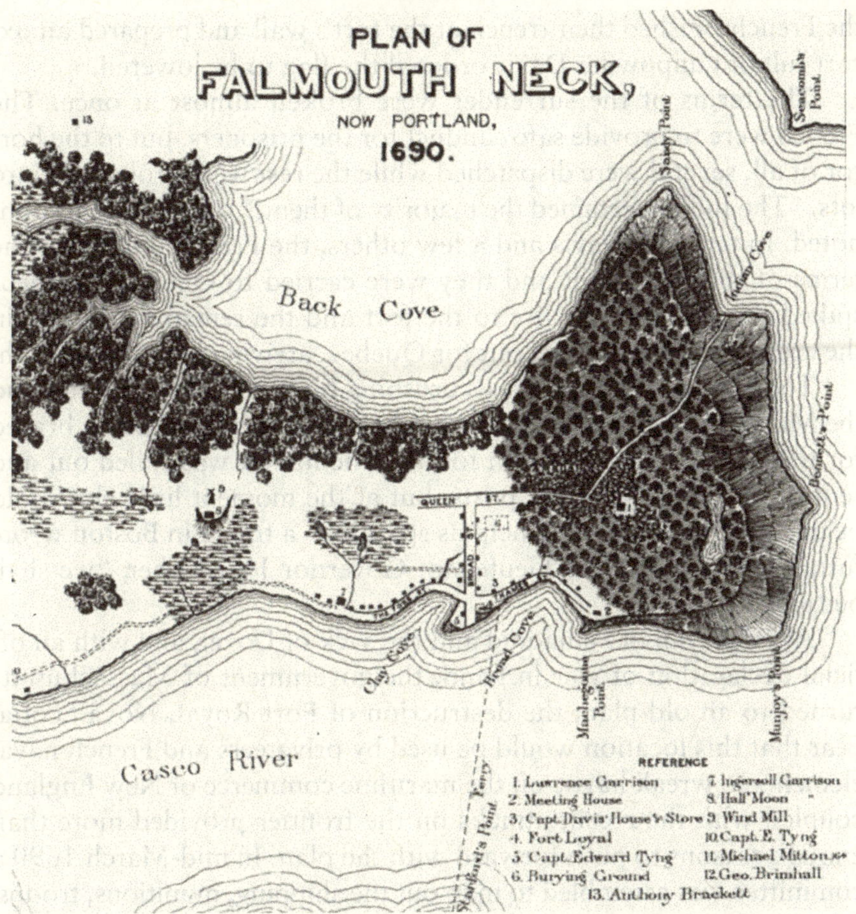

Falmouth Neck circa 1690. Fort Loyal (point 4) is the rectangular box just below the junction of Queen St. and Broad Street. (Hull, John, *The Siege and Capture of Fort Loyal* [1885])

explosives to breach the structure. While half his force probed and sniped at the fort's defenders, the rest of Portneuf's detachment made good progress on their siege trench using captured tools.

For Davis the advanced state of the enemy's siege works and his perilous position forced him to request a parley the evening of May 28. Portneuf informed the English officer that his terms required the English to surrender the fort, its guns, and supplies in return for quarter. The English officer asked for six days to consider the terms, but Portneuf was not interested and gave him that evening. Both sides resumed a steady fire upon one another the next morning, but when the French finished their trench at the fort's wall and prepared an ox-cart full of gunpowder Davis ordered the flag to be lowered.

The terms of the surrender were broken almost at once. The French were to provide safe conduct for the prisoners, but to the horror of all, several were dispatched while the rest were broken off into lots. "The Indians retained the majority of them," one French account noted. In terms of Davis and a few others, the French did honor the terms of the agreement and they were carried to Quebec. Portneuf spiked the cannons, set fire to the fort and the remaining homes in the area, and on June 1 set out for Quebec, arriving later that month.

The loss of Falmouth was a crushing blow for New England and the Maine frontier. Towns from Saco to the outskirts of Boston braced for the raids that would soon follow. The militia was called out and sent to bolster the frontier posts, but at the moment little else could be done. "Unless the King help us speedily," a friend in Boston wrote future New Hampshire Lieutenant Governor John Usher, "we shall be ruined."[6]

After the fall of Pemaquid and the sack of Dover, and with an official declaration of war in hand, the government of Massachusetts turned to an old plan, the destruction of Port Royal, Nova Scotia. Fear that this location would be used by privateers and French naval elements to wreak havoc on the maritime commerce of New England coupled with the recent attacks on the frontier provided more than enough reasons to push forward with the plan. In mid-March 1690 a committee was assembled to map out the shipping, munitions, troops, and provisions needed for the expedition.[7]

A few days later the task took on more meaning when news of the attack on Salmon Falls arrived. Preparations were accelerated, and not long after the recruiting officers began beating their drums. Command of the expedition was given to Sir William Phipps who commanded the 42-gun frigate *Six Friends*. Phipps, born on the Maine frontier, was a well-known ship captain and adventurer, but with no military background to speak of he was an odd choice. He had married a wealthy widow and used this modest wealth to finance a series of treasure-hunting expeditions. After several dismal attempts, in 1686 Phipps located and salvaged over £200,000 from a sunken Spanish treasure ship off the coast of Haiti. Not only was Phipps now a rich man, but the king's portion of the take was sufficient to earn him a knighthood, the command of a frigate, and a colonial appointment as well.

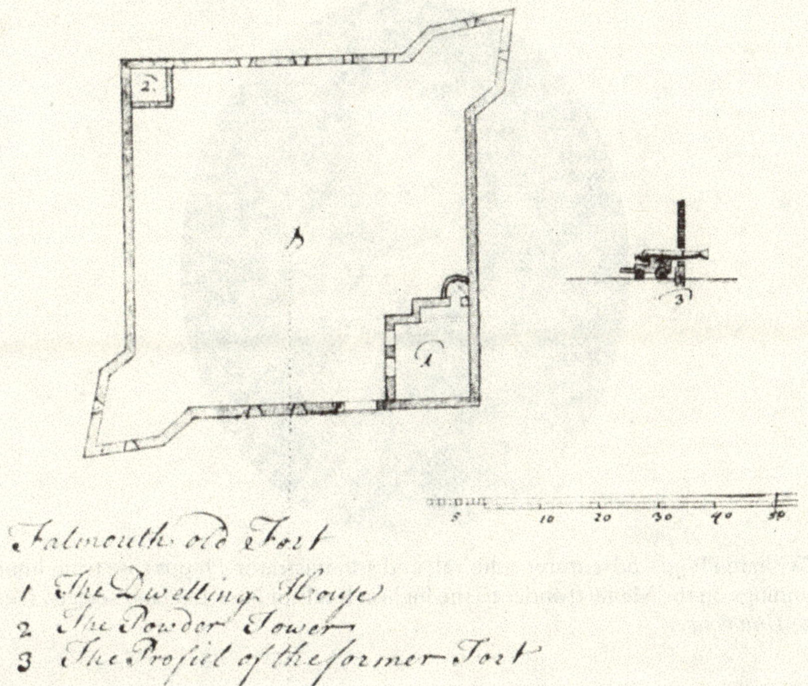

Fort Loyal at Falmouth, c. 1690. This small two bastioned fort, about 50-feet to a side, had firing ports cut in the walls for the structure's eight cannons. (*The Crown Collection of Photographs of American Maps, III, plate 164*)

Over seven hundred men volunteered for the expedition, and seven vessels were assembled, the largest of which was the *Six Friends* and the smallest being the two-gun *Mary Anne*. The fleet departed Boston on April 28, 1690, and set course for the coast of Maine. Phipps's first target was not Port Royal but Castin's stockade trading post at Penobscot. After arriving in the vicinity scouts returned with news that Castin was gone, but the post was currently occupied by two hundred or so Wabanaki. Phipps ordered an attack, but the weather deteriorated to the point that it was not until the evening of May 4 that the troops went ashore only to find a few moments later that the fort was deserted. The next day was spent destroying the stronghold and welcoming a pair of colonial companies that arrived in two small vessels.[8]

From Penobscot, Phipps set sail for Passamaquoddy Bay where he spent a few days raiding French settlements in the area before setting a course for Port Royal. On the morning of May 9 the small

Sir William Phipps, adventurer, admiral, and administrator. Phipps rose from humble beginnings on the Maine frontier to the highest levels of New England society. (*Salem State University*)

flotilla entered the Basin and dropped anchor before Port Royal. Phipps immediately began landing men, while under a white flag an envoy in a small boat carried a summons for the fort to surrender.

The governor of Acadia, Louis-Alexander de Menneval, was in an impossible position. The fort's garrison of seventy-two men was short on powder and arms, and the fort itself was in such bad repair that an engineer had recently been dispatched to build a new one. To make matters worse, the stronghold's eighteen cannons, in anticipation of the new structure, were not mounted, meaning that there was nothing he could do before the pair of 42- and 20-gun English warships anchored not far away. With no hope of timely relief Menneval accepted Phipps's surrender summons, as he claims, under honors of war, meaning he and his men were to keep their arms and be transported back to Quebec as part of the agreement.

If this was the case, Phipps did not live up to his end of the bargain, as Menneval, his garrison, as well as two French missionaries were immediately taken prisoner. Phipps and his men then set themselves to ransacking the fort and the nearby buildings. The zeal for this task even reached the fort's church, as by Phipps's own admission, "we cut down the cross, rifled the Church, pulled down the high altar,

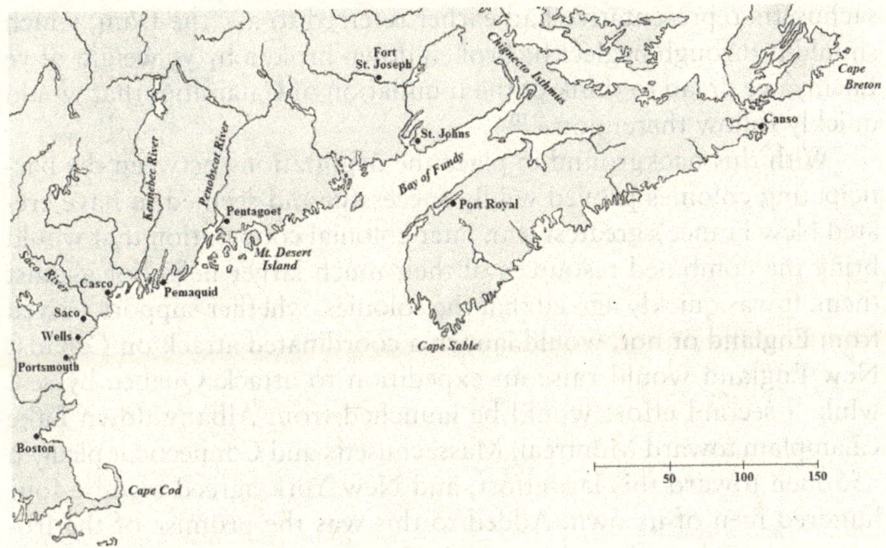

Nova Scotia and the Gulf of Maine. (*Author*)

and broke their images." When this was done the fort was demolished, its guns loaded aboard the fleet, and the inhabitants forced to swear an oath of allegiance to King William. The 20-gun sloop *Porcupine* was dispatched to raid French coastal settlements in Acadia, while Phipps and the rest of the fleet took their prisoners and plunder back to Boston.[9]

News of the destruction of Fort Loyal would dampen the celebrations a few weeks later, but greater plans to strike back were already in the works. In late March Massachusetts governor Simon Bradstreet took the lead and invited representatives of the New England colonies, New York, New Jersey, Maryland, and Virginia to meet in Rhode Island on the last Monday of April in order to discuss "Uniting and combining as one to withstand and Oppose the common Enemy." The venue would be shifted to New York City where the interested parties convened on May 1.

The meeting was opened with a discussion of the state of affairs, which was quickly summarized with a retelling of the northern colonies' woes under the relentless assault of French and Indian war parties. The perilous nature of the Maine and New Hampshire frontier was reiterated, as was the need to secure Albany, which one Massachusetts representative had earlier referred to as "the Dam, which should it through neglect be broken down broken by ye weight of ye Enemy, we dread to think of the Inundation of Calamities that would quickly follow thereupon."[10]

With this background in place the negotiations between the participating colonies proved wildly successful and seemed to have created New France's greatest fear, inter-colonial cooperation that would bring the combined resources of their much larger neighbor against them. It was quickly agreed that the colonies, whether support arrived from England or not, would launch a coordinated attack on Canada. New England would raise an expedition to attack Quebec by sea, while a second effort would be launched from Albany down Lake Champlain toward Montreal. Massachusetts and Connecticut pledged 355 men toward this last effort, and New York agreed to raise four hundred men of its own. Added to this was the promise of the Iroquois to join the effort with up to 1,800 men. The twin attacks would overwhelm the forces of New France, leaving it in English hands by the end of the year. Not long after it was agreed that General Fitz-John Winthrop of Connecticut would lead the Lake Champlain expedition while Sir William Phipps would command the seaborne attack on Quebec.

In late August with both Phipps's and Winthrop's campaigns well underway, Massachusetts governor Simon Bradstreet and his council turned their attention to the Maine-New Hampshire frontier. It was agreed to strike back at the Wabanaki Confederacy, and Major Benjamin Church, who had recently led an expedition along the Maine coast and had an excellent reputation as a woodland fighter, was chosen to lead this expedition. After securing transport Church arrived in Portsmouth, New Hampshire in early September 1690. Some three hundred militia and volunteers had rendezvoused here and by mid-month had landed near the ruins of Castin's fort. Striking inland Church did manage to overrun a partially abandoned Wabanaki village and free half a dozen English prisoners. He also managed to ambush and scatter a small French and Indian war party, but more importantly he and his men were ambushed while encamped at Cape Elizabeth in bad weather. Church's men eventually extricated themselves and put the smaller enemy party to flight but at the cost of over thirty casualties from the engagement. The expedition returned to Ports-mouth on September 26, having accomplished little else for their efforts.

Major Benjamin Church. Considered the first American Ranger, Church would lead expeditions against French and Indian targets in King William's War and Queen Anne's War. (*New York Public Library*)

Whatever disappointment that came from this venture would be transplanted a few months later by much worse news as both Phipps's and Winthrop's campaigns had failed. The former had reached the French colonial capital but were short on powder from the failure of a supply ship to arrive in time from England. Troops were landed above the town, but unable to provide covering fire from a lack of powder, and with ice already forming on the vessels of the fleet, it was agreed that it was too late in the year to conduct a siege and Phipps abandoned the effort. On Lake Champlain, Winthrop, whose forces were decimated by smallpox, which kept his Iroquois allies from joining him, could only manage a small raid on La Prairie across the river from Montreal.

The financial loss from the failed expeditions crippled Massachusetts. The ventures were financed in part with the assurance that the booty obtained would cover the costs. As there was no booty to speak of, the entire bill fell upon the colony. There was not enough money to pay Phipps's men, which threatened to create another problem as many of them hung around Boston in hopes of obtaining at least some of their pay. Paper money was issued for the first time in the colony in an attempt to alleviate the fiscal problems, but it proved nearly worthless.

The Massachusetts and New Hampshire frontiers were fortified with troops, but there was no way to pay them. Even if they all stayed at their posts despite this, it was not likely to make much difference. There was no way to know when or where a French and Indian war party might strike, and it was simply impossible to fortify and garrison the entire frontier. Even the seaports down the east coast were in peril should a French fleet arrive in North American waters. Taken together with the colony's financial woes, a smallpox epidemic brought by Phipps's returning troops set off a wave of despair. Fortunately, Church's expedition had paid one dividend that lifted the colony's spirits. Although the expedition had failed to secure its goals, the prisoners taken were eventually exchanged for English captives, and perhaps just as importantly, a temporary truce was agreed upon by both parties until May 1691.[11]

Three

THE RISE AND FALL OF PEMAQUID

IT WOULD NOT BE until June that the French and Wabanaki raids returned with a failed attack on Wells before falling upon nearby York with more success. Massachusetts attempted to be proactive and dispatch a two-hundred-man expedition under Captain John March along the Maine coast, but this proved to be a repeat of Church's effort, complete with another ambush of the colonial forces. It also did nothing to stop the raids along the frontier. Exeter, Berwick, and Rye, New Hampshire, were struck by war parties, but in general the government of Massachusetts was relieved that no major attack had materialized. As for the current raids, given the colony's fiscal resources little more could be done but attempt to weather them.[1]

In England, Phipps spent the early summer personally reporting the details of his failed campaign to King William and then pressing the monarch to allow him to lead a second effort against Quebec. Phipps requested a ship-of-the-line to escort the New England fleet, a hundred cannons, powder, and two thousand small arms to see this task through. The king showed interest in the scheme and asked Phipps for more information, but given the time of the year, this request meant that it was unlikely that the expedition would go forward. The prodding by the adventurer turned admiral did have some positive effects. Two hundred barrels of powder and ten siege guns were forwarded to Boston, and at Phipps's urging, it was agreed to assign a frigate to patrol New England waters to counter the growing number of French privateers. Although a second expedition against the capital of New France was not to be, the Board of Trade and the Admiralty had taken notice of a memorandum Phipps wrote concerning the ability of the New England colonies to provide all the major needs of the English navy. Taken together, when the new royal charter was completed for Massachusetts, Phipps seemed the obvious choice and was appointed governor in late November 1691.[2]

Beyond coping with the outbreak of witches and warlocks in Massachusetts, Phipps faced a number of serious military issues when he took office in May 1692. After squashing the witch hunting fervor through use of his royal authority the governor pursued one of his primary orders, that of rebuilding the fort at Pemaquid. A number of colonial leaders questioned the wisdom of his rebuilding the Maine outpost. Although a new fort could certainly be built at Pemaquid, its isolated location would make it difficult to support, as the only practical avenue to do such was by sea. Undeterred, Phipps raised a force of 450 men, gathered together the necessary materials, and set sail for the Maine coast in early August 1692. The flotilla briefly stopped at Falmouth to inspect the ruins. The dead, still scattered about the town after its capture several years before, were buried, and the fort's great guns, which had been left behind by the victorious French and Indian war party, were recovered. As half of his force turned toward the task of constructing the new fort at Pemaquid, Phipps detached Major Church with the rest of the troops to attack nearby enemy villages. Church accomplished little, but his efforts did seem to screen Phipps's work at Pemaquid, as no attempt was made to disrupt it.[3]

In October the English flag was raised over Fort William Henry as the structure was christened. Given the abundance of nearby rock, and the desire to build as secure of a fortification as soon as possible, it was agreed to construct the fort of stone. Unfortunately, limestone was nowhere to be found in the vicinity. Instead, a mixture of clay and sand was used as a substitute. It was a mistake that weakened the structure, and in the estimation of Royal Engineer Colonel Wolfgang Romer, who visited the site after the conclusion of the war, led to the fort's early demise. The resulting structure was essentially a

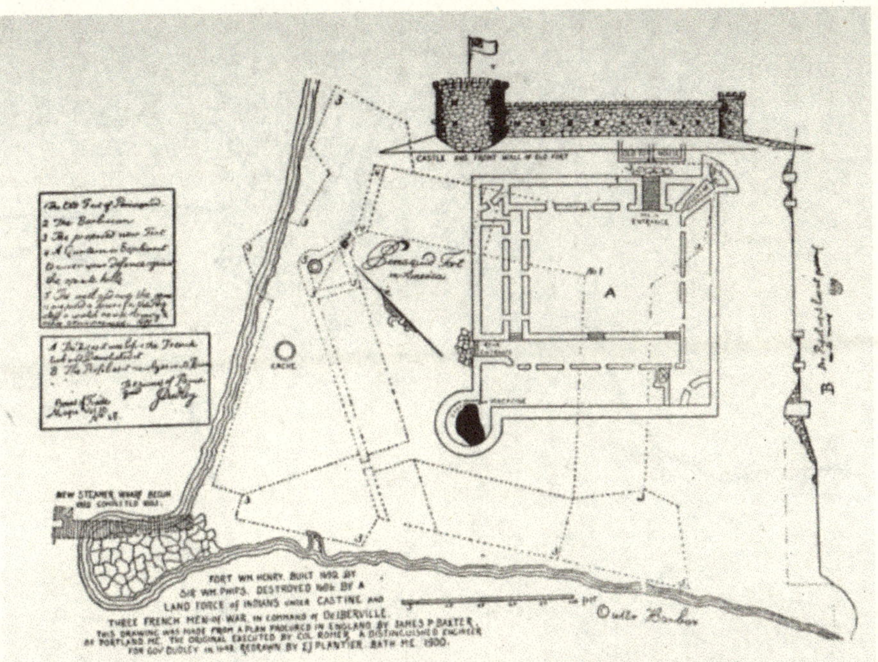

Fort William Henry at Pemaquid. The broken lines are the trace of a new fort proposed a few years before the start of Queen Anne's War. (*The Crown Collection of Photographs of American Maps, III, plate 159-160*)

stone square, about 185 feet to a side. The seaside walls were six feet thick and twenty-two feet in height with a three-story cylindrical bastion occupying the western corner. The walls facing the landside of the fort were slightly shorter with a smaller bastion occupying the eastern corner of the structure. The interior of the fort was also bisected with 108-foot walls to create something of a keep. Twenty-eight gunports were cut into the walls and tower to allow the fort's fourteen cannons to be brought to bear, with the largest guns, six 18-pounders, positioned to defend the seaside walls of the structure. With the weather deteriorating and little else to be accomplished, Phipps left Captain John March and sixty men to garrison the fort and departed with the rest for Boston.[4]

The rebuilding of the fort at Pemaquid certainly strengthened the Maine frontier, but there were greater worries that had to be addressed. Most of the New England seaports, including Boston, were vulnerable to an attack. An actual invasion was unlikely given the population density of the area, but a raid intent on burning the town

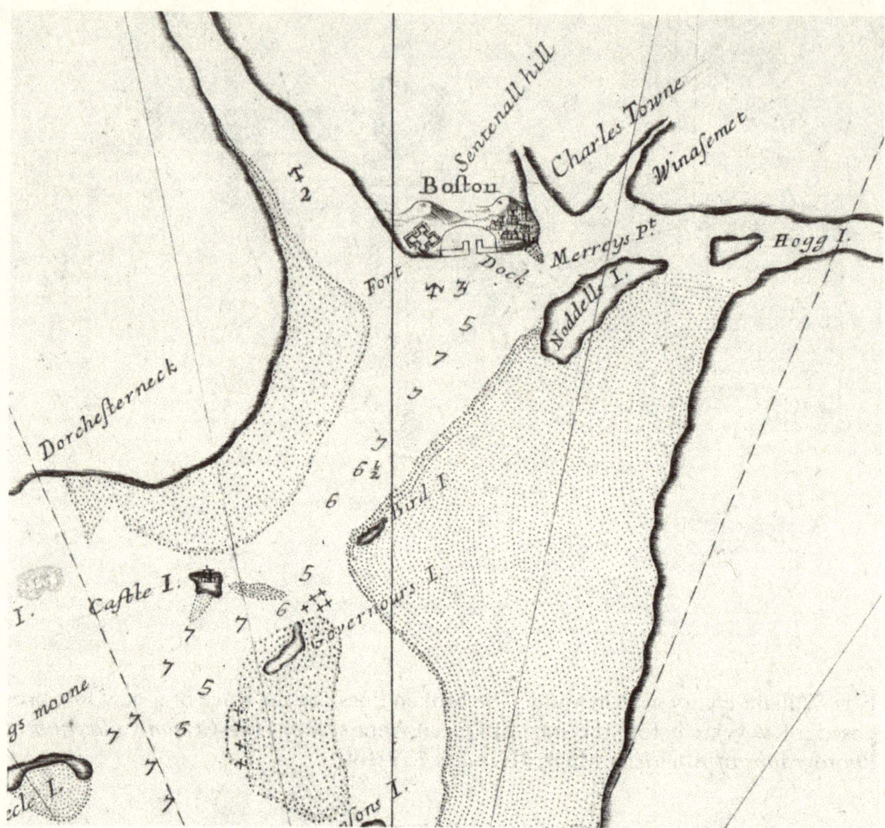

A portion of a c. 1689 map showing the approach to Boston Harbor between Castle Island and Governors Island. (*Norman B. Leventhal Map Collection, Boston Public Library*)

and the shipping in the harbor was possible. This threat came in two forms, a raid by privateers or a French naval attack. The first of these possibilities would be aimed at smaller coastal communities, as these raiders would be reluctant to challenge the fortifications of some of the larger towns. Even here some of the smaller fortifications, such as those at Salem and Marblehead, were likely to dissuade this type of attack given that the raiders were motivated more by profit than military objectives.

The real fear was a descent on the coast by elements of the French navy. In this instance, even the major fortifications, such as Castle Island in Boston Harbor or Fort William and Mary at Portsmouth, would be called into question. In fact, French planners had considered just such an action. Early in the conflict a joint attack on Albany and

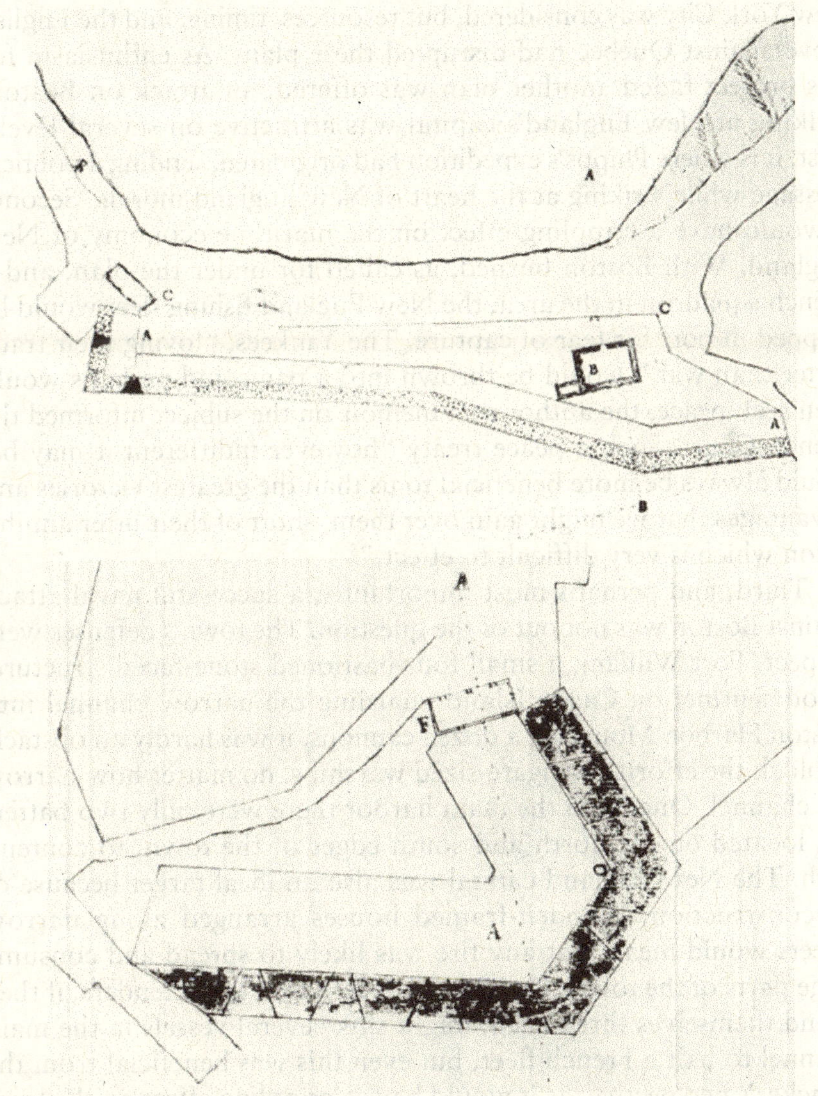

Top: The South Battery of Boston, 1705. Started in 1665, the base was reported to have been formed with 10-ton stones and the walls made of brick and stone. The firing ports through the wall are shown to the left. "A" is the battery, "B" is the battery's stone magazine and storehouse, which given its location would be subjected to bombardment, while "C" is a palisade that enclosed the works. (*The Crown Collection of Photographs of American Maps, III, plate 189-190*)
Bottom: The North Battery of Boston, 1705. Built around the same time as the South Battery, the firing posts for the half-a-dozen cannons can be seen in the drawing. "A" is the battery which on the drawing was noted to be in poor condition, while "F" marks the battery's watchtower. (*The Crown Collection of Photographs of American Maps, III, plate 191-192*)

New York City was considered, but resources, timing, and the English move against Quebec had disrupted these plans. As enthusiasm for this project faded another plan was offered, an attack on Boston. Striking at New England's capital was attractive on several levels. First, it is where Phipps's expedition had originated, sending a political message while striking at the heart of New England morale. Second, it would have a crippling effect on the maritime economy of New England. With Boston burned, as called for under the plan, and a French squadron in the area, the New England fishing fleet would be trapped in port for fear of capture. The Yankees, "loving their trade better than war," would be thrown into a panic and perhaps would even seek peace, the author of a memoir on the subject informed the French Court. Such a peace treaty "however indifferent it may be, would always be more beneficial to us than the greatest victories and advantages that we might gain over them, short of their utter annihilation which is very difficult to effect."[5]

Third, and perhaps most importantly, a successful naval attack against Boston was not out of the question. The town's defenses were suspect. Fort William, a small four-bastioned stone-faced structure, stood sentinel on Castle Island guarding the narrow channel into Boston Harbor. Mounting a dozen cannons, it was hardly an obstacle to block the efforts of frigate-sized warships, no matter how narrow the channel. Once into the main harbor there were only two batteries, located on the north and south edges of the town, to contend with. The New England capital was also an ideal target because of its construction. Wooden-framed houses arranged along narrow streets would mean that any fire was likely to spread and consume large parts of the town. There was concern that the defenders, if they found themselves threatened, might sink several vessels in the main channel to halt a French fleet, but even this was beneficial from the attacker's perspective, as it would have a crippling effect on the local economy. The plan also made sense in terms of what was required to maintain the defenses of the colony. Frontenac and the leadership of the colony agreed that, at minimum, a squadron of four forty-gun frigates were needed to keep the mouth of the St. Lawrence free of English privateers and challenge any future attempts by the English to launch an attack on Quebec. These vessels could cruise the Nova Scotia and New England coasts in search of prizes and even make up part of the squadron sent from France to undertake the attack on Boston.[6]

As work continued to strengthen Castle Island, in late 1692 the Massachusetts Council, fearing an attack bent on burning the town, passed legislation entitled, "An Act for Building in Stone or Brick in the town of Boston and Preventing Fire," which called for all future buildings within the town to be constructed of stone or brick with slate or tile roofs. An alarm system had also been agreed upon. As the garrison at Castle Island, typically a company, were most likely to spot the enemy first, they were to raise a pair of flags and fire two cannons. If the observation came from elsewhere three shots were to be fired in rapid succession or a beacon fire lit. Whichever the case, the town's militia was to immediately assemble at their designated points, while riders were dispatched to neighboring communities with the news.

While French naval threats remained along the New England coast, for the Maine, New Hampshire, and Massachusetts frontiers relief came when a truce was negotiated between the New England colonies and the Wabanaki in the summer of 1693. Although neither side believed it would last, both were exhausted and agreed to the ceasefire. The peace was broken the following year, when in July, French and Wabanaki war parties devastated the townships of Durham and Groton, New Hampshire. Smaller raids followed, but by the summer of 1695 the Wabanaki attacks had greatly diminished. The reason was simple. The French had not been able to supply the confederacy with the goods they required to carry on the fight. The lack of Wabanaki activity during this time was also the result of an active English naval presence along the coast of Maine and Acadia, as well as the reestablishment of Fort William Henry at Pemaquid, which the Wabanaki had begun negotiating with to obtain the items the French could not supply.

This collusion became the French focus not long after the attack on Durham. In making a case to the minister of the marine for an expedition against Pemaquid, the French governor of Acadia, Joseph Robineau de Villebon, saluted the foresight of his English adversaries. "They judged very correctly that in building Pemaquid, they were depriving our Indians of the power of going freely coastwise on their expeditions; embarrassing them in an extraordinary degree in hunting Deer which were very abundant thereabout, and that the Indians, finding themselves thus straitened, would be obliged to enter into negotiations, as has in fact been the case." Seizing Pemaquid would not only recement the Wabanaki-French alliance, but it would also remove the strongest English position along the Maine coast, opening up a large stretch of the coastline with its excellent harbors for French use. To accomplish the task the governor called for three ships, a pair of frigates, and a fly boat to land troops. A force of a hundred soldiers along with a like number of sailors from the fleet would be joined by Villebon and two hundred Wabanaki once they landed. With a force this size it would take little to invest the fort, and from there the governor estimated that a battery of four 18-pound guns and a pair of mortars would be sufficient to reduce the stone fortress, especially when supported by the cannon onboard the frigates.[7]

A more pressing problem was the English naval activity, but there was little Villebon could do in this regard. A pair of frigates had routinely fitted out in Boston each year to cruise the Maine-Acadia coast in search of prizes. The warships, coupled with a number of privateers, had a devastating effect on the Acadian fishing fleet and often intercepted French supply vessels. It appeared to the Wabanaki that the English ruled the seas, and that was why the French could not supply them. The sight of more New England fishing vessels in the area, coupled with the activity of two New England frigates, the *Sorling* and the *Newport*, only seemed to reinforce the Wabanaki's position.

On July 8, 1695, this changed when Captain Simon-Pierre Denys de Bonaventure arrived at St. John (New Brunswick) in the damaged frigate *Envieux*. Bonaventure informed Villebon that he had arrived at Pentagout on June 19 where he had been informed by Father Thury that a 40-gun English frigate had been seen at St. John. After taking on provisions, he sought out the enemy warship, and around three o'clock on the afternoon of July 5 he found his quarry. The 36-gun frigate *Sorling* was an even match for the Frenchman. The two vessels dueled for five hours, exchanging broadsides and trying to maneuver to rake the other from stem to stern. Bonaventure had severed the *Sorling*'s main topmast and part of the Englishman's mizzenmast had splintered upon a direct hit and fallen on the aft deck. The *Envieux* was struck hard as well, but Bonaventure believed that if the last enemy broadside had not cut a number of his lines and damaged his mainmast that he would have taken the enemy vessel. Bonaventure unloaded his supplies and made repairs before setting sail for Quebec on July 21. The timing proved fortunate, as not long after both the *Sorling* and the *Newport* arrived at the St. John River looking for the French warship.[8]

Pierre Le Moyne de Iberville. (*National Archives of Canada*)

The French supplies seemed to have had the desired effect on the Wabanaki, and Bonaventure's actions certainly questioned any perceptions they had regarding English naval dominance, but this did not translate into what Governor Villebon had hoped. Small bands of Wabanaki did strike at isolated targets along the frontier but not in the numbers needed to alarm the English, and soon the season for such things slipped away.

When Villebon's call for an expedition against Pemaquid arrived in Paris, he found a receptive French court. Should the Wabanaki Confederacy collapse or agree to a long-term peace treaty the region would prove vulnerable to the New England colonies. This would mean the possible loss of the Acadia fishing industries, and likely, the extensive fishing interests in Newfoundland as well. Given the circumstances and consequences there was general agreement among the king's ministers to go forward with the governor's proposal. This consensus was aided in part by inserting the projected attack on Pemaquid into a larger scheme that called for seizing all of Newfoundland and then expelling the English from Hudson Bay.[9]

Execution of this broader plan was given to Pierre Le Moyne de Iberville. Iberville was one of eleven brothers, sons of the Montreal legend Charles Le Moyne. Like his older brothers, St. Helene and

Maricourt, Pierre learned his woodland skills from his father during the latter's many fur trading expeditions, and like his father, he would have a long connection with the *Compagnie de Nord*. It seems that Iberville had decided on a naval career early on, for he frequently sailed his father's trading vessel on the St. Lawrence and as a young man had visited France. His first official opportunity to serve New France came in 1686, when alongside his older brothers, he was appointed a lieutenant in Captain Pierre de Troyes's expedition to James Bay. His woodlands knowledge and abilities were instrumental in navigating the eighty-five-day voyage north from Montreal to the Hudson Bay Company posts. After serving with distinction on this front for several years, Iberville returned to Quebec in time to participate as second in command in St. Helene's attack on Schenectady in 1690. After this he returned to his interest in seeing Hudson Bay secured for France.[10]

Iberville was given a pair of thirty-four-gun frigates, the *Envieux* and the *Profond*, along with the transport vessel *Wesp*. His orders directed him to set sail for Spanish Bay, Cape Breton, and from there sail to St. John and rendezvous with Governor Villebon's forces. Here he would offload supplies and munitions needed by the governor to reestablish a fort at the mouth of the St. John River. Once this was complete the combined forces would lay siege to Fort William Henry at Pemaquid. Upon the capture of the English fort, Iberville was to set sail for Placentia, Newfoundland, and there join forces with Governor Jacques-François de Monbeton de Brouillan for a descent upon the English-held eastern coast of the island. Brouillan was to command the naval element of the expedition while Iberville, accompanied by his Canadians and some sixty Micmac volunteers, would command the land forces. With this task complete and the English settlements on this island destroyed, if time permitted, the young mariner was to set sail for Hudson Bay and attack the English trading post on the Nelson River. To assist in these plans the court had sent letters to Villebon, Frontenac, and the governor of Placentia, Brouillan, informing them of the project. Frontenac in particular was to raise a company of eighty Canadians who would accompany Iberville on his mission to Newfoundland, while Villebon and Brouillan were to organize their forces so as to be ready to cooperate with Iberville's detachment.

It was an ambitious plan that required four separate parties, three of them in the New World, to meet a rigid timetable, and it was riddled with questions concerning command and the responsibilities of the various elements involved. The problems started almost at once. Iberville's squadron, which was loaded with provisions, gifts, and artillery for the new fort at St. John, was late getting out of La Rochelle. The tender *Wesp* was sent on to Quebec to collect the company of Canadians who were to rendezvous with the expedition at Placentia, while the *Envieux* and *Profond* steered a course for Cape Breton and dropped anchor at Spanish Bay on June 26, 1696. Letters from Governor Villebon awaited the vessels. Three English warships were patrolling the mouth of the St. John River and had effectively blockaded the intended landing area. Iberville stayed at Spanish Bay only long enough to make minor repairs, replenish the crew's provisions, and take on a number of Micmac and Abenaki recruits. On July 4, everything having been seen to, he set sail in search of the English warships.[11]

The poor weather slowed Iberville's approach, and on the morning of the fourteenth the fog was dense enough that he dropped anchor off the northwest coast of Nova Scotia, some twenty miles from St. John. The weather started clearing that afternoon, and around two o'clock lookouts pointed to three English warships on a course for St. John. The vessels proved to be the frigate *Sorlings*, which Captain Bonaventure had fought the year before, along with the 22-gun frigate *Newport* and a small tender. Captain Fleetwood Emes of the *Sorlings* had stationed his flotilla near the St. John River in expectation of intercepting the seasonal French supply fleet. Now, as his lookouts pointed to two large ships at anchor, Emes ordered the squadron to steer for the vessels, while he and his officers eyed the craft closely. Both French vessels weighed anchor, and a pair of duels began as the *Sorlings* bore down on the *Envieux*, while the *Newport* targeted the *Profond*. In an attempt to make himself look like an unarmed merchantman Captain Bonaventure ordered the gunports closed on the *Profond* and raised an English flag to make the vessel look like a prize in tow by the *Envieux*. The French warships, however, could only carry on the masquerade for so long. When the ploy was discovered, the *Newport* unleashed a broadside but soon found itself the target of far more cannons and a huge volume of musketry from the *Profond*'s crew as well as the Micmac and Abenaki on board. The *Sorlings* and the *Envieux* circled about in a twisting affair of passing broadsides for the next several hours, repeatedly scoring hits upon one another.

Seeing that he was outgunned by the pair of French frigates, Emes ordered the squadron to make sail to the southwest. The decision to retreat came too late for the *Newport*. Iberville and Bonaventure, keeping the weather gauge in their favor, exchanged fire with the English frigate. Badly outgunned it was only a matter of time for the *Newport*. It had been hit several times between wind and water, and there was five feet of water in the hold. Iberville's ship scored the decisive blow when a broadside from the *Envieux* brought down the *Newport*'s main mast. With the loss of maneuverability, his ship taking on water, and two enemy frigates firing upon him, Captain Wentworth Paxton ran the vessel ashore and struck his colors. Not happy with just the *Newport*, Iberville ordered a prize crew onto the captured vessel and then, along with Bonaventure in the *Profond*, set out after the fleeing English squadron. The *Sorlings* and the tender were fortunate as fog banks and misty rains rolled in, covering their escape.[12]

While the *Envieux* and *Profond* briefly chased the retreating English warship, their new prize, under the command of local pilot and corsair, Jean Baptiste, made sail for St. John. Unfortunately, the tides and poor weather, coupled with the ship's impaired performance, resulted in Baptiste running it up onto the rocks at the mouth of the St. John River. At length the *Newport* was freed, and soon all three French vessels dropped anchor at St. John. The supplies destined for Villebon were unloaded over the next few days, including an impressive array of artillery for the new fort. Attention was also turned toward repairs on the *Newport* and a crew for the prize. With these matters seen to, some fifty Wabanaki were taken onboard, and the three vessels set off for Pentagoet. Here Iberville finished the repairs on the *Newport* while he waited several weeks for Castin's Native allies to appear. By the end of the first week of August Castin had assembled 240 Wabanaki and 25 colonial marines. When added to the hundred or so Wabanaki already onboard, and a detachment from the warships to man the artillery, it put Iberville's numbers close to

Opposite: A portion of a 1761 map of the confluency of the St. John River and the Bay of Fundy in modern day New Brunswick. The fort denoted by "A" is Fort Frederick, built in 1758, but the location had previously hosted several French forts along the same pattern since the 1640s. Iberville was carrying supplies and cannons for the newest version, which Governor Villebon erected in 1698. Called Fort St. Jean, Villebon abandoned the post a few years later because of supply issues and cost. It would not be the last fort at this location. (*Norman B. Leventhal Map Collection, Boston Public Library*)

HARBOUR
High Water Mark
Low Water Mark
High Water
Low Water Mark
Sandy
dry at Low Water
Low Water Mar

five hundred men, or about five times that of the English garrison of Fort William Henry.[13]

The force departed in two detachments with Castin and his Native contingent travelling to Pemaquid by canoe, while the rest of the expedition sailed aboard Iberville's warships. The fleet anchored about a league from the English fort a few hours before sunrise on August 15. Iberville summoned the stronghold's commander, Captain Pasco Chubb, to surrender, but the latter replied that he would not yield even "if the sea were covered with French vessels and the land with Indians." The French commander had expected as much, and while the opening formalities of the siege were being enacted his men had been busy landing cannons and marking out trenches to approach the fort.

The French pressed their siege trenches forward throughout the morning to the flash of musketry and thunder of cannons as the defenders attempted to undermine their efforts. By afternoon a firing battery of two large mortars and two twelve-pound cannons had been erected a few hundred yards from the fort. A little before two o'clock a call rang out, and one of the mortars let out a hollow thump as its bomb arched through the air clearing the fort and exploding behind it. The next shot was long as well, but after that the crew found the range, and several rounds fell within the confines of the stronghold. The point being made, Castin ordered the guns to stop firing and sent a surrender demand to Chubb. The French envoy met with Chubb and a few of his officers outside the fort and informed the English commander that, if the fort was not surrendered by the time the next mortar was fired, "he did not know whether there would be man, woman, or child saved; for the Indians would come in upon us if our walls were breached, and would give no quarter."[14]

The threat resonated with the English, but to convince Chubb of the futility of resisting he was invited to send an envoy to the French camp. The English commander agreed and sent a sergeant from the garrison. The man returned an hour later to report that the French had a battery of two mortars and twelve-pound cannons. Six more cannons had just been landed and would be in position within a day or two. The enemy appeared to be six hundred strong, five hundred Wabanaki and a hundred French, and this did not include the crews on the warships which numbered several hundred.

Chubb, later claimed by many to be a marginal officer, was in a predicament. It is true that he had a new stone fort to stand behind, with over a dozen guns mounted on its ramparts, and a garrison of ninety-two men, forty of whom had just arrived from Massachusetts. They were well provisioned and sufficient in number to guard the walls of the structure. If determined, there is little doubt that the English garrison could have seriously contested the French siege, but part of the problem was the enemy had attacked in a direction where only one cannon could be brought to bear against them, and after firing this gun a few times the ramparts beneath it began to crumble. To make matters worse, the enemy had cut them off from their water supply, and with news that the French warships had beaten off a New England fleet in the area there was little hope of timely relief.

In the end, Chubb surrendered the fort on the condition that the garrison would be allowed to keep their personal possessions and would be carried back to Boston where they would be exchanged for French and Indian prisoners being held there. Iberville agreed to the terms and marched the garrison out as prisoners of war. The gates were opened and the fort ransacked. A half-dead Wabanaki was found in the fort's jail, which set off a furor among Castin's allies. Fortunately, Iberville had been wise enough to immediately ship the garrison off to a small island in the bay where he could keep a close guard over them. When everything of value had been taken efforts turned toward destroying the fort by pulling down its walls and putting everything that would burn to the torch.[15]

News of Fort William Henry travelled the length of New England like a shock wave. The fort, reputed to be one of the strongest in North America, had fallen in less than twenty-four hours. Captain Chubb, who along with the rest of the garrison was returned when Iberville held up his end of the surrender, was accused of treason and thrown in jail. The militia was called out, and there was fear that Iberville's next target would be Portsmouth, but at least in this regard Governor William Stoughton of Massachusetts was fortunate. The frigates H.M.S. *Arundel* and H.M.S. *Oxford* had just arrived at Boston with a number of merchant men in tow. Stoughton contracted a large merchant ship fitted out with thirty-six guns, and along with the *Sorlings* and the *Province Galley*, sent the two Royal Navy warships out in pursuit of Iberville. The hastily constructed English fleet nearly accomplished their task. They surprised the French who were lying at anchor with the captured *Newport* at Mount Desert Island. Had the wind not suddenly died off, Iberville might have had a serious dilemma on his hands, but instead he used the cover of darkness to slip away. He was briefly sighted the next morning, but foggy weather ended any hopes of a pursuit.[16]

The New England response to the fall of Fort William Henry came quicker than anticipated. This was in part because, earlier in the year, the Massachusetts Assembly had sanctioned another eastern expedition under Major Church. This was to be Church's fourth expedition of the war, and this time he approached the matter differently. Throughout the spring and earlier summer Church travelled from New Hampshire to Connecticut recruiting men for the venture. He also recruited a large number of Bay Indians to man the whaleboats he had constructed for his force. In the past the major had been frustrated by his enemy discovering his movements before he was in a position to strike. By employing the whaleboats, he could have the major vessels carrying the expedition anchor out of sight, while his forces moved forward undetected. The boats would also give his war party the ability to navigate the inland waterways in search of his quarry, which would not only make his movements faster but offer the opportunity to strike with the element of surprise.

On August 22 Church and his four hundred men boarded three brigantines and set sail for Winter Harbor. The detachment found no enemy activity in the area, and after a fruitless ascent of the Penobscot River in search of a reputed Wabanaki village, Church was for attacking the rumored enemy fort at St. John. The ships' captains, however, were not so keen on the idea. They might well find a French warship or a privateer at St. John, and the brigantines were not sufficiently armed, being fitted out primarily as transports. Instead, a compromise was struck and the detachment set sail for Chignecto in Acadia. Here they burned and plundered several French villages and skirmished with French settlers.[17]

With their task in Chignecto complete, the expedition seems to have had a change of heart and set sail for St. John. The ships hid at a nearby island while Church and some of his men landed on the west bank of the St. John River. Fanning out into the woods the detachment advanced until they were opposite the old French fort on the east bank. From their vantage point they saw a dozen men at work erecting new fortifications. After monitoring the enemy's activities for a while Church withdrew. The next morning his entire force, including the transports, moved forward at sunrise and seized the partially completed fort. The surprise was near total, and most of the work crew scattered into the woods leaving Church with a single wounded prisoner. After being treated for his wounds, the French corporal proved of help by showing Church where the fort's heavy cannons were buried. There was some discussion of moving upstream and attacking Governor Villebon's Fort St. Joseph (near modern-day Fredericton, New Brunswick), but this was dismissed when it was revealed that the water level in the St. John River was currently too low for the boats. Satisfied with his take of twelve French cannons and a number of other stores, Church spent the next few days loading everything onto the boats for a return trip to Boston.

The detachment had barely put out to sea when they encountered the Royal Navy frigate *Arundel*, the *Province Galley*, and a small sloop. On board were a hundred men under the command of Lieutenant Colonel John Hathorne. Hathorne had orders from the governor placing Church and his men under his command for an attempt on the new fortifications at St. John and Fort St. Joseph farther upriver. With Church having dealt with Fort St. John, Hathorne ignored the low water levels and ordered the expedition up the St. John River.

By the morning of October 18 Hathorne's and Church's men were encamped on the south bank of the Nashwaak River within musket range of Fort St. Joseph. With the thirty-yard-wide ribbon of water between the two parties a brisk exchange commenced with the French side occasionally punctuating their effort with one of the fort's cannons that sent grapeshot tearing through the woods like a cloud of angry bees. The fort's fire, quite intense at times, still did not prevent the English from erecting a redoubt, and by nightfall a battery of three three-pound cannons had been raised on the south bank of the river.[18]

It was an uneasy night for the attackers as Villebon prevented them from lighting fires by directing volleys of grapeshot toward any sign of light. At daybreak the firing began again. Around eight o'clock the English brought their new battery into play, adding to the cacophony. One of the English cannons proved too exposed, and its crew were quickly chased away by musket fire. The other two guns required a more concerted effort on the part of the defenders, but within a few hours one had been dismounted and the other abandoned by the bombardment. The firing remained steady from both sides until nightfall. Shortly after sunset the English lit a large portion of the shore on fire, and as Villebon immediately suspected, withdrew down river. By October 21 it was over. Hathorne's troops had returned to their vessels and the fleet had put back out to sea for Boston. Fort St. Joseph had proven too difficult. The problem was, as Church had stated, the water level was unusually low for this time of year. This limited the approach toward the fort, particularly from the logistics side, but more importantly it limited what artillery could be brought before the structure. Had it been possible to carry a battery of 12-pounders upriver, the siege of Fort St. Joseph likely would have ended much differently.

1697 would prove to be another difficult year on the New England frontier. Starting with a major attack on Haverhill, Massachusetts, in March, almost a dozen French and Indian raids had killed, wounded, or captured over a hundred colonists, and with few exceptions the enemy had suffered little in the way of losses. When coupled with the panic set off by rumors of a French fleet in North American waters and its intent to burn Boston, it had been an unsettling time for New England. Fortunately, on December 10, good news arrived. A peace treaty had been signed at Ryswick. The war was over.[19]

Four

THE KING'S ENGINEER

In early 1697 a petition came before the British Ordnance Board for a military engineer to serve in North America. King William's War had clearly demonstrated the vulnerability of the New York and New England frontiers and the need for a professional engineer to rework these defenses into a coherent system. To fulfill this request the board, who managed England's artillery trains and engineers, selected a German-born engineer by the name of Wolfgang William Romer. There was little question in terms of Romer's qualifications. The fifty-seven-year-old colonel had served in a dozen campaigns and sieges on the Continent before coming to England in 1689 with the future king, William of Orange. Romer's senior standing quickly translated into an engineering warrant, and he spent the next two years campaigning in Ireland as part of William's efforts to subdue the Emerald Isle. In 1692 he was appointed chief engineer for Sir Martin Beckman's St. Helen's artillery train, destined to operate against the coast of France, and the following year he was named chief engineer of the ordnance train destined to operate in the Mediterranean under the command of Richard Coote, Lord Bellomont. Filling various posts over the next few years, by 1697 Romer was listed as extraordinary engineer, second only to the chief ordnance engineer Sir Martin Beckman, but oddly, with a significantly higher salary than his superior.[1]

Now carrying a warrant as chief engineer for North America, Romer accompanied the newly appointed governor of New York and New England, Lord Bellomont, to the colonies in 1698. The two had worked together in the past, and Bellomont clearly held a high opinion of the engineer's talents. Shortly after their arrival Bellomont directed Romer to conduct a survey of the fortifications of New York, starting with those of the Upper Hudson Valley. Pleased with the engineer's report and his suggested corrective actions, the following spring he dispatched Romer to view the fortifications on Castle Island in Boston Harbor. From there he was to travel to the Piscataqua River in New Hampshire and Pemaquid on the coast of Maine to "take the plans of all three forts and make such observations as will be proper of their scituations, importance and what the charge may be of building good substantial forts."[2]

In June 1699 Romer submitted a brief report on Castle Island to the governor. The fort at the location was clearly in need of a major overhaul, and to this end the engineer had already begun drawing out new works to strengthen the location, but in his opinion,

> Although the whole Castle Island were made one entire fortification and in condition to defend itself against a year's siege, as according to the new design it might, yet this could only serve the inhabitants of Boston and neighbourhood to secure their riches, but could not hinder but that an enemy might blockade and commit all manner of outrages even to bombarding, except the coming in at the passages from the sea be secured, and by that means an enemy be forced to stand off to sea.[3]

What was ultimately required was to prevent an enemy fleet from establishing itself in Nantasket Harbor from where they could assert control over the surrounding islands, land troops at their leisure, and block access to any fleet looking to relieve the town. To prevent this Romer submitted a plan which not only called for the reconstruction of the fort but for the establishment of a pair of fifty-gun batteries positioned on points of land "regulated so that they may make good defence in front, flank and rear."[4]

With this first task accomplished Romer travelled to Fort William and Mary at the mouth of the Piscataqua River along the coast of New Hampshire. Here he spent the better part of July examining the

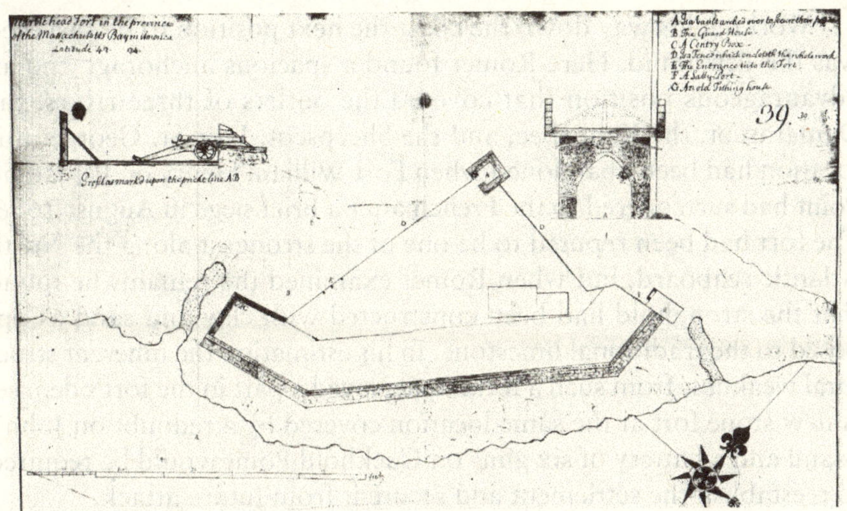

A 1705 plan of the battery at Marblehead. This was one of several small fortifications that Wolfgang Romer inspected on the Massachusetts coast. (*The Crown Collection of Photographs of American Maps, III, plate 191-192*)

fort and a number of islands that dotted the mouth of the river. He found the fort itself, located on Newcastle Island (Great Island), positioned correctly but in its present condition "uncapeable of defending the entrance into that noble & important River not being sufficient to endure three or four days attack of an Enemy." The engineer laid out a set of plans for a new fort, but to ensure the safety of the harbor and the nearby town of Newcastle, he concluded that Clarke Island to the east and Wood Island to the west should both be armed with a battery of cannons while a stone fortification in the form of a tower should be placed at the point of nearby Fryer's Island.[5]

By late August Romer was on his way to examine Casco Bay, Pemaquid, and the mouth of the St. George River to determine the nature of these harbors and what would be required to fortify these important locations. The voyage took nearly two months and was one of the most extensive the engineer would make in North America. He started with the outlet of the St. George River, deserted since King William's War and at that time the boundary between Maine and New France. The entrance to the river was tricky enough that, in his opinion, a simple redoubt holding a battery of guns located at the neck of what he called Bellomont Bay would suffice to guard the river.

Working his way down the coast the next position to be surveyed was the Pemaquid. Here Romer found a spacious anchorage and an advantageous position that covered the outlets of three rivers, the Damarascot, the Kennebec, and the Sheepscot. Like St. George, this location had been abandoned when Fort William Henry on Pemaquid Point had surrendered to the French after a brief siege in August 1696. The fort had been reputed to be one of the strongest along the North Atlantic seaboard, but when Romer examined the remains he found that the stronghold had been constructed with clay and sand as opposed to the traditional limestone. In his estimation the inherent structural weakness from such a technique played a part in the fort's demise. A new stone fort at the same location covered by a redoubt on John's Island and a battery of six guns on Cuckhold Point would be required to reestablish the settlement and secure it from future attack.

Romer's next stop was the Kennebec River. There was an excellent anchorage at this location, and the river was navigable for miles into the interior. Like the other settlements along the Maine coast, this one had also been abandoned during the last war. The engineer examined the ruins of two palisade forts, one on Damaras Island and another upriver at the deserted hamlet of Newtown, and concluded that a new fort would be required at Newtown, and at a minimum, a redoubt was required on Sagadahock Island to guard the entrance to the river.

"I find Casco Bay the noblest, as I do the country about it the fertilest that's in all New England," Romer wrote of his next stop a dozen or so miles down the coast. He was particularly careful in his sounding of the bay and seemed to delight at the multitude of small islands that dotted it, repeating the colonial tale that there were as many of these as days of the year. As with the previous locations the fort here had been destroyed in the last conflict. It amazed the engineer that such a badly placed, poorly built, and ill-kept wooden structure could inspire the confidence to build the nearby town of Falmouth, which, like the fort, now lay in ruins. "'Tis great pity that so fine a country should be deserted," he concluded. From Casco Bay he stopped at Winter Harbor on the Saco River and then made a brief visit to the villages of Wells and York before returning to Boston in late October.[6]

Romer would spend the next year meeting with the Iroquois and working on the defenses of New York, but talk of war between England and France was to make him an extremely busy man. A week after Bellomont's death on March 5, 1701, he was ordered to inven-

A portion of a 1770s map showing the location of Newcastle, New Hampshire, Kittery, Maine, and Fort William and Mary at the entrance to Piscataqua Harbor. While Romer called for an armed stone tower across the channel from the fort on what was known as Fryer's Island at the time, and a battery of guns on Wood and Clarke Islands, as for the positioning of Fort William and Mary he would later write, "No place I have seen in my Travails being naturally better scituated & more suitable for defence." (*William L. Clements Library, University of Michigan*)

tory the stores of Fort William Henry in New York City. This was barely completed when he left for Boston to start work on the new fortifications on Castle Island. The task was to prove particularly trying for the engineer. Much of this stemmed from the major technical challenges, the time table imposed by the threat of war, and a myriad of logistical issues confounded by unfamiliar colonial practices. But just as much, if not more, of his frustrations seem to have come from his interactions with those around him. Of particular annoyance was the new commander of Fort William, Captain Elisha Hutchinson who, Romer complained to the Massachusetts Council, was obstructing his efforts.

> I am of the Opinion, that Work will Suffer very considerably, unless it be managed according to reason, & I may have full power to command all those w^h are imployed in that work. Nor do I expect that Coll Hutchinson as Capt^ne of s^d Castle, should have ye least power to contradict me in my business there, as I do not pretend to have any thing to do with those w^h are under his immediate Command.[7]

The engineer, who had served in sieges alongside King William, was not in the practice of taking commands from colonial captains, nor from amateurs in the field of military fortifications. He demanded that the council immediately resolve this issue,

> Otherwise I shall not continue any longer on s^d Work, nor answer for it; but be obliged after I have publickly aquitted my self of all ye damage wch may happen thereunto, to take my leave thereof. For I am unwilling to submit my self to ye directions of raw & unexperienced people, w^h many of them pretend to be my friends, but hate me in their hearts, as I have found by grievous experience during my Slaving & toyling in s^d Work.[8]

Apparently Romer's coarse German tongue, fueled by his frustration, had also led to a number of other complaints. Samuel Sewell, a member of the Massachusetts Council, went down to the fort in an attempt to diffuse the situation. A sympathetic Sewell spoke with the offended workers on the subject, informing them that the council had not ignored their grievances but that, for the moment, they should focus not on the engineer's cursing but on his directions. The problems between Hutchinson and Romer persisting, the entire council visited the fort the following month where an agreement was reached giving the engineer direct control of the resources assigned to him, along with basic military judicial powers.[9]

By fall Romer found himself pulled in several directions at once. In addition to the work on Castle William the town of Salem required his services to rework the dilapidated fort that covered the town, while those of Marblehead, Gloucester, Plymouth, and Hull wished to have the engineer examine their old works as well. At the same time Lieutenant Governor John Nanfan, who had temporarily succeeded Bellomont, sent request after request for Romer to report to

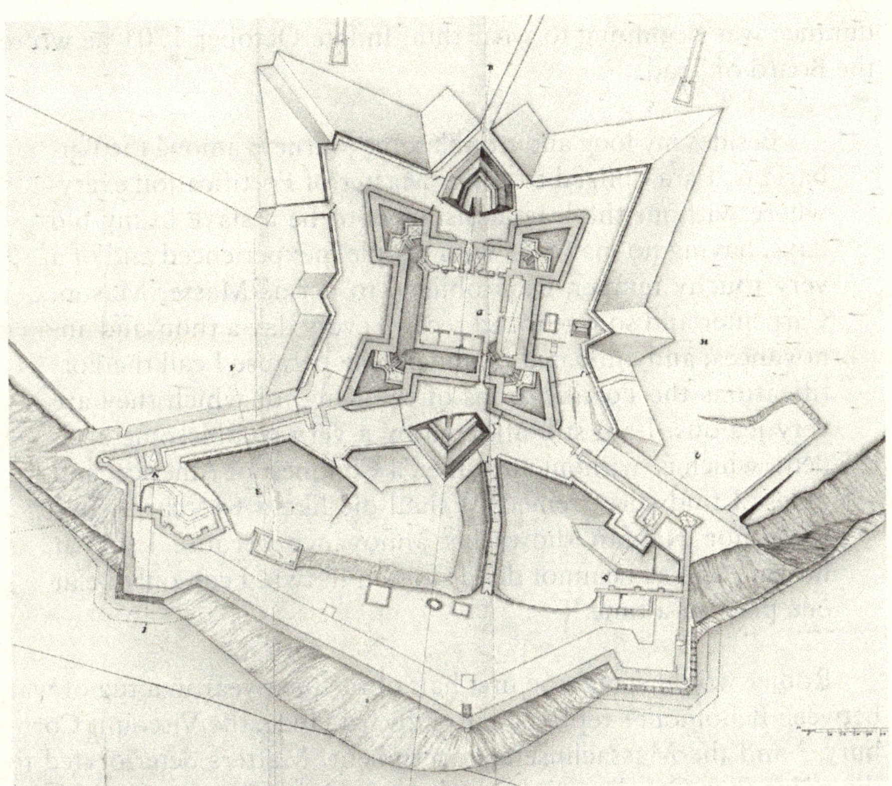

A plan of Castle William, 1705. The fortress took Romer nearly five years to complete, but when it was finished it guarded the entrance to Boston for nearly a century. (*Norman B. Leventhal Map Collection, Boston Public Library*)

Albany to begin work on the new forts along the New York frontier. The Massachusetts Council, however, insisted that the engineer could not leave at this critical point, to which Romer, realizing that there was no one to whom he could hand the project over, concurred. Letters had also arrived from the Board of Trade notifying him of Bellomont's replacement, Edward Hyde, Lord Cornbury, and requesting that he meet Cornbury in New York upon the latter's arrival to brief him on the status of the colony's defenses. With this also came depressing news that his stay in America would be extended indefinitely, or at least until Cornbury no longer required his services.[10]

With little in the way of help, save his twenty-one-year-old son, John, whom he had brought over from England to teach him his trade, and suffering from a hernia he had developed during his travels on the New York frontier, the old colonel's temperament and endurance was beginning to wear thin. In late October 1701 he wrote the Board of Trade,

> Besides my long and troublesome journeys among the Barbarians, I am obliged to act as Master of Fortification everywhere without the least assistance, to be a slave in my old days, having no manager, with people inexperienced and of a very touchy temper, I am obliged to act as Master-Mason, Carpenter and so forth, and receive every day a thousand annoyances, and am hated by the people because I call the Fortifications the Fortifications of the King, of which they are very jealous. I am still afflicted by a very troublesome accident, which is, without any other, a Conquest of America, and unless I find some remedy, I shall die like a wretch. Lieut.-Governor Nanfan shows his annoyance because I am at Boston, and as I cannot divide myself in two, I can only be at one place at a time.[11]

Romer would spend the first half of the next year in a tug of war between Bellomont's replacement, Edward Hyde, the Viscount Cornbury,[12] and the Massachusetts government. Matters deteriorated to the point that Cornbury informed the engineer that he would have him arrested if he did not report to Albany to continue work on the fort there. He then audited the engineer's accounts and found a trifling discrepancy for which he demanded immediate repayment. Fortunately for the engineer, he was to have few dealings with Cornbury in the future, primarily because, in late 1702, orders came from Whitehall directing the governments of Massachusetts and New Hampshire to raise the fortifications Romer had recommended at Pemaquid and at Fort William and Mary. With the outbreak of war between France and England the fortifications at both sites, and the repair of those along the Massachusetts coast, had taken on a higher priority.[13]

Romer spent the first half of 1703 finishing the works on Castle Island. Although the effort was projected to have been completed by midsummer a number of items, such as the fort's barracks, guard rooms, and the gun platforms, delayed the completion. By September the efforts on Castle Island had progressed to the point that the new governor of Massachusetts and New Hampshire, Joseph Dudley, was able to dispatch Romer to Casco Bay with orders to raise a fort there capable of taking a garrison of five hundred men. Romer first stopped at Salem and Marblehead, and after doing what he could for these fortifications he proceeded on to Casco. The efforts at Casco Bay did not take the engineer long, and by the end of the month the governor was happy to report that a new palisade fort, complete with bastions, had been erected on the site fit for six hundred men. The trip, however, took its toll on the engineer, and not long after he reported to New Hampshire to begin work on Fort William and Mary he contracted a "distemper," which, combined with his previous untreated ailments, greatly slowed his routine.[14]

After a winter's interlude, the status of Fort William and Mary was reviewed, and with the spring thaws work started once again on the structure. Romer pushed hard to complete the modifications to the structure, and as with his efforts at Boston, he soon found himself at odds with his colonial workforce. In June the lieutenant governor and commandant of the fort, John Usher, attempted to remedy this problem by reminding the New Hampshire Council of the importance of the task and their obligation to support Colonel Romer who "has constantly been at the Fort from morning to night to put the same in a defensive posture." The plea initially yielded positive results, and by mid-July Dudley reported that the project was progressing well under Romer's hand, although the engineer was clearly "uneasy with a difficult and poor people." Whatever burst of momentum that was gained, however, had fizzled away by September. In the middle of that month Romer sent a letter to the New Hampshire Council pleading with them to forward the supplies and the laborers he had requested. But in what was a growing problem the engineer pointed out that just sending men was not enough. What was needed were individuals "that understand workmanship" and would do their duty with the zeal he had shown toward his own work. Too often the laborers assigned to the project would not do what was required of them, and when the engineer pressed them on the point, they displayed a "Rude and Unmanerly behavior," toward him.

This lack of discipline and Romer's limited authority over his workforce clearly frustrated the colonel and, from his perspective, threatened the entire project. Part of the problem was that much of the labor force working on the fort was impressed. Such men, paid nothing for their effort, showed little inclination toward discipline or the task at hand, typically looking only to finish out their time in the most minimal fashion possible. Those individuals with the skills Romer was looking for demanded a high wage for their efforts, and because of

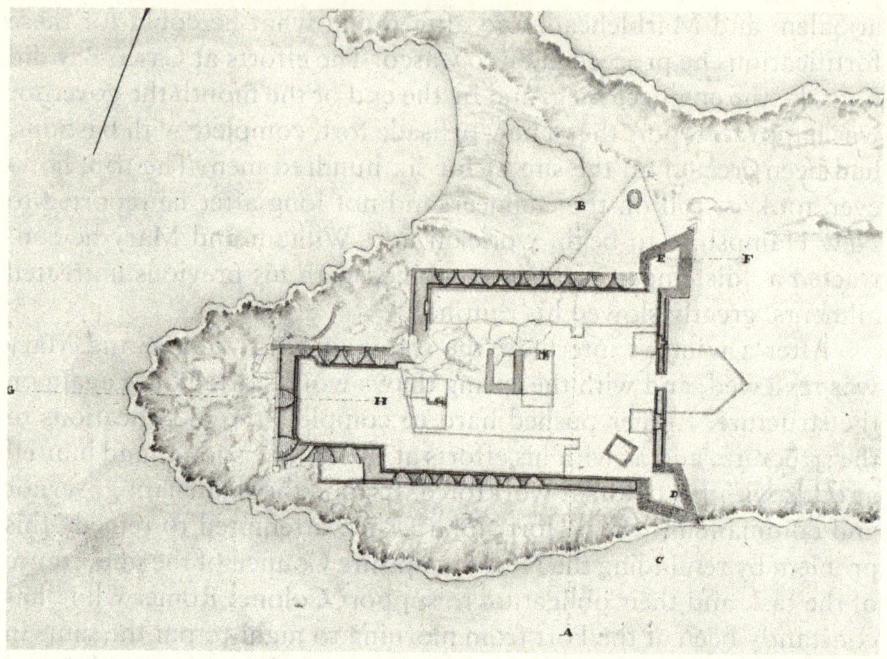

Fort William and Mary on Newcastle Island, c. 1705. Note the cannon firing ports in the fort's walls. The lighter traces were Romer's recommended changes to the structure. (*Norman B. Leventhal Map Collection, Boston Public Library*)

their skills they typically possessed the means to pay their way out of impressed service. Missing the point, the New Hampshire Council responded to Romer's plea by ordering the provincial sherriff to impress the number of laborers Romer had requested. As might be expected, this failed to solve the issue, and with the severity of winter soon at hand, work on the fortification was suspended for the year.

With the stoppage Romer turned toward administrative matters, compiling a list of the guns and ordnance required for the posts from Boston to Casco Bay, which totaled some fifty-nine cannons of various calibers. To go with these, he also requested that a pair of master gunners be sent over from England, one to be stationed at Castle William and the other at Fort William and Mary. The remainder of his time was spent redrawing prints that had been lost while crossing the North Atlantic.[15]

Farther south, along the coasts of Rhode Island and Connecticut, blockhouses or redoubts for a few small guns were erected to protect the local harbors. These crude fortifications were designed to discour-

A profile of one of the fort's walls showing the structure's earth and stone construction. (*Norman B. Leventhal Map Collection, Boston Public Library*)

age raids by privateers and seldom mounted a cannon larger than a 6-pounder. Assisted by a good watch, a ready militia, and the maritime resources in the harbor, which in times of conflict would typically include a few armed privateers, this approach was pursued by many communities. New London was a good example. As early as 1680 the idea of fortifications for this seaport had been brought before the Board of Trade in London. "The harbor lyeth league up the (Thames) river, where the town is," the governor wrote in response to a query from the board.

> Ships of great burden may come up to the town, and lye secure in any winds; where is great need of fortification, but we want estate to make fortification and purchase artillery for it, and we should thankfully acknowledge the favor of any benefactors, that would contribute towards the doing of something towards the good work.[16]

While aid from England was not forthcoming after four French privateers briefly bombarded the harbor in late July 1690 and raided nearby Fisher's Island, the colony took it upon itself to act. The following year an earth redoubt holding a battery of half-a-dozen six- and four-pound cannons was raised to cover the harbor. This position would soon decay after King William's War only to be revived during Queen Anne's War and then left to fall into ruin once again after news of the Treaty of Utrecht arrived in the colony. The matter would not be seriously addressed again until 1739 when rumors of war between Spain and Britian began to circulate in the colony. By now the harbor was essentially defenseless against a sudden attack. A petition by the citizens of the town on January 7, 1740, noted that, "There is no fort erect'd in any port of Haven upon all the Sea Coast thro out this Colony, nor a vessel of force to Guard ye Same." As to New London itself, the document made clear that the "weak & undefenced State & Condition of the Town & port afors'd Renders us Easie Prey to the violence & Invasion of our Enemies & will in all Reasonable Construction Invite their attempts against us." In response to this request, the old battery at the eastern end of the harbor was ordered to be rebuilt and furnished with cannons. A second battery would also be raised at the head of the harbor to catch any intruder in a crossfire. While this work occurred it does not seem to have been executed in the spirit first put forward, given that when King George's War started there were only three small guns in the eastern battery, which one witness referred to as "signal guns" due to their diminutive size, and four more in an earth battery set up in the town. While the aid sought from Britian never materialized, much to the delight of the town's citizens neither did an attack during King George's War or the French and Indian War that followed.[17]

Newport, Rhode Island, which would soon establish itself as one of the central hubs of American privateering, was more proactive and built an earth fort on nearby Goat Island in 1702 to cover the anchorage to the east. Named after Queen Anne, the fort was to have mounted a dozen cannons, but one witness claimed a few years after its construction that there were fifteen cannons in the fort, 9- and 6-pounders. Work moved slowly with monies being appropriated in 1705 to finish the structure, but when completed, whatever its failings, it still made Newport one of the better defended New England ports. While Queen Anne's War continued a reasonable garrison was keep at the fort, which provided the manpower to deal with the main-

A portion of a 1711 map of New England showing Narragansett Bay from Newport to Providence. (*Norman B. Leventhal Map Collection, Boston Public Library*)

tenance of the structure. However, with the Treaty of Utrecht in 1713, this garrison was reduced to a handful of caretakers, and by the spring of 1721 the fort was in desperate need of repairs. The agreement was to rebuild the structure in stone, but funding and progress was slow, and as late as June 1731 one officer at the fort reported that, "We are now at work constantly upon the fort wall, with about five or six hands, and hope to have the wall up this summer." This same officer then explained part of the delay. "We find it very difficult to get stones, which makes us go on slowly."[18]

In 1727 the colony turned its attention to the fort's armament. The current dozen or so cannons on hand from the previous structure were temporarily mounted, but they were too old and too small to deter an adversary looking to force its way into the roadstead. To address this shortfall the colony petitioned London for twenty heavy cannons to arm the fort. With peace reigning in North America and Europe between the Spanish, British, and French this matter was not addressed, although the colony made several attempts through their London agent, Richard Partridge, to convince the Board of Trade otherwise. Finally, having received no assistance in this area from London and with Fort George nearing completion, in the spring of 1735 the colony authorized Partridge to purchase smaller cannons on the open market. In this task Partridge was aided by the fact that the general peace meant that the cannon foundries could quickly fulfill the order for twenty-four twelve- and six-pound guns. After chartering transports, Partridge forwarded these on to Newport.

With the outbreak of the War of Jenkin's Ear in 1739, a garrison of fifty-three men was thrown into Fort George, and two years later the fort was expanded to take on an additional ten guns and a newly constructed circular brick powder magazine. The matter of heavy cannons for the fort would appear again before the Board of Trade, but it was not until the fall of 1744 that an attempt was made to address the problem. Partridge once again requested twenty heavy cannons for Fort George, pointing out that a new stone fort that the colony had built with £10,000 of its own money would mean nothing without a battery of heavy cannons. When the Board of Trade contacted the master of the ordnance regarding the desired artillery, they discovered that the ordnance department had never supplied the colony with cannons or "Military Stores of any kind whatsoever." This was enough for the board to recommend that the requested twenty-four-pound and eighteen-pound cannons be sent along with an ample supply of shot and artillery stores.

It seemed the cannons would soon be on their way, but the ordnance department pointed out that they did not have a plan or profile of the fort by which to judge what would be necessary to properly defend the structure. This, in turn, led the board to request a plan of the fort before the matter proceeded any further. This issue was eventually resolved, but it was not until early 1746 before the heavy guns reached the fort. That fall, in response to rumors of a large French fleet operating off the Atlantic coast, there was discussion about erect-

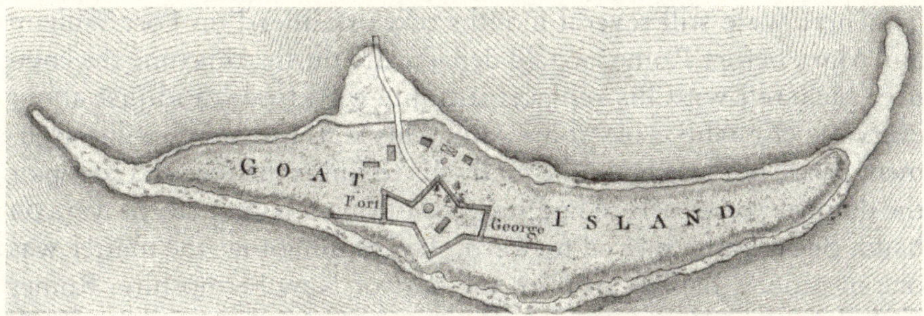

A 1777 sketch of Goat Island and Fort George. Located at the western end of Newport Harbor, the fort was briefly renamed Fort Liberty in the opening years of the American Revolution, before being captured by the British and returned to its former title. Note that north is to the left in this image. (*Norman B. Leventhal Map Collection, Boston Public Library*)

ing another battery of guns on Goat Island, but many opposed the effort. The current fort, armed with a powerful combination of twenty-five 24-pounders and twelve 18-pounders, was more than enough to repel privateers, and another six-gun battery located nearby would make little difference if an enemy fleet appeared. In addition, by this point in the conflict Newport was a central point for privateers, meaning that there was always a sizable number in harbor that would add to the port's defense. In either case it did not matter, as like New London, no serious attack ever materialized against the port.[19]

If Colonel Romer had been given orders to survey the vulnerable Connecticut and Rhode Island coastline certainly more clarity would have been brought to resolving its defensive issues, but as it was the colonel's time in North America was coming to an end. The Board of Ordnance sent a letter dated August 8, 1704, informing Governors Cornbury and Dudley that the engineer's replacement, Captain John Redknap, would be dispatched as soon as arrangements could be made for his departure. In March 1705 Captain Redknap arrived along with Romer's orders to return to England. This was perhaps for the best, as the old campaigner's patience, fractured by the colonial environment and his nagging ailments, was reaching a breaking point. "My pen is not able to expres the calamityes and contempts I have suffered and do still suffer," a grateful Romer wrote the Board of Trade upon receiving news of his recall, and in something of a summation of his relations with his colonial employers he added, "I wish Capt. Redknap may be happyer and meet with better treatment in advancing our Great Queen's service."[20]

There were still several months of work ahead on Fort William and Mary before Romer would depart, and during this time the engineer bickered with his replacement, his workforce, and just about everyone else who crossed his path. This is not to say that his arguments were not justified. The materials to finish the fort and to repair the damage the structure had suffered during a winter storm were on hand, but nothing moved forward. Ascertaining that the matter was one of money, or lack of it on the part of New Hampshire, Romer took the extraordinary step of offering to pay for the remaining work out of his own pocket. Having received no reply to two of these offers the colonel launched a tempest upon Governor Dudley in early June regarding the current arrangements, the work still to be performed to make the fort defensible, and Captain Redknap's new control and apparent lack of concern over the state of the fortifications. Clearly wanting to finish what he had started, Romer again offered to pay for the remaining work, writing Dudley that,

> I thincke yor Excellecy could not have a better opportunity as now before you, to finishe ; and yor Excell^{cy} must be sensible of it, considering that in this joncture it is of the higest necessity, to secure that place by the chevaux de frise ag^{t} surprise: item, ye ravelin before the gate & couvering of ye same, & by that means to macke a good correspondency for a relieff, if occasion should offer ; & lyckwyse the brustwork of ye whole poligon towards the neck, together with ye centry boxes & the settling of all that belongs to ye preservation of ye well, soe that a high flood mae not corrupt ye same in tyme to come, is at present all of the greatest necessity & my duty soe to lay before yor Excell^{cy}. [21]

Had Romer left it with this sound argument he might have made a better impression on the governor, but instead he continued on, pointing out how he had endured numerous and unjust difficulties in the service of his task, how in doing so he had submitted to "slavish service in obeiing & submitting to yor Excell^{cys} orders & commands," and how he did not deserve "suche hard indurations as no notice taken of my proposals." In the end, he informed the governor, if his offer were rejected, "then I shall leave Capt Redknap in his good oppinion, & in a more weiser & better conduct to his quietnes, & shall be glad to see that hee (according to his oppinion) can & mae do better service then I have donne."[22]

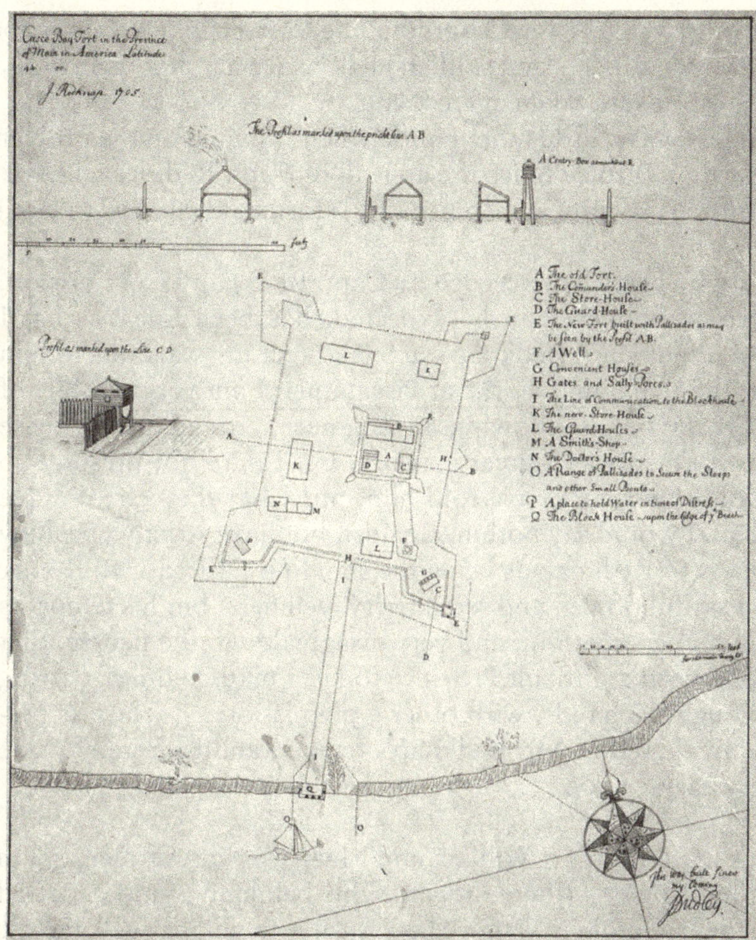

Fort Casco designed and built by Wolfgang Romer around the original fort in the fall of 1703. Like many of Romer's works the drawings have been redone by Captain John Redknap and/or have Governor Dudley's name attached. This is because the original sets were either lost in transmission to England, or were thrown overboard by Romer when he was captured on his return voyage to England. (*The Crown Collection of Photographs of American Maps, III, plate 167*)

Dudley was taken aback by the tone of the letter and, after commenting on Romer's "huffing all mankind in these Provinces," made it clear that at the moment the monies required were not available and that per the directives of the Ordnance Board, and Romer's own wishes, Captain Redknap was now in charge. He then pointed to a long-standing problem with the engineer. "I will now tell you plainly that your angry & harsh treatment of every body these three years since my arrivall (the Ln[t] Governour, the Councellors & Comissioners of the Works, officers and soldiers) has been such that there is an universall displeasure taken against you."[23]

Dudley was a little more politic when bringing up the problem to the Board of Trade. "Since the arrivall of Capt. Redknap, I have had some difficulty with Col. Romer," he informed the board in late July,

> who being superceeded by Capt. Redknap's Commission, perhaps sooner than he expected, has been uneasy, that I would not since Redknap's arrival direct my warrants to him for the remaining works at Piscataqua. I am very sensible of H.M. favour in allowing an Engineer's attendance in these Governments at a great expence, but I dare not presume to imploy two, as I have told him, but what they could agree upon, I would say nothing against, but have strictly given my orders to Redknap as being the standing Officer. Col. Romer is a skilful officer, and served very well here, but his temper is harsh and superiour, and very disagreable to the people, that it has been a difficult Province to keep matters quiet, passing through his hands, with other Commissioners, which is perfectly altered in Mr. Redknap's temper, and is thereby made very easy.[24]

The matter of Fort William and Mary would resurface, but in the meantime Romer gathered together his belongings and departed for England in October 1705. The return trip might well have been thought an extension of the engineer's previous frustrations. A few weeks out he was forced to throw six years' worth of his papers overboard when his ship was taken by a pair of French frigates that eventually carried him to St. Malo. He was soon released on his parole and returned to England in order to negotiate his exchange. It would seem Romer's talents were thought highly enough of that the standard offer of twenty seamen for a colonel was turned down by the French commissioner. The English government agreed and offered General Marquis de Levy, or naval captain Chevalier Nangis to complete the transaction. Although it is unclear which of the two choices were ultimately accepted, Romer was officially exchanged in 1708.[25]

Five

QUEEN ANNE'S WAR

It would not be for almost a year after news arrived of Queen Anne's War, as the War of Spanish Succession was known in North America, that hostilities broke out on the Maine and New Hampshire frontiers. The renewal of the peace treaty between New England and the Wabanaki Confederacy in the summer of 1703 worried the governor of New France, Philippe Vaudreuil, the Marquis de Vaudreuil. What the marquis feared was that the Wabanaki dependency on cheaper and more plentiful British trade goods would only increase the ties between the two. Believing that such a scenario would threaten French holdings in Acadia, Vaudreuil pushed the Wabanaki toward war. It did not take much. Fiery orations by Jesuit Father Sébastien Rale, one of several missionaries to the Wabanaki, pointed out that many of the old animosities remained unresolved and that the colonial towns expelled from the coast during King William's War had returned. Backed by speeches from chieftains from the Abenaki missions in Canada, and the words of Lieutenant Alexandre Leneuf de Beaubassin of the colonial marines, who Vaudreuil had sent to the region to organize an attack, the tide quickly shifted to striking at the English.

The planned assault would fall upon the Maine frontier from Wells in the south, to Falmouth in the north. When Beaubassin tallied his forces, he found himself with close to five hundred Wabanaki and a score of French at his disposal. The numbers and element of surprise gave Beaubassin and the Wabanaki sagamores an opportunity to launch a coordinated blow against the English settlements by breaking into smaller parties for simultaneous attacks along the frontier. With the plan agreed upon, by the first week of August war parties began to trace their way through the dapple-lit forests of Maine toward the coast.

On the morning of August 10 war parties struck at Wells, Cape Elizabeth, Purpooduck, and Cape Porpoise with devastating effect. They would also strike at Saco but showed no interest in challenging the fort there, or at Winter Harbor where the inhabitants had managed to reach the wooden Fort Mary and from there hold off the attackers. Smaller hamlets and isolated homesteads were also attacked. In general, the assault had proven highly successful, but one important element still remained, an attack on Casco. The old fort at this location had been destroyed early in King William's War and after the conflict was replaced with a wooden palisade known as Fort Casco. This structure operated as a trading post and a place of refuge for the citizens who had returned to the town. Here the Wabanaki opted for deception rather than ambush. The fort's commander, Major John March, and his garrison of three dozen had been on alert when a runner notified him that three chieftains carrying a white flag were outside the main gate. Standing on the fort's parapet March recognized the three chieftains as Moxus, Wanongonet, and Escumbuit. At first the commander considered sending an envoy out to meet them, but the trio appeared unarmed, and there were no signs of any war party, so he went out to speak with them accompanied by a pair of guards and two elderly citizens of the town by the names of Phippenny and Kent.

The sentries in the guard towers and along the fort's walls watched as the main gate opened and March's party approached the Wabanaki chiefs. The major and his men had just come to a stop and saluted the trio when the sagamores produced tomahawks from under their clothing and attacked the Englishmen. Unarmed and unprepared, both the elderly Phippenny and Kent fell to a few quick blows, but the attackers did not find March as easy a target. A large man noted for his great strength, the major disarmed one of the chieftains and kept the trio at bay with his newly acquired tomahawk. One of March's guards tried to come to his aid, but a shot rang out from a nearby ambuscade striking him down.

The unequal contest soon broke up as the Wabanaki retreated at the sight of a squad of soldiers rushing through the main gate toward them. The garrison's quick actions had saved their commander, and now together they manned their posts and braced for the coming storm. However, the French and Indian war party showed little interest other than occasionally sniping at the fort. The nearby town was ransacked and burned, but no serious effort was made to challenge the stronghold. Over the next few days March understood why. Bands of French and Wabanaki began converging on the location. Finally, Beaubassin appeared, bringing the besiegers' numbers to five hundred or so.[1]

The French lieutenant also brought direction and energy to the siege. The harassing fire on the fort was increased, and a captured sloop and a pair of shallops now fired on the water side of the fort. More importantly, a sandy bank along the water side approached close to one of the fort's walls. Using this embankment as shelter, Beaubassin set crews to work digging trenches toward the wall. Progress was slow, but after two days the attackers were almost close enough to storm the fort from their sap.

For March there were few options. His garrison was exhausted after being under fire six days and nights, his supplies were failing, and there was nothing he could do to stop the French fieldwork from advancing. If relief did not come in a day, or maybe two, he would be forced to surrender the fort or face annihilation. March and his garrison would not have to wait long for an answer. The following morning a vessel could be seen entering Casco Bay. The sight caused all to pause, and the firing slackened as eyes focused on the distant sail. Speculative whispers and occasional pointing continued until the fifty-foot ketch entered the Casco River and approached the fort. Any doubt was soon dispensed by a thunderous cheer from the ramparts and a groan from Beaubassin.

With the flag of St. George flying from the main mast the commander of the Massachusetts warship *Province Galley*, Captain Cyprian Southack, ordered his gunners to their posts and shifted course to make a pass on the captured French sloop and shallops. The Wabanaki watched, contenting themselves with a few long-range shots at the warship, when suddenly, five columns of blue smoke rippled down the side of the ship. A wave of grapeshot and ball quickly convinced those onboard the captured vessels to abandon ownership, but Southack was hardly finished. He next turned his attention to the hundreds of canoes that lined the shore. Round after round of grapeshot ripped through the fragile craft and served as a deterrent to anyone foolish enough to risk trying to save the flotilla. Beaubassin watched, kicking at the ground and shaking his head as the cannons onboard the *Province Galley* slowly asserted control over the area. It was over. With the French works exposed to the warship's guns, and his supplies dwindling, Beaubassin called off the siege. The next day the French and Wabanaki departed, most on foot, as some two hundred of their canoes had been destroyed.[2]

The timely relief of Fort Casco was one of the few things to go right for the denizens of the Maine frontier. Seven other towns had been attacked and close to 175 settlers had been taken or killed. Scores of homes had been burned and most of the livestock slain. Relief would come but too late in most cases. Columns of smoke and shattered refugees were all to be found. Apart from Fort Casco, the French and Indian attack had gone as planned. There had been little in the way of casualties among the raiders, and the results of their efforts were clear; the Maine frontier was in shambles, and Governor Vaudreuil now had his war.[3]

For the next six months French and Indian war parties raided the Maine, New Hampshire, and Massachusetts frontiers. There was little the New England colonies could do. Patrols were sent out and garrisons in the small towns and hamlets increased, but it did little to stop the onslaught. Rumors soon arrived of a raid on Newcastle, New Hampshire, and an attempt to seize Fort William and Mary in the spring of 1704. These fears soon disappeared as a colonial force under Colonel Church began gathering at Newcastle. With the influx of these troops and a pair of frigates anchored in the harbor there was little to worry about in terms of French and Indian raiders. Church was to look for enemy forces along the Maine coast before turning his attention on French Acadia. With several troop transports carrying 550 men and three warships, the 14-gun *Province Galley*, and a pair of Royal Navy frigates, the 32-gun H.M.S. *Gosport* and the 48-gun H.M.S. *Jersey* acting as escorts, Church had a force of close to two thousand men. With such a powerful detachment at his disposal he wanted to besiege Port Royal, but Governor Dudley made it clear that without explicit orders from London, an attack on Port Royal was off limits. It would prove to be a missed opportunity.[4]

Church and his 550 volunteers arrayed in a flotilla of whaleboats departed Newcastle in early June, and after a few weeks of minor op-

The McIntire garrison house in South Berwick, Maine. This Queen Anne's War structure was common among many of the towns of New England. These local strongholds acted as a place of refuge against French and Indian raids, and were designed with an overhanging top floor to allow the defenders to fire down along the length of the building's walls. It would not be uncommon to see a gated wooden palisade erected around the structure. (*Library of Congress*)

erations that resulted in nothing but a few French captives, they set course for Port Royal where the detachment's three warships had been ordered to rendezvous with them. When Church and his men arrived in the basin before the fort they marveled at the tall British warships bristling with heavy cannons and could not imagine how the small low-lying French fort on the eastern end of the waterway could survive a bombardment by these vessels.

When this force arrived on June 22 Governor Brouillan, in command of the French fort, called out the militia and sent a pair of emissaries to the English to ascertain their intentions as well as stall for time. Additional detachments were sent out to monitor any English landing and to dispatch a warning if this were to occur. Trenches were dug by the garrison and several small cannons placed to discourage an approach on the fort, but the stronghold was ill-prepared to handle a siege, and none of the militia Brouillan had called out had yet appeared. Fortunately for the governor, there would be no siege. Church knew that his orders did not allow for an attack, and he did not press the point. The old colonel berated the French envoys and threatened to turn the fort's garrison and nearby town over to his Indians once he seized it. He then warned them that their raids on the New England frontier would not go unchallenged. If they did not stop, he would return with a thousand men and burn down the entire colony.[5]

Brouillan dismissed the rhetoric and waited for an attack while his troops, a few hundred with the militia that had responded, continued their fieldworks and filled sandbags. On the evening of July 4 Church and his council of war met and concluded that, regardless of the colonel's orders, with the addition of the local militia the fort was too strong to attempt without siege guns. Church would spend a few more days in the basin launching small raids on the nearby French settlements. By this point in the siege Brouillan's troops were so weary that he had to stop work on the fortifications. "If in that time the enemy had pressed him closely," a French witness noted, "he would have been very embarrassed, it not being possible that people who are 15 days without sleep and working all day are well able to make war." Instead, on the morning of July 7, Brouillan and his officers watched in disbelief as the English fleet raised anchor and departed into the Bay of Fundy. Church would launch a few more minor raids on the Maine coast during the return voyage, but by mid-July he was back in Boston.

Dudley would be severely criticized for the restrictions he placed on the expedition, but more importantly the effort did nothing to slow the attacks on the New England frontier. Fortunately, Dudley had managed to negotiate a prisoner exchange and a ceasefire with Governor Vaudreuil in the spring of 1705, which, temporarily at least, stemmed the flow of raiders. The ceasefire, however, was a local arrangement between the two colonies and did not lessen the possibility of a French naval attack against New York City, Boston, or a major New England port. With Colonel Romer's departure, responsibility for the fortifications of these strategic locations fell on his replacement, Captain John Redknap. While Governor Dudley may have been relieved to see the irritable Romer depart, there would come a point where he would regret the loss of such an experienced engineer, especially one who had conducted over twenty sieges.

Redknap's first order of business was to take over work on Fort William and Mary. In early June 1705, Governor Dudley ordered the engineer to repair the fort's barracks and a pair of angles that had

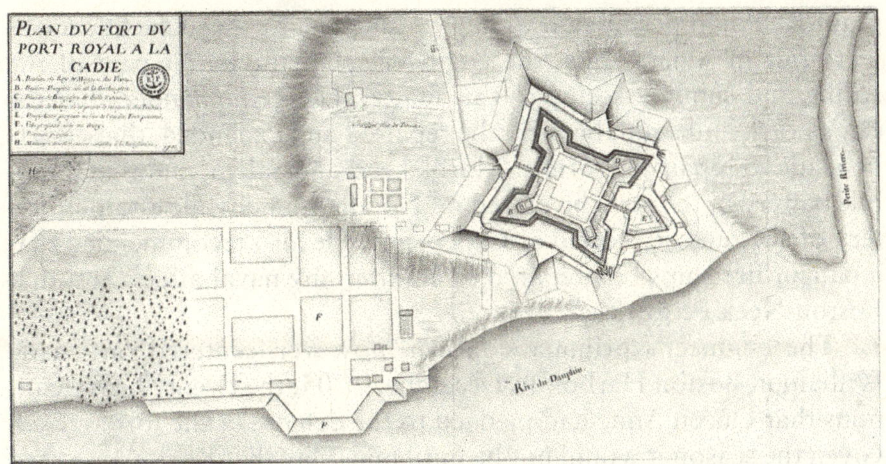

A 1702 map of the French fort at Port Royal. (*Achives Nationales, France*)

been damaged by spring storms and rising floodwaters. Beyond this, there were still half a dozen pressing issues with regard to finishing the structure, the most important being the erection of a *chevaux de frise* about the fort to prevent it from being taken by surprise, the construction of a ravilen to protect the main gate, and finishing the breastwork along the landside of the fort. The tasks proved easy, as there were no funds available to do anything of significance. With work stopped, Redknap spent most of the year copying the plans of the existing fortifications along the New England coast, which were later transmitted to England. If anything, this work proved useful in acquainting the new engineer with the details of the fortifications recently erected and those proposed by Romer. This was especially true with the proposed fort at Winter Harbor, Maine, which the government of Massachusetts was anxious to build in order to abandon the dilapidated structure at Saco. Redknap was ordered to lay out plans and construction costs for this new fort after having visited the area.[6]

In the spring of 1706 Redknap returned to work. The engineer's efforts became of more concern when reports arrived that a French fleet led by Iberville was planning an attack on either Boston or New York City. The reports were enough for the governor of New York, Lord Cornbury, to summon Redknap to New York City to oversee work on the defenses there. Redknap was prepared to leave, but with their own defenses in question the Massachusetts Council refused to grant Redknap permission to depart until their coastal fortifications were put in order. Thus, the engineer spent the better part of the spring and summer seeing to this matter. He recommended that the city's north and south batteries be repaired and expanded, that efforts be made to repair the forts at Marblehead and Salem, and that a mobile battery of ten guns be placed on Noodle Island while another battery of six guns be erected at Cape Anne. He also recommended that a pair of fire ships be prepared to counter any naval attack and that Boston Neck be fortified.

The engineer's primary concern, however, centered on Castle William in Boston Harbor. In December 1705, the twenty heavy cannons that Queen Anne had pledged to the defense of the fort arrived. Given the season it would not be until mid-May that Redknap started work on mounting the guns. By the first week of August he was nearly finished with the task. He then turned his attention to finishing the outlying works of the castle and repairing the damage wrought by the spring and winter storms. By fall he was able to report to the Massachusetts Council that most of this work was finished, but in pushing forward these efforts there had been little time to see to the other proposed works around Boston, and as such, nothing was accomplished in this area.[7]

In September 1706, Redknap finally secured permission from the Massachusetts Council to travel to New York. When he arrived, he found the city transformed. A wooden stockade had been run from the East River to the Hudson River on the north side of the city supported by a number of redoubts, three batteries totaling thirty-seven guns had been placed on the East River, and three more batteries totaling seventeen guns had been placed along the Hudson River. Another battery of eleven guns was erected below Fort William Henry, and the fort itself had been put into the best possible state of repair.[8]

While no naval attack came on the eastern seaboard in 1706, it was clear with the return of French and Indian raids along the frontier that the ceasefire was over. Although Dudley did not accomplish all of his goals during these negotiations, he had bought New England eighteen months of relative peace—time which was spent strengthening its defenses, raising men, and recovering from its losses. With Castle William and Fort William and Mary in a defensible state, Dudley set his sights on Quebec. His dealings with Vaudreuil during the peace and prisoner negotiations had pointed out to him how weak French Canada was. English privateers had intercepted their supply ships,

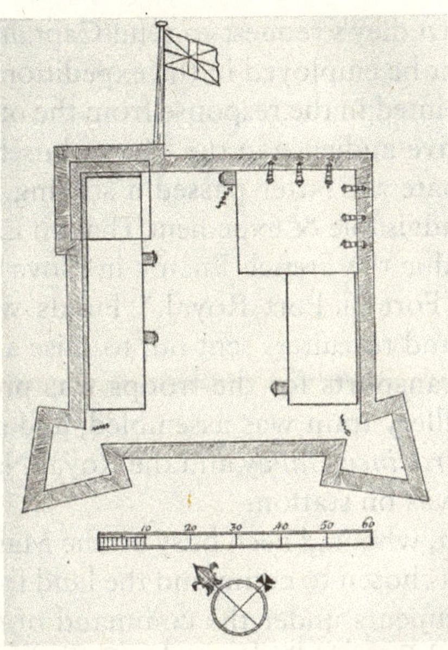

A plan of John Redknap's proposed fort at Winter Harbor. (*Massachusetts Acts and Resolves, VIII (1703-1707), p. 523*)

and uncertainty among their Native allies had further stretched their resources. Now seemed the time to strike. "If H.M. would be graciously pleased to give us but 4 ships of war and mortars," he informed London, we would remove "all the French from Canada and Port Royal."[9]

The response the governor received from London in the spring of 1707 made it clear to him that, with the current commitments in Europe, a campaign against the French colonial capital was unlikely. With an attack on Quebec off the table Dudley turned to an old idea, the capture of Port Royal. He wrote Cornbury and the New England governors with a plan to lay siege to Port Royal and officially solicited their aid. If the town could be taken, he pointed out, it would deprive the French navy of one of their primary anchorages in the region, and thus, lessen the likelihood of an attack on either Boston, New York, or some other location along the eastern seaboard. Most agreed with Dudley's arguments, but this did not translate into material support for the idea. Connecticut refused to participate, and the best Rhode Island and New Hampshire could do was a company of troops each and an armed schooner or two. Governor Cornbury of New York wrote back that he was not in a position to support the enterprise, but he did honor Dudley's request to send Captain Redknap back to Boston so he might be employed in the expedition.

While disappointed in the response from the other colonies, Dudley found a receptive audience in the Massachusetts Assembly. After a few days of debate the latter passed a stirring resolution, stating "That it is highly advisable & expedient That an Expedition be forthwith made to subdue the French Enemy in Nova Scotia, & particularly to take the Fort at Port Royal." Funds were appropriated, contracts signed, and recruiters sent out to raise a thousand men for the expedition. Transports for the troops was procured from local merchants, an artillery train was assembled, and an escort arranged consisting of the *Province Galley* and the Royal Navy frigate H.M.S. *Deptford*, which was on station.

Colonel March, who had been busy on the Maine and Massachusetts frontiers, was chosen to command the land forces, which would consist of two regiments under the command of Colonel Winthrop Hilton and Colonel Francis Wainwright. Captain Charles Stucley of the *Deptford* would command the naval portion of the expedition, and when he arrived from New York, Redknap was commissioned commander of the ordnance with the duty of seeing to the actual details of the siege and the deployment of the expedition's artillery, which consisted of eight field pieces and two small mortars. "I also desire and direct you to advise and assist at the council of war," Dudley's warrant to the engineer spelled out, "taking the third place at the board."[10]

By mid-May the forces had been assembled and loaded onto the awaiting transports. The flotilla set sail on May 12 and after an uneventful voyage dropped anchor in the Port Royal Basin on May 26. Although the troops and their supplies were landed with little in the way of opposition, the expedition quickly began to flounder. Lieutenant Colonel Samuel Appleton with 320 men had landed on the north shore of the basin so late in the day that the detachment made little headway through the "hideous woods and fallen trees across our way, which sometimes we climbed over, at other times crept under."[11]

The expedition's commander Colonel March personally led the main detachment of 750 men who landed on the south shore a few miles below Goat Island. The broken, marsh-laden ground, coupled with the dense debris on the forest floor, slowed the colonial advance. By nightfall March was forced to make camp half a dozen miles from the fort, while Appleton's men plowed through the forest until they

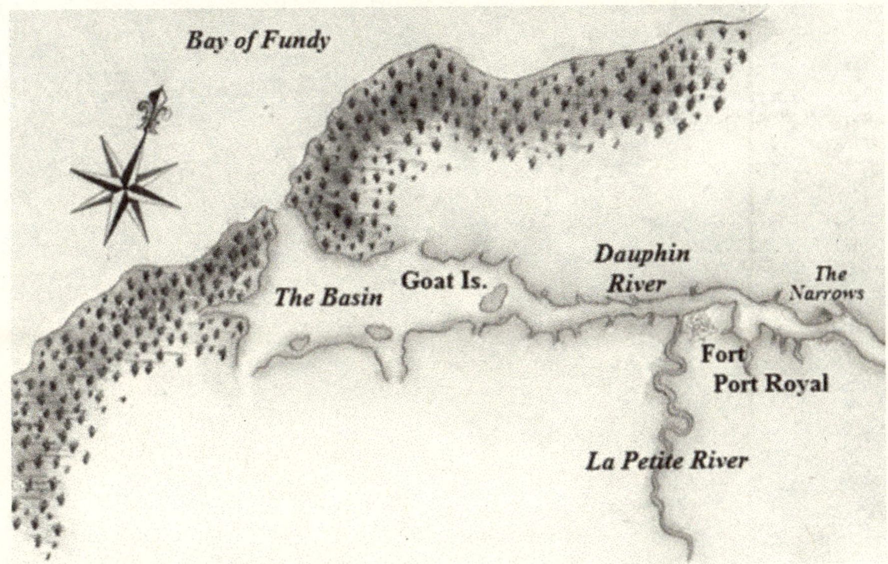

The area around Port Royal. (*Author*)

too were forced to make camp still miles from their objective. It had been an exhausting and somewhat confused advance, but as the army made camp March was quick to realize two things. First, it could have been far worse if the enemy had contested his landing, and second, he was in position to invest the French stronghold the next morning.[12]

Six

THE SIEGES OF PORT ROYAL

Early on the morning of May 26 a breathless runner found the new governor of Acadia, Daniel Subercase, in Fort Royal. He reported that fifteen enemy ships had been sighted near the entrance to the basin. The information sent the old soldier into motion. The drums beat the garrison to arms, while he sent orders for the militia from the nearby villages to report to the fort. He then sent the messenger back with orders for the observation party to send updates on the flotilla's progress. When enough troops had arrived, the governor formed small detachments of forty to fifty men and sent them out in search of the English on both sides of the Dauphin River. The rest of his troops he set to work digging trenches, making gabions, and repairing the structure's weather-damaged walls. Once the militia was assembled Subercase had close to five hundred men. Fortunately, sixty Canadians had arrived the day before to bolster his numbers. Vaudreuil had sent them to help man a privateer that was being dispatched to the port, but at the moment Subercase had them digging trenches.

The next morning both Appleton's and March's detachments encountered Subercase's advanced guards. After a brief exchange of gunfire Appleton pushed aside a French detachment and marched to a point opposite the fort, "a little more than a musket shot over the North (Dauphin) River." March ran into a similar-sized enemy detachment at a small stream crossing. The French fired a few volleys, and upon hearing far too many fired in return, retreated to Allen Brook, or the La Petite River as it was called at the time. Here they were met by another detachment of fifty men who lined the east bank of the tidal waterway. Shortly thereafter Subercase arrived with another 120 men to shore up this position.

March's men pushed forward and were greeted by a volley from Subercase's detachment. The fire halted the English advance, but it would not be for long. As the two sides exchanged fire it became clear to the French governor that he was badly outnumbered. Matters would only get worse as a good number of his militia bolted after the opening shots. Subercase had his horse shot out from under him, and after he was helped to his feet, he realized that it was only a matter of time before the English crossed the brook farther upstream and outflanked his position. With little choice he conducted an orderly retreat back to the fort, burning any buildings that might be of use to the enemy along the way before taking up a position in front of the stronghold. The trailing English came to a halt a few hundred yards away, content with their accomplishment.[1]

At this point Captain Charles Stucley, commander of the 50-gun frigate *Deptford* and naval commander in charge of the flotilla, took Redknap and Captain Ebenezer Wentworth in a small launch to within cannon shot of Fort Royal. After this reconnaissance it was agreed to land the artillery at Appleton's camp on the opposite side of the river. Over the next few days Redknap marked out the ground in advance of the artillery's landing. The engineer was clearly not happy with the arrangement. According to an account attributed to Arthur Jefferies, a former commissary under Colonel March, "Coll Rednap being ashore mark'd out his ground & had begun to make some provision to raise his Batteries &c But placed as difficultly as possible might be, His Fretfull, spitefull Temper all ye time he was ashore sufficiently shewed his dislike to undertake w^{t} he was sent about."[2]

Jefferies was correct in his assessment of the engineer. The ground Redknap had selected for the expedition's artillery was a poor choice. The majority of Fort Port Royal's cannons were directed to control water access to the Dauphin River, and the fort itself was strongest

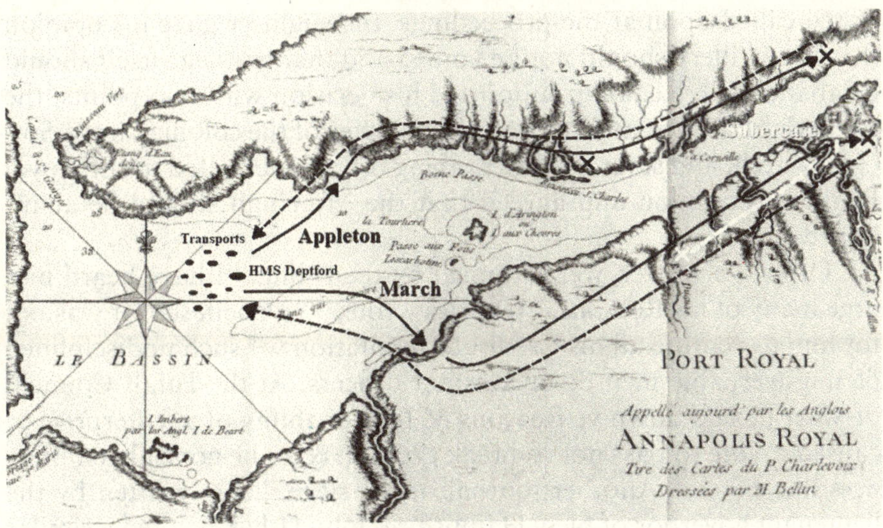

March's siege of Port Royal. (*Author*)

along the shoreline. This meant that the location Redknap had selected was a position that would be subject to a severe bombardment while the trenches were dug and the firing platforms erected. This concentrated French firepower also seriously threatened the landing of the artillery and the vessels that would conduct the landing operations. If Redknap initially missed his error, the French gunners soon pointed it out, firing cannon balls and dropping mortar rounds into Appleton's camp over the next few days.[3]

During this time March proved content in sniping at the fort and burning down nearby homes. Subercase and his garrison watched as the English lit fire after fire, sending columns of black smoke high into the air and creating an eerie glow at night. The governor fired a few cannons at the enemy more in an attempt to display his vigilance than a chance of causing harm. The truth of the matter was that he was short on powder and did not dare do more. To conserve what supplies he had, the garrison was told not to fire unless he gave the order, which he only intended to do if the English stormed the fort. As it was Subercase had to abandon his encampment in front of the fort, and now, along with the rest of his men, he waited behind the structure's walls to see what the English would do next.

On May 31 a council of war was held, likely at Redknap's urging, to discuss the landing of the artillery and the expedition's options.

When called upon at the proceedings, the engineer gave his opinion that the artillery should not be landed and that the siege itself should be abandoned. Redknap supported his decision with two points: the strength of the fort and the unruly character of the colonial army. Stucley, March, and several other ranking officers defaulted to the Royal Engineer's opinion and agreed that the campaign should be abandoned.

Others, however, were stunned by the ruling. "I have heard him urge many of his Reasons," Jefferies wrote. "Ye Cheifest Y^{t} it was not for him to venture all his Creditt & reputation wth such undisciplined & ungovernable men & unconstant officers. At the Fatall Councill of Warr he laid down ye Reasons & Improbability of ye enterprise & caused a Vote to pass not to break ground, & so be gone ab^{t} o^{r}. buisness like Fools." Another journal of the siege, likely written by the lieutenant governor of New Hampshire, John Usher, painted a similar response to the decision to abandon the attack on the fort.

> The ground Col. Rednap marked out impossible for our artilery to be thither broughtt. Fr. never exspected us there, butt on other side the ground seizable. And now our greatt and fatall Councill satt to finish all. Col. Rednap opinion being asked declared nott to break ground (though our artilery there) by reason of disobedience and insufficiency of our men, nott being persons proper for him to venture his reputation on, and reply was made, our orders are otherwise then to send : this point gain'd, caused a consentt in all others. Adieu Rednap and Secritry, scared outt of there witts.[4]

Jefferies and several others claimed that such a decision was rash and that the artillery could easily be landed without danger at another location. For a moment, this new opinion held sway over the council of war, but with Redknap still objecting, the determination of the expedition's leadership wavered and then finally defaulted to their original position. After spending several days killing the local livestock, tearing up fences, destroying crops, and burning as many structures as could be found, the New England forces embarked for Casco Bay satisfied that they had crippled French efforts in the region.[5]

Subercase was stunned when he saw the English withdraw to their ships and sail out to sea. With every advantage before them the enemy had withdrawn without firing a single cannon at the fort, and in their haste, they had left a large number of tools and supplies behind. The governor and several around him speculated that one of the French deserters had spread a rumor that the governor had started, that five hundred Wabanaki and a hundred French were on their way to relieve the fort. Whatever the reason, it hardly mattered from the governor's perspective. French casualties had been light, a few killed and a handful wounded or taken prisoner, and while the town had been plundered and burned, Port Royal and Acadia still remained in French hands.[6]

The fleet returned to Caso Bay while Redknap and a delegation from the aborted expedition returned to Boston. The news had travelled quickly, and upon the latter's arrival they were greeted with jeers. A crowd of women brandishing wooden swords and mocking the party with chants of "Port Royal, Port Royal," met the delegates at Scarlet Wharf and followed them to the town hall chanting their insults to the beat of a small drum they had procured. Over the following days Governor Dudley listened to the reports and read the letters from those on the scene. The witnesses broke down into two camps: those in favor of Redknap's opinion and those who opposed it.[7]

In his own defense Redknap pointed to the strength of the enemy position. "The Fort of Port Royal," the engineer began his report to the governor,

> is a Fortification of Four Bastions a halfe moone, wth some other out workes, which have been newly made, there is eighteen pieces of Cannon, mounted upon the Ramparts, twelve and eighteen pounders, the Ditch is between twenty four and thirty foot broad, seven foot deep, the Ramparts about eight foot height from the surface of the earth. There is a Battery of twelve pieces of Cannon, six twenty four pounders and six thirty six pounders, wth one Morter, but these do not add much to the strength of the Fort, they being designed only to command all Vessels that pass up that River, it will be very difficult to bring them Guns upon the Ramparts, there are eight pieces four pounders, and eight Pateraroes belonging to the Galley wch may be mounted on any of the works, and there is no want of ammunition in the Garrison.[8]

According to a number of deserters, Redknap added, the garrison was close to six hundred men, and reports were that they were expecting reinforcements from the surrounding settlements any day. The expedition was outgunned, and had less than the recommended three-to-one advantage in manpower. Coupled with a raw colonial army, it was a recipe for disaster. "I think it impossible to have done more," Redknap wrote to the Board of Trade of the incident, "unless we had had cannon and morters superiour to theirs, to have thrown away the Country people in assaulting the place to no effect (would) had been much worse. . . If we had sustain'd so great a loss upon any settlement of this province, then they would make a clamour of our being undone."[9]

Although there were dissenters who pointed to the intrepid work done by the New England soldiers in forcing the French back into their fort, Governor Dudley had already received a letter from his son alluding to the lack of discipline within the colonial ranks. As such, he accepted Redknap's assessment of the situation.[10]

Questions seemed to linger, however, as to Redknap's abilities, and such questions are understandable. Certainly, Redknap's selection of where to place the expedition's artillery was questionable, and his approach to rectifying the error, via a council of war's opinion that the campaign be abandoned, is somewhat suspect given this error. In the end, however, Redknap's seemingly self-serving stance may have been the right decision. The expedition had badly underestimated the strength of Fort Royal, and the English artillery was too small and too few in number to challenge the guns of the fort. More importantly, it was clear the Royal Engineer believed that any siege of the French citadel would be a long one, something that the inexperienced colonial army was ill-prepared to deal with.

Dudley, however, was not interested in giving up so easily. Several of the more aggressive commanders urged the governor to order the fleet back for a second attempt on the French stronghold. Governor Samuel Cranston of Rhode Island agreed and even went further by suggesting that matters before the fort not be left to a council of war, which "may againe prove of Ill consequence." After reading the reports from the commanding officers and speaking with the members of the delegation, the governor ordered the troops back to Port Royal and promised to send them whatever reinforcements he could obtain. The thought was not to attack the fort but to cut off its supplies in hopes that it would be forced to surrender. Returning would also offer an opportunity to launch raids into the interior of Acadia with the aim of burning villages and destroying livestock. Lastly, returning offered a chance to undo the political damage that was now on display as clusters of women and boys paraded about waving their toy swords and mock flags to the music of an *ad hoc* marching band.

A large merchant ship, the *Ruth*, was converted into a frigate and loaded with provisions and munitions, as well as two newly raised militia companies, and dispatched to the fleet riding at anchor in Casco Bay. With these reinforcements came orders to make a second attempt on Port Royal and a directive that frowned upon councils of war, placing instead all decisions in the hands of Colonel March.

March's force had only suffered around fifty casualties; hence the inclusion of the reinforcement increased his numbers. A 24-gun warship had been added to the expedition, ample provisions had been distributed, and there was a sufficient supply of powder and shot. On paper at least, March's force was stronger, and now armed with more intelligence concerning the terrain around Fort Royal, and a feel for the strength of the French garrison, it appeared that an opportunity existed to correct any earlier mistakes. The naval force would block any aid coming to the fort by sea, while the army surrounded the stronghold, devastated the local countryside, and slowly starved the French garrison into submission.[11]

The only problem was that most of the army had little faith in their leaders, and most of their leaders had little faith in the decision to return. The men distrusted their officers and distrusted the redcoats even more. In the same vein the colonial officers questioned their unruly men and resented Stucley and Redknap, who looked down on them and blamed the colonials for their own poor decisions and lack of commitment. Matters were also complicated by the term of the troop's enlistments, which was to be ten weeks. It was rapidly approaching eight, and if the force was to return to Port Royal the expedition would certainly go well beyond the agreed upon time, which might create other problems.

March ordered the fleet to sail on July 17, but it was stopped by a wholesale desertion the night before. Well over a hundred men had disappeared from the camp along the shores of Casco Bay. When combined with a rash of earlier events, it left March in the position that the new companies did not even cover his losses from desertion. Not that the rest of the men were enthusiastic about returning. "The soldiers are utterly adverse and will at best be but passive in returning to Port Royal," one witness wrote his wife, "just as prisoners are transported." When the fleet set sail near the end of July Colonel Elisha

Hutchinson reported March's strength at "743 officers and soldiers, sick and well." He then echoed the earlier statement: "They are so extremely dispirited, that we cannot look upon them equal to 300 effective men."[12]

The fleet did not sail directly for Port Royal but for Passamaquoddy where Dudley had ordered a series of attacks made on the French traders and settlers in the area. The army lingered at this location for over a week, which did nothing to improve morale. March resigned, claiming that both his spirit and health were broken. Command now passed to Colonel Wainwright, one of the officers who had urged Dudley to launch a second attack. The fleet finally set sail and on the morning of August 10 entered the Port Royal Basin. The following morning whaleboats and small launches carried the troops ashore. The landing spot was an orchard about two miles below the fort on the opposite side of the river.

Subercase and his officers watched Wainwright's landing with their spyglasses from the fort's ramparts. The group exchanged observations and estimates of the enemy's numbers. While hardly pleased to see the English reappear, at least Subercase had been reinforced in the interim. Not long after the English retreated a French privateer entered Port Royal Harbor. The sight of the vessel and its crew of 150 was a welcome one for the beleaguered garrison and the local citizens. The vessel carried provisions and powder. It also carried news that a sizable English force was preparing to return. Subercase believed the reports and used the increased manpower to further strengthen the fort and its outworks, which included erecting a redoubt at the Allen Creek crossing.

The morning after the landing the French governor and his officers listened to scouting reports and watched the English column thread its way along the opposite shore toward a series of clearings across from the fort. The first clearing, a musket shot from the fort, proved too difficult to hold as the garrison poured small arms fire onto the attackers and the fort's cannons swept their ranks with grapeshot. The attackers fell back to a second clearing a little below the first but still within musket range. It still proved too close and, on the twelfth, while Wainwright was landing his supplies, this position was abandoned as well. The next morning a large French and Indian war party crept through the woods toward Wainwright's position. Around 8 a.m. this detachment began skirmishing with the English advanced guard. The firing would continue off and on until

Annapolis Royal (Port Royal) in quieter times. Positioned on a bluff, the fort is seen in the center of the image. The waterway to the right is the outlet of Allen Creek (Petite River). The waterway to the left leads to the town and the anchorage. (*Norman B. Leventhal Map Collection, Boston Public Library*)

nightfall. Most of this accomplished little, but around 4 p.m. one detachment of nine English soldiers foolishly marched into the woods at the urgings of "a mad fellow" and were quickly surrounded and cut to pieces by the French and Wabanaki.

It proved an uneasy night broken by the occasional shot that alarmed all. The next morning Wainwright seemed to have grasped how dismal his situation had become. He was penned into an area near the shore. "Indeed," he wrote of his situation, "the French have reduced us to the same state which we reduced them, at our last being at Port Royal." What was much worse was the growing sick rolls. Violent fluxes, swelling throats, and those so filled with terror that they were unable to function were decimating his ranks such that "in a short time, there will not be men well enough to carry off the sick."[13]

It would get no better. While the colonel formed plans with his officers on what to do next, the French stepped up their attacks. Raiding parties sniped at the sentries while the fort's cannon and mortars rained shot and explosive rounds down on their position. On the sixteenth the English were forced to move their camp a mile downriver, out of the range of Fort Royal's guns, but it was a temporary stay. An attack by a French and Indian war party forced Wainwright to move once more, this time under the protection of the fleet's guns back to the original landing zone. Here the troops entrenched for three days.

Finally, on the twentieth, Wainwright left a small force to guard the current encampment, and under the protection of the fleet, crossed the river to the south bank pulling his boats ashore on the edge of a large orchard. The men landed without difficulty allowing Wainwright to quickly organize his ranks for the upcoming march. The columns had barely cleared the fencing at the inland edge of the orchard when a rolling volley erupted along the nearby tree line. The echo of the first shots had barely faded when another volley followed, this time punctuated with the sound of war whoops. In the woods before them was Baron St. Castin and a hundred French and Wabanaki furiously reloading their muskets as the English launched a scattered response at them. Castin called out, and a third barrage was launched at the enemy ranks.

Thus far Wainwright's men had stood their ground and were ready to push forward on the enemy position, but orders came for them to fall back. News travelled quickly and Subercase, seeing an opportunity, sent Captain Louis-Simon Le Poupet de La Boularderie forward with 150 men to support St. Castin, before following himself a few minutes later at the head of another 120 men. The three French detachments surged forward like waves behind the retreating colonials.

The tables quickly turned when a handful of English officers rallied their troops and set up a firing line. This time it was St. Castin's turn to face an unexpected volley, which tore through his ranks and stalled his charge. Another volley cut through the French and Indian line sending them reeling backward toward the woods. Shouts came from the English officers followed by a "huzzah" as the New Englanders launched themselves forward in pursuit.

Both parties soon encountered Boularderie's men pushing their way through the thickets and underbrush. The arriving French merged with some of Castin's men, and fired on the charging English, but it was not enough. The two lines collided and the matter briefly turned into a hand-to-hand melee before a wounded Boularderie sounded the retreat. The English followed and now collided with Subercase and a number of rallied French troops in the woods near the English column's earlier position. This time the English had seen enough. They exchanged fire with the French and then slowly withdrew in an organized fashion to their boats. By now Subercase had seen enough as well, and although he sent detachments to harass the enemy's withdrawal, for all practical purposes the battle was over.[14]

So too was the second siege of Port Royal. The English fleet sailed away the next day to the cheers and defiant shouts of the defenders. Perhaps not unexpectedly, the second attempt on Port Royal proved even less successful than the first affair. English losses, some sixteen killed and a score wounded, were not much different than the first attempt, and yet almost nothing was accomplished, leaving one to ponder, given the severe morale and leadership issues that existed, why it was even attempted?

For the French it was a major victory. Their losses were small, with three killed and fifteen wounded, and little additional damage had been done to the surrounding countryside and communities. Subercase, who had proven his resolve in the first siege, had seized the initiative from the start of the second siege and did not let go until the English had departed. He had used his resources wisely and pressed the besiegers at every opportunity. The king was impressed with the governor's actions and awarded him a pension for his conduct and bravery.

For Dudley things were not so simple. While the two expeditions were a blow to his reputation, he focused on the expedition's accomplishments and avoided pointing fingers at several suspect officers, even though there were serious questions to be asked. In the end, the governor had learned an important lesson from the undertaking; he would need help from England to subdue the French stronghold on Nova Scotia. The intercolonial rivalries, logistical entanglements, and a general lack of experience among colonial field officers convinced him to pursue this approach. In mid-October 1707, he sat down and wrote a letter to the Board of Trade. "I hope," he wrote on this idea, "to lay the whole matter before Her Majesty as to obtain the assistance and cover of some shipps and force from home, which may remove this troublesome neighbor."[15]

Seven

THE CAPTURE OF PORT ROYAL

It would not be until the spring of 1709 that the idea of attacking Quebec would once again take form in the New England colonies. Led by Massachusetts agent Samuel Vetch, who had spent a good deal of time in Quebec during the ceasefire and prisoner negotiations a few years before, the plan was essentially a copy of the effort made during the opening years of King William's War. An Anglo-Iroquois expedition under General Francis Nicholson would advance down the Champlain Valley to attack Montreal while a British fleet carrying siege artillery and five thousand regulars rendezvoused at Boston with colonial forces, before ascending the St. Lawrence and laying siege to Quebec.

This time London agreed to support the expedition, which from a practical point of view seemed to mark the last days of New France, but affairs in Europe intervened and the promised British fleet was diverted to Portugal. For Dudley, Vetch, Nicholson, and everyone else involved in the campaign of 1709, it had been a calamity. The colonies had not been notified of the change of plans until October, meaning that they had kept large numbers of men in the pay of the colony for much of the year. The annual costs for defending the frontier and seaboard were close to £30,000, but with the additional troops raised for the aborted expedition this sum had doubled. Still, the colony had cheerfully paid this, Dudley informed the Board of Trade, "in hopes, Her Majesty, if the war continue, will be pleased to revive that expedition in the Spring."[1]

The Massachusetts Assembly asked Nicholson to travel to London and make the case for resuming the expedition next spring. Peter Schuyler also travelled to London accompanied by several Iroquois sachems. They, too, looked to plead the case for renewing the campaign in the spring of 1710. These endeavors appeared fruitful when Secretary of State Charles Spencer, the Earl of Sunderland, revived the campaign. This time, however, at Nicholson's urging, he included an attack on Port Royal before a descent on Quebec. He sent Nicholson back to Boston in May with orders to raise the colonial contingent, while a British fleet and five regiments of regulars under General Richard Shannon would be assembled and dispatched to Boston in a few months. If all went well this British force would combine with its colonial counterpart, advance on Port Royal, and after its capture set sail for Quebec. The secretary, however, wisely realized that Shannon's troops might not arrive in time and gave Nicholson a sizable detachment, which when combined with the colonial efforts in Boston would still be able to seize Port Royal.

Nicholson dropped anchor in Boston Harbor on July 15. He immediately called together the governors of New England and New York and read them his orders. Few had faith that a British fleet would appear, but at the very least it seemed that Port Royal was to be dealt with. To ensure this part of the plan Nicholson brought with him a regiment of Royal Marines, the 50-gun warships H.M.S. *Dragon* and H.M.S. *Falmouth*, the 36-gun frigate H.M.S. *Feversham*, the 32-gun frigate H.M.S. *Lowestoft*, and perhaps more importantly, the bomb ship *Starr*. This force alone was enough to take Port Royal, but to ensure success, it was to be augmented by a thousand colonial troops provided for by the New York and the New England colonies via a quota Sunderland had laid down.

It was a tall order to muster so many troops this late in the year, but Governor Dudley was able to report in early September that nine hundred men had been assembled at Boston, enticed in part by the advancement of a month's pay and an agreement that they could keep their government-issued arms after the campaign was over. Transports, and particularly provisions and the siege guns, took longer than expected. The provisions were eventually had at inflated prices, while the two Royal Engineers on the expedition, Captain Alexander Forbes and Captain Redknap, who was serving as a volunteer, built field carriages for ten heavy guns taken from Castle William and Fort William and Mary, which were to act as the expedition's siege train.

A change in English government brought a new secretary of state, William Legge, the Earl of Dartmouth. The delays and inevitable confusion such a transfer of power brings meant that Dartmouth did not consider the British component of the campaign until July. At this point it was a question of whether or not the fleet could reach Quebec and seize the city before the St. Lawrence began to ice over. After consulting with someone familiar on the subject, who demonstrated their lack of expertise by informing the new secretary of state that operations before Quebec were possible up through November, Dartmouth ordered the five regiments to Portsmouth and directed the navy to provide the transports and warships for the expedition.[2]

These forces had yet to be assembled when, in late August, Dartmouth realized that the delay was likely fatal to the campaign. Still hoping to salvage some victory from the effort he wrote the colonial governments expressing his regrets that plans to dispatch this force had been laid aside due to contrary winds and other important services. Plans for an expedition next year were being considered, but in the interim the attack on Port Royal should proceed with the forces on hand in Boston.

The message would not arrive in time, but it did not matter. By late September it was agreed that, even if the British fleet did arrive, it was too late to attack Quebec. As such, Nicholson and the colonial governors decided to move forward with the attack on Port Royal. The troops were embarked as well as any last-minute supplies, to include fifty barrels of powder for the siege train, and on September 29 the fleet of half a dozen warships and thirty transports raised sail. Six days later the flotilla dropped anchor in Port Royal Basin having already suffered their most significant loss in the campaign when the small schooner *Caesar* ran aground near the entrance to the river and was dashed against the rocks by wind and wave with the loss of twenty-six men.[3]

For Governor Subercase, the flotilla was an ominous sight. He had perhaps three hundred men at his disposal, assuming that at least some of the local militia would respond to his call in such a one-sided affair. His fort was a crumbling mess, covered with patches and makeshift sandbag solutions. He had not been properly supplied in several years and was short on almost every element needed to defend the stronghold. The commandant had continually requested men and supplies but at the same time sent back seventy men that Vaudreuil had sent a few months before because of an inability to feed these reinforcements.

Whatever the case, it was perhaps for the best. The next morning English detachments came ashore on both sides of the river. On the south shore Colonel Robert Reading and Captain Redknap came ashore below the fort with two hundred marines, while on the north shore Vetch and Captain Forbes landed with a company of grenadiers. With both sites secured Nicholson gave the order for the main army to land. Colonel William Tailer's and Colonel Shadrach Walton's provincial regiments were sent to the north shore while the rest of the army led by Nicholson landed on the south shore a few hours before sunset. After marshaling their forces, both detachments advanced to the beat of the drum.

Even if he had wanted to, Subercase did not dare oppose the landing, fearing that many of his men would desert at the first opportunity. Instead, he trained the fort's guns on the advancing columns. The cannon balls tore through the foliage, and one passed quite near Colonel Reading at the head of his regiment, but did little else. At dusk both Vetch's and Nicholson's detachments halted for the night. The former was almost directly across the river from the fort, while the latter had taken a position on the west bank of the Petite River.[4]

Subercase had sent out several patrols that skirmished with Nicholson's men throughout the evening, but when dawn came the English formed their ranks and advanced to within three-quarters of a mile of the fort. The stronghold's guns barked in defiance, and scattered musket fire came from the nearby houses, but it did little to dissuade the enemy who encamped for the evening. Nicholson sent an advanced guard forward with orders to push in the enemy pickets and entrench themselves four hundred paces from the fort. This they accomplished under a hail of grapeshot and small arms fire, which accounted for half a dozen casualties.

As Nicholson's men dug in, the hollow thump of mortars could be heard coming from the river. The bomb ship *Starr* had moved forward and now began dueling with Subercase's guns. No damage was done on either side, but the effort did allow Nicholson to land his artillery without any interference. Later in the evening Vetch and Forbes

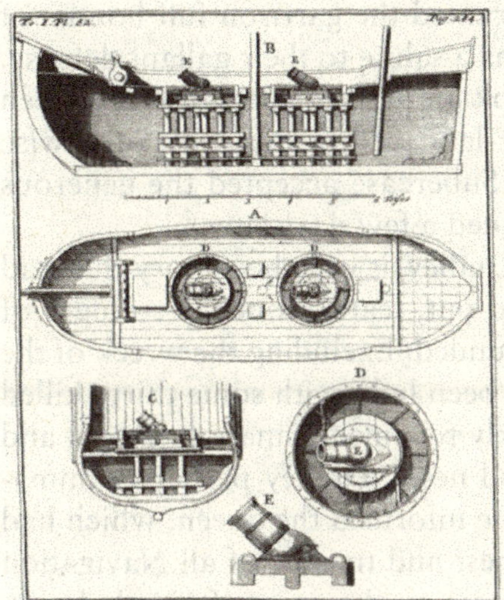

A diagram of an eighteenth-century bomb-ketch, such as the H.M.S. *Starr* used in Nicholson's siege of Port Royal. (*Memories d'artillerie* [1741])

led a detachment of a hundred men to Spur Point directly across from the fort. The plan was to plant a dozen small Coehorn mortars at this location to bring the fort under a constant fire, but the distance was found to be too great and the ground unsuited for the guns.

Morning brought rain and fog, which only covered the English efforts to land supplies. Subercase kept up a sporadic fire and dueled with the *Starr* later that evening, but beyond causing a handful of casualties there was nothing he could do to prevent the enemy from raising batteries for the siege guns they had brought ashore. This task was hampered by rainy weather for several days, but by October 12 Forbes and Redknap had set up three batteries of guns only a few hundred yards from the fort's walls. In keeping with tradition, a chorus of trumpets and drums filled the air for a few minutes before the command to fire echoed from each of the batteries. Cannon balls struck the stronghold's walls, sending up clouds of dirt and masonry, while mortar rounds burst overhead and within its confines.[5]

Nicholson halted the barrage after a few volleys and under a flag of truce sent Colonel Tailer with a surrender summons. The militia within the fort had already petitioned Subercase to surrender, and with nothing to be gained by continuing the one-sided affair, he agreed to seek terms. Nicholson granted the garrison full honors of war and transport back to France as a salute to their gallant defense. As for the local citizens, if they took an oath of allegiance to Queen Anne, they were free to keep their land and possessions; otherwise they had to depart within a year. Subercase accepted the generous terms, and the capitulation was signed a few days later.[6]

For the English and especially Dudley, it was the victory that had eluded them for years. As it turned out, fears about the strength of the French stronghold proved unfounded. Excluding the wreck of the *Caesar*, Nicholson's casualties had been light with some thirty killed or wounded. Port Royal was quickly renamed Annapolis Royal and heralds sent out to spread the good news. Dudley perhaps summarized the victory best. Port Royal, he informed the queen, which had "been these seven years the great pest and trouble of all Navigation and Trade of your Majesty's provinces on the coast of North America" was no more.[7]

On the French side, there was criticism regarding Subercase's release of the reinforcements sent to him by Vaudreuil, but given the circumstances the latter admitted that it would not have changed the outcome. "I am fully convinced, My Lord," Vaudreuil wrote the minister of the marine, "that, whatever resistance he could make, having only the garrison with him, he would be overpowered by superior force. This is a justice that I feel obliged to render him; but nevertheless, I cannot help complaining of the little attention he has paid to the reiterated notices I sent him that he was to be besieged." Indeed, the warnings were crucial, but outnumbered ten to one in a fort that was falling down around him, short of food and powder, and surrounded by a garrison that might desert on a moment's notice, perhaps what is more surprising is that Subercase was able to secure any surrender terms at all.[8]

The seizure of Port Royal did not end the conflict between the British colonies and New France. The next year the invasion plan of 1709 was revived, and this time the British fleet, under Admiral Hanoveran Walker, arrived at Boston in June. With Nicholson once again in position to advance down Lake Champlain and Walker's fleet, which included thirteen ships-of-the-line, having departed from Boston in late July, it appeared that New France was doomed. However, lack of experienced river pilots and a strong storm wrecked a portion of Walker's fleet on the lower St. Lawrence. Even though the fleet still remained strong enough to have captured Quebec, without

Fort William and Mary, the site of the 1713 Anglo-Wabanaki Peace Treaty. (*Norman B. Leventhal Map Collection, Boston Public Library*)

pilots Walker dismissed any further attempts to reach the French colonial capital and returned to Britain. Nicholson had no choice but to abandon his effort after the news reached him, which ended the campaign.[9]

Small raids would still occur until news of a truce arrived in October 1712. With both sides exhausted and reports that the Wabanaki were looking for peace, Dudley arranged a meeting with the sagamores at Portsmouth in July 1713. The result was a treaty that brought an end to the fighting between the two sides, and less than a month later official news arrived announcing peace in Europe. Queen Anne's War had ended and on terms beneficial to the north British colonies. The Iroquois were officially recognized as British subjects, and Nova Scotia, vaguely defined according to its ancient limits, was ceded to Britain. French holdings in Newfoundland and on Hudson Bay were also turned over to British control, but Cape Breton Island to the northeast of Nova Scotia would remain French. This last point was punctuated almost immediately as French forces began work on one of the largest fortresses constructed in North America.[10]

Eight

THE LONG PEACE

The Treaty of Utrecht brought an end to the War of Spanish Succession and its American counterpart, Queen Anne's War. The ink on this document had barely dried when the sound of hammer and saw could be heard coming from French-held Cape Breton Island. The idea of a fortified naval port on the island had been broached half a dozen years before, but with the challenges already imposed by Queen Anne's War, the matter was put aside. Now there was no choice in the matter. Unlike the British colonies to the south, Canada was not self-sufficient, and if it was to maintain its lifeline with France as well as a market for its primary export, furs, it had to control the Gulf of St. Lawrence. The loss of Port Royal as well as part of Acadia under the Treaty of Utrecht, coupled with the loss of Placentia, Newfoundland, the primary port of the seasonal French fishing fleet, had now made a fortified post on Cape Breton Island a necessity.[1]

An initial settlement, which also acted as a new home for the displaced Placentia fishing fleet, was erected at English Harbor, soon to be renamed Louisbourg. While efforts progressed to establish a settlement at Louisbourg, a decision as to whether or not this location, Port Toulouse, or Port Dauphin would be the agreed upon fortified port still lingered. With a number of conflicting reports before the French court regarding the costs involved in fortifying the three posts,

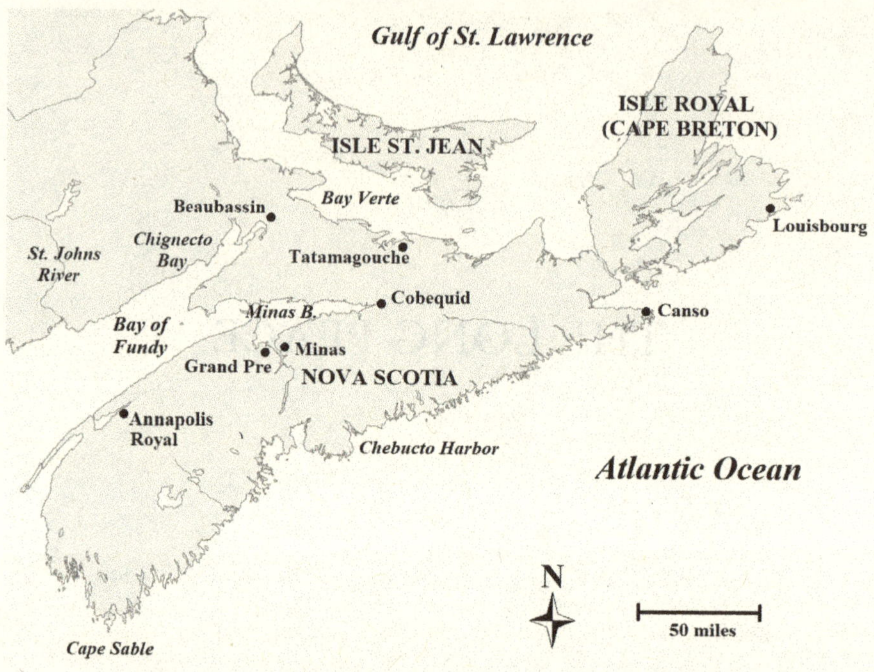

Nova Scotia and Cape Breton. (*Author*)

it was agreed to dispatch a senior military engineer to take charge of the project. The task fell to Jean-François de Verville. Commissioned in the prestigious Royal Engineers in 1704, Verville had fought in a number of engagements in Spain and Germany during the War of Spanish Succession, earning a coveted Cross of St. Louis and knighthood in the process. He was wounded at the siege of Landau during the Rhine campaign of 1713 and later would be stationed in Flanders before being nominated for the position of Director of Fortification for Isle Royale (Cape Breton) in June 1716.

Verville's first order of business was to survey the three primary ports on Isle Royale before returning to France with an estimate of the cost to secure each. By late 1716 the engineer had accomplished this task. He first recommended that Louisbourg be the center of the fishing trade and the colonial capital. Fortification work should start here, with Port Dauphin and Port Toulouse being given secondary considerations.

At Louisbourg, Verville's projected fortifications began with the town and anchorage situated along a peninsula on the western edge

A 1719 plan of Louisbourg Harbor and the proposed fortifications. Key: A. Dockyard, B. the Town, E to G. Landside wall, H. King's Bastion, I. Island Battery, K. Royal Battery. (McLennan, J. S., *Louisbourg, from its Foundation to its Fall, 1713-175*, p. 50)

of the harbor. To guard the landside approach to the town the engineer took advantage of a series of hills at the base of the peninsula to erect bastions and interconnecting curtain walls, which would stretch over a thousand yards from the sea to the harbor (G to E on map). The bastions would double as barracks for the six companies of troops assigned to the port, and a ditch would be dug in front of the works, the resulting dirt from this being used to form a glacis and covered way.

The Island Battery (I) near the narrow entrance to the harbor was the primary line of defense against naval forces looking to force entry and attempt a landing. As such, a masonry redoubt capable of holding a score of heavy guns was to be erected here. Behind this, at the head of the bay (K), Verville called for a redoubt and a battery of heavy guns that could not only target the narrow entrance and support the Island Battery but bombard any intruders that made their way into the upper harbor. Known as the Grand or Royal Battery, the position would become a fixture in the defenses of Louisbourg even though isolated, and with suspect landside defenses, it was of questionable use. There were other issues Verville addressed. He called for state officials not to be involved with the fishing trade, and he complained of the slow progress made by the garrison on the current defenses, recommending that a contractor be employed to construct the proposed works.

It is clear that the engineer's opinion carried a great deal of weight, in part given the status French engineers had amassed under the leadership of Vauban and in part as a result of his own reputation. The use of masonry construction would be costly, as there was no nearby quarry or brickyard, meaning a source would either need to be found or everything would have to be imported. Fortunately, limestone was discovered at nearby Canso, which would simplify logistics and reduce the costs for this important component. The French authorities accepted Verville's opinion and approved his plan in July 1717.[2]

As the fortress of Louisbourg began to move forward a number of British governors of Nova Scotia began to express concerns. First, although the Treaty of Utrecht granted Britain control of Nova Scotia as defined by its ancient limits, the reality was that the British only controlled two places in Nova Scotia: Annapolis Royal and the fishing village of Canso on the eastern tip of the island. The rest of the peninsula was still occupied by the French Acadian citizenry and their Micmac allies. Second, by treaty, the French citizens had one year to decide whether to take an oath to the British sovereign and stay or depart for French territory. This time had passed, but there was a debate as to whether they should stay or go. If they left, would it not simply increase the power of Louisbourg? On the other hand, if they stayed without taking the oath, could they be trusted to stay neutral in any future conflict between Britain and France?

These problems would haunt the British governors of Nova Scotia for a generation. Even with their pleas ignored by the British government, the countryside filled with potential enemies, and a French naval fortress being constructed nearby, the period between 1713 to 1744 was generally peaceful. There was one major exception, Dummer's War (1722–1725) or the Fourth Anglo-Wabanaki War. The conflict pitted the much-weakened Wabanaki and their pro-French Native allies against their old New England adversaries. New France, while promoting the conflict and supplying the Wabanaki with material aid and a few volunteers, was officially neutral.

Given that the Wabanaki could barely field five hundred men, the scope of the conflict became limited to Maine, New Hampshire, and Nova Scotia. The coastal fortifications were not seriously contested, as the Wabanaki had agreed to try and magnify their numbers by conducting numerous smaller raids and avoiding situations where they

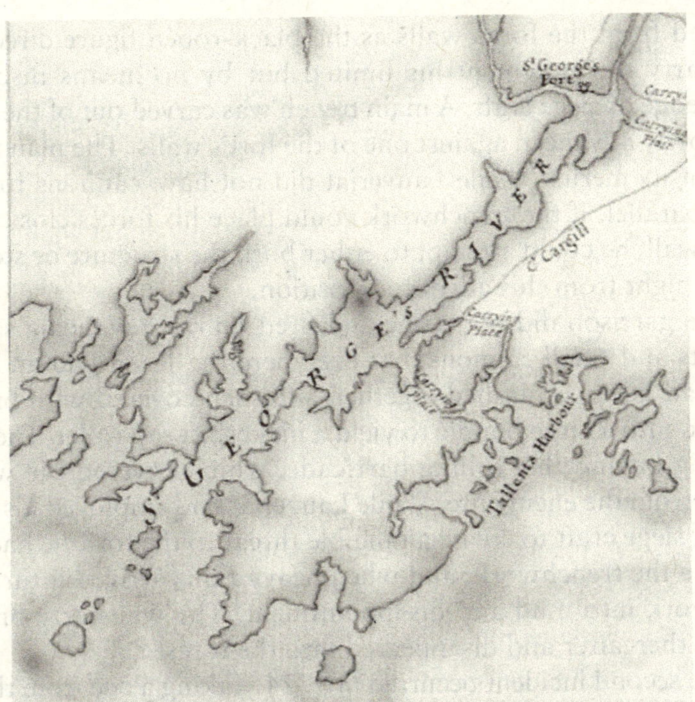

A 1759 map showing the St. George's River and the location of St. George's Fort. (*Norman B. Leventhal Map Collection, Boston Public Library*)

might suffer large losses. In general, this meant that, if fortifications were encountered and they could not be surprised, a few shots might be fired at the garrison and the structure invested, but no serious attempt would be made to capture the stronghold. There were, however, a few exceptions to this, both concerning attacks on Fort St. George's in modern Thomaston, Maine. St. George's Fort had been constructed on the east side of the St. George's River by erecting a pair of blockhouses near the river's edge and then enclosing them along with the garrison's barracks and the old trading post with palisade walls. A small harbor and the clusters of homes comprising the nearby hamlet were the only other structures for miles.

The first attack on the fort occurred in late June 1722 when a war party of Penobscot quickly overran the settlement of St. George's (Thomaston, Maine) and laid siege to St. George's Fort for twelve days, "being very much encouraged by the influence of the Friar that was with them." In fact, it was Jesuit Father Étienne Lauverjat of the Penobscot mission at Pentagoet. Under drizzling skies, the garrison watched from the fort's walls as the black-robed figure directed the war party to implement his limited but by no means insufficient knowledge of siege craft. A main trench was carved out of the ground and slowly advanced against one of the fort's walls. The plan was not without its merits. While Lauverjat did not have cannons to erect a firing parallel, if the trenchwork could place his forces close enough to the wall, he could attempt to either burn the structure or storm the fort at night from this advanced position.

The garrison did not panic and fired on the advancing sap with muskets and small cannons, but even here the Jesuit had an answer. Logs had been cut, lashed together, and then covered with branches and tied into a large bundle to yield a makeshift sap roller. The trench was dug behind this rolling barricade, which covered the working parties from the enemy fire. While Lauverjat had employed his knowledge of siege craft to create a tangible threat to the fort, he had failed to brace the trenchwork, and when heavy rains arrived it turned the hard work into mud and disappointment. The war party broke up shortly thereafter and disappeared into the forest.[3]

The second incident occurred in 1724. Taking a cue from the Micmac success in Nova Scotia the year before, the Wabanaki along the Maine coast began targeting fishing vessels that summer, and just as in Nova Scotia they found immediate success. Waiting along the shores of several harbors they watched the English ships drop anchor for the evening or send boats ashore to dry their catch. That night the war party would quietly take to their canoes, often helped by wind and rain, and crept alongside the fishing vessels. Once aboard, a handful of shots and war whoops followed, and within a few minutes it was over. The tactic proved so successful that, by midsummer, the Wabanaki were in possession of close to thirty vessels along the coast of Maine, one of which was a large Marblehead schooner armed with a pair of swivel guns.[4]

Using this recently acquired naval power the Wabanaki descended on St. George's Fort. Late on the afternoon of July 21 the sentries notified the fort's commander, Lieutenant William Canady, that five vessels were approaching and that an Indian delegation was coming ashore under a white flag. Canady met with the Wabanaki envoy a little before sunset. The envoy, using a captured fisherman as an interpreter, demanded the surrender of the fort, offering to send the garrison back to Boston in one of their captured vessels. Canady refused and informed the spokesman that he would fire on the vessels if they approached any closer. The Wabanaki signaled for the ships to stop, but already closer than Canady was comfortable with, a warning shot from one of the fort's cannons brought them to a halt. The meeting soon broke up, and after dark the Wabanaki invested the fort, making their presence known with shouts and the occasional shot.

The next morning negotiations resumed, which led into a brief conversation on land rights. When Canady proved defiant, the spokesman threatened the garrison with no quarter if the Wabanaki were forced to attack. Canady informed him that, if they wanted the fort, "you must take it by force of Arms which you nor all ye Indians in the Eastern Country can do." A few more words passed between them before the Native ambassador threw up his hands and departed. The garrison watched as the enemy sailed a pair of small vessels into a cove and began loading them with wood and other combustibles. Late that afternoon the two fireships, bellowing smoke and flames, approached the fort under full sail.

The intent was to burn the fort's blockhouse near the shoreline, and according to the fort's commander, the unexpected attack almost succeeded. The fort's cannon scored a hit on the first vessel, which likely damaged its steering, as the abandoned craft sheared away, and with the help of the tide, went harmlessly ashore. The second vessel, however, was more problematic. Although striking the ship several times with the fort's guns, it did nothing to halt its progress, and it passed near enough that Canady noted, "we had ye good fortune to escape." There was another attempt at negotiations and several unsuccessful efforts to seize the handful of British vessels in the harbor, after which the Wabanaki abandoned the siege and sailed away.[5]

These nontraditional attempts to destroy St. George's Fort, coupled with the unexpected Wabanaki maritime threat and the small raiding party philosophy, allowed the vastly outnumbered confederacy to keep New England off balance for almost three years. "It is surprizing to think that so small a number of Indians should be able to distress a Country so large and populous," Samuel Penhallow wrote of the conflict. Even so, numbers simply overwhelmed the Wabanaki, who sued for peace in 1725. The treaty would bring a generation of peace to the region. From 1689 to 1725, New England had been at war with New France and/or its allies for twenty-two years, almost two-thirds of this period. Generations of French, English, Wabanaki, and Iroquois had only glimpsed fleeting periods of peace, and all welcomed the opportunity to put aside their arms.

For New France, New England, and Nova Scotia this period was an opportunity to turn toward defensive measures and secure their current claims. Foremost among these was Louisbourg. For the growing colony the years following the Three Years' War were filled with trade, a good portion of which was illegal, pirates, internal command disagreements, and the threat of war with the English. By 1726 Louisburg, counting the garrison, numbered some 1,300 inhabitants, which would swell to several times that number when the seasonal fishing fleets appeared. Perhaps just as importantly, thirteen other settlements had been established along the coast that harbored another 2,200 denizens. Commerce was steadily increasing, as that year ninety-six vessels arrived from France, Canada, and the West Indies with another twenty-two calling upon the smaller ports along the coast. With the confines of the French and British navigation acts restricting commerce and profits, a robust illegal trade appeared, a good deal of which was between New England and Louisburg.

Throughout this period work on the fortifications pressed forward, although not always at the desired rate. Verville's initial plans for a defensive work at the head of the harbor called for a small battery with the guns fired *en barbette*, that is, over a parapet, but he was to change his mind. In 1723 the engineer addressed this matter in a paper outlining the construction of a much larger structure, which would become the Grand or Royal Battery. The proposed fortification had two functions. First, working with the guns of the Island Battery, it was to prevent an enemy vessel from forcing its way into the harbor. Second, should an enemy vessel gain entrance to the harbor, the cannons of the Royal Battery were to deny it a safe anchorage, especially to the northeastern portion of the harbor. In Verville's opinion, this task called for a large battery of thirty heavy guns and would dictate the layout of the stone fortification to accommodate the desired firing patterns. There was yet another element that dictated a large structure, the likelihood of an attack from the landside. There were plans for a glacis and a covered way fronted by a *cheval-de-frise* on this side of the structure, as well as provisions for several cannons and a pair of flanking towers on either end of the structure. Even with these defensive provisions, it was clear that the battery would require a sizable garrison to prevent an enemy force from simply storming the structure from the landside while the battery's cannons were engaged.

The earthwork was started in 1723, and for the next few years stone was hauled to the location and lime kilns erected before work

A 1745 plan of Louisbourg. (*William L. Clements Library, University of Michigan*)

began in earnest. By the summer of 1728 the fortification was pronounced complete. Of course, there were still many items to perfect and the violent nor'easters that travelled the region guaranteed that there was always work to be done. As such, it would not be until 1732 that the Royal Battery took on its regular garrison.[6]

The Island Battery was the key to the harbor's defenses, and it was not until August 1, 1722, that Verville could report that the excavation of the site was underway. The work was "pushed with vigor," and by December seven cannons had been mounted at the makeshift works. The following year brought more clarity to the project. Verville laid out a battery for thirty-eight heavy cannons, ten of which were focused on vessels approaching the harbor's entrance, four on vessels in the harbor, and the rest on the narrow straits between the island and the lighthouse peninsula. An elevated twenty-three-foot-thick wall was raised running along the east-west length of the island with a turnback to the south at either end to capture a tall rocky bluff to the south, which formed a natural fourth wall facing the sea and greatly hindered any bombardment from that direction.

Ramparts and firing platforms would be fashioned for the predominantly northern- and eastern-facing cannons, which fired *en barbette* over a two-foot parapet, while barracks, storehouses, and the powder magazine were laid out in the interior.

Work began on this project not long after, but by mid-November 1724 the wall was not complete. While all involved realized the importance of this battery, manpower shortages, bad weather, and high seas had stunted the effort, bringing all work to a halt until spring. Little was accomplished the next year as manpower and resources focused on the Royal Battery. In fact, it would not be until December 1730 that the Island Battery's powder magazine was finished, the platforms constructed, and the cannons mounted along the ramparts. There was still a cistern to construct and a number of items to finish within the interior leading to the official declaration of completion in June 1732. Even so, like most North American fortifications, it would always be a work in progress.[7]

By 1738 work on the fortified town on the southern shore of the harbor had been declared complete. The landside defenses consisted of a series of stone bastions built on a string of small hills and connected by thirty-six-foot curtain walls that stretched from the harbor's edge to the seashore. At the western end of this chain was the Dauphin's Bastion, which guarded the most commonly used gate into the town. Next was the largest of these bastions. The King's Bastion was the centerpiece of the line, behind which the four-story-tall stone citadel was erected, which housed the governor and part of the garrison. The Queen's Bastion was next before the line terminated at the Prince's Bastion on the sea side of the peninsula. To further brace this line a large ditch, glacis, and covered way, supported by a *cheval-de-frise*, protected the outer walls from an infantry assault, should one dare risk such a proposition in the face of dozens of heavy guns mounted along the ramparts, although at this point there were only a few actually mounted. From the Prince's Bastion the shore acted as a defense, allowing for a smaller wall from this strongpoint to the Maurepas Bastion, which covered the eastern seaside approach and enclosed the town.

Inside these walls a hospital had been erected, an ordnance park laid out, barracks constructed, and government buildings raised. Scores of smaller stone and wood buildings, which housed the 1,500 permanent inhabitants, filled in the intervening spaces, and church bells rang periodically from several locations. Streets lined with shops

A view of the entrance to Louisbourg Harbor. (*Norman B. Leventhal Map Collection, Boston Public Library*)

and rows of homes spoke to the colony's rapid progress, but perhaps a better indicator was the fact that, by the early 1740s, the town boasted two dressmakers and a hairstylist from Paris.[8]

The garrison now consisted of eight companies of the Free Companies of the Marine, a little over five hundred men at full strength. This was supplemented by two companies of the Swiss Regiment Karrer, which had been raised in response to a shortage of marines. Together these troops would number over six hundred men, but neither were ever at full strength, and with detachments at several outposts on the island it placed the effective force at Louisbourg at less than five hundred men. In a time of crisis, the garrison would be augmented by some three hundred to four hundred militia and whatever naval personnel or fishermen happened to be in port, likely doubling or tripling their overall numbers. While over a thousand men guarding a fortified city supported by a complex of heavily armed stone fortifications might appear sufficient, the quality of the troops would have more bearing on the outcome than numbers. Of particular importance at Louisburg was the lack of skilled gunners. With the works in a constant state of construction, and shortages a way of life, there had been little time to drill the gun crews, many of whom were only vaguely familiar with the loading, aiming, and firing of a cannon. The governor had attempted to rectify this problem in the spring of 1736 when he drafted two men from each company to train and serve as artillerymen. Although they were not officially a *Compagnie des Bombardiers*, as was commonly seen in fortifications along the French coast, St. Ovide was looking not only for the same function but, just as importantly, the same appearance so as to change the perception of "foreigners, who say openly that though we have many cannon, we have no one to serve them."[9]

By the early 1740s what was once just shorelines of forest had been transformed into a sprawling set of defensive works and a major naval base that would stand guard at the entrance of the Gulf of St. Lawrence. The town now stood enclosed by siege-level defenses and bastions mounting heavy cannons. The channel into the harbor was an eight-hundred-yard expanse flanked on either side by two peninsulas. The southwestern peninsula was formed by a rocky shoal that stretched from the mainland to a small island. Here the Island Battery now mounted a score of heavy guns focused on the passage, with another half-dozen aimed out to sea. A lighthouse towered over the rocky shore of the northeast peninsula. Erected in 1734, it was claimed that the beacon could be seen for over fifteen miles. In 1736 the structure burned down, but another was soon raised in its place. Originally a battery of cannons was considered for this location, but at this point it had not been started. Instead, work was concentrated on the Royal Battery at the northwestern edge of the harbor. A self-contained fortress in its own right, the stronghold's three-dozen 42-pound cannons were aimed directly ahead at the main channel, creating a deadly crossfire with the Island Battery. Here there was still more work to be done. The landside defenses of the Royal Battery had not been finished, leaving the position vulnerable to an infantry attack. Even so, the three fortified positions guarding the harbor could bring over a hundred cannons to bear against an attacker. Backed by a garrison that would do its duty, and hopefully a French warship or two that happened to be in the harbor, attacking Louisbourg would be viewed as a difficult proposition for any army.[10]

In Nova Scotia defensive measures were moving in the opposite direction. A string of governors complained about the fort at Annapolis Royal and the fort at Canso. The former, originally built by the French, spent most of its existence in a state of disrepair. The cause seemed to be a poor application of the stone facing, which allowed water to enter and erode the earth ramparts. Subercase had complained of this, and now Governor Richard Philipps wrote the Board of Trade in February 1724 that the fort was slowly falling apart under the ravages of the seasons, leaving "breeches in the ramparts sufficiently wide for 50 men to enter abreast." The magazine was not secure, the barracks were near collapse, and many questioned the wisdom of even firing a cannon for fear of bringing down more of the wall. Even the most basic elements to defend the fort, from shovels to ramrods for the cannons, were in short supply, and the garrison needed almost everything from arms to clothing. After inspecting the structure, Philipps noted that "A thorough repair thereof is by no means adviseable, in regard that a new fort of smaller dimension may be built at less expense, which the circumstances of that post will admit." Plans were drawn up, but nothing came of the effort. By 1727 matters had become so bad that the lieutenant governor and his officers paid for the construction of wooden palisades to close the gaps in the fort's walls. Sixteen of them then signed and sent a petition to the Board of Trade regarding "the increasingly ruinous condition of the magazine and fortifications."[11]

Although there was a battery of twelve cannons at Canso, the earth fortifications on which they were mounted were crumbling, and the makeshift barracks were incapable of serving the large garrison required to defend the location. Beyond money and material for new fortifications and repairs, manpower was just as important. Philipps noted that the nine companies of his 40th Regiment numbered only 360, which was well below establishment and barely enough to secure Canso and Annapolis Royal, much less enforce British rule throughout the predominantly French-populated colony. Major Paul Mascarene, when submitting his plans for a new fort at Annapolis Royal, spoke to the necessity of seven hundred to eight hundred men to accomplish this task. It was clear that the colony desperately needed men and money to put it on a secure footing. Neither would appear, and in 1734, Mascarene, now lieutenant governor, informed the Board of Trade in London of the "naked and defenseless" condition of Canso, the colony's primary fishing port, noting that there were not even barracks for the four understrength companies stationed there. Should the French move against this location, he simply did not have the manpower or resources to stop them.

There appeared some hope for the defenses of Annapolis Royal when Royal Engineer John-Henri Bastide arrived in 1740 with orders to construct a new fort. After a quick survey of the decaying French structure, he understood why Mascarene had called for a new stone fort. Bastide and Mascarene selected a site for the smaller fort and detailed the material and labor requirements as well as preparations to land and transport the materials. It appeared that a new fort would be built, but just as before it was an illusion. Funding and material delays, as well as the lack of a proper dock to land the stone, nor the funds to build one, not only left the project in limbo but left Nova Scotia in a nearly defenseless state.

Along the New England coast, the peace meant that many of the old settlements along the Maine coast had been reestablished and new ones had appeared. This was not surprising given that the northern New England colonies which bore the brunt of these early conflicts, New Hampshire and Massachusetts, which included Maine, had nearly doubled in population from 1720 to 1740, and by the start of King George's War would be close to two hundred thousand inhabitants. While this perhaps speaks to the prosperity that the peace had brought, very little of this was directed toward the old coastal fortifications.

As in Nova Scotia, peace had brought disinterest in these subjects. Jonathan Belcher, the governor of both New Hampshire and Massachusetts, wrote London in March 1731 that "There is one Fort or Place of Defence, called Fort William and Mary, situated on the Great Island in New Castle, which commands the Entrance of Piscataqua river, but is in poor low circumstances, much out of repair, and greatly wanting of stores of war, there not being one barrel of gun-powder at this time in or belonging to that Garrison." Not that matters improved over the years. Most of the funding for the fort was spent on repairs, and the garrison petitioned for a wage increase on several occasions. In May 1737, responding to a query from the Board of Trade, Governor Belcher noted that "Fort William and Mary has 45 guns, many of them honeycombed and unfit for service, without powder, ball and other warlike stores, the walls with the other works and carriages in a ruinous condition." He informed the board that a bill had been put forward to repair the stronghold, but at the moment the garrison consisted of "a captain, a gunner, and one sentinel."[12]

Castle William and some of the smaller fortifications also suffered from this trend. The garrison of the castle and their pay had been established in December 1726. It would consist of one captain, one lieutenant, one gunner, six quarter gunners, one sergeant, three corporals, twenty-five sentinels, a drummer, and a chaplain. The captain was ordered to be at the fort at least three days a week while his lieutenant

Lt. Governor Paul Mascarene. (*Los Angeles County Museum of Art*)

would reside at the fort and was only to be absent with the captain's permission. While having a clear understanding of the garrison's costs, maintaining a stone fortification on the scale of Castle William at the edge of Boston Harbor, subject not only to the seasonal changes but repeated strikes by violent storms, proved more expensive than first thought. Underfunded, the fort fell into disrepair, and its garrison, like that at Fort William and Mary, petitioned the government for relief and their backpay in 1733.

The next year, at the urging of Belcher, the assembly voted £2,000 to finish needed repairs on Castle William and the sea battery next to it, and to raise a new battery of heavy guns on the eastern side of the island to better control the approaches to the main channel. Belcher wrote the secretary of state, Thomas Pelham, the Duke of Newcastle, on the status of the fortifications and the projected work.

> Here is, my Lord Duke, in this harbour, about three miles below the town a very regular fortification on a place called Castle Island, and to which a new addition is now making for the entertainment of twenty large cannon, and then Castle William (so it is called) will be capable of mounting 120 guns;

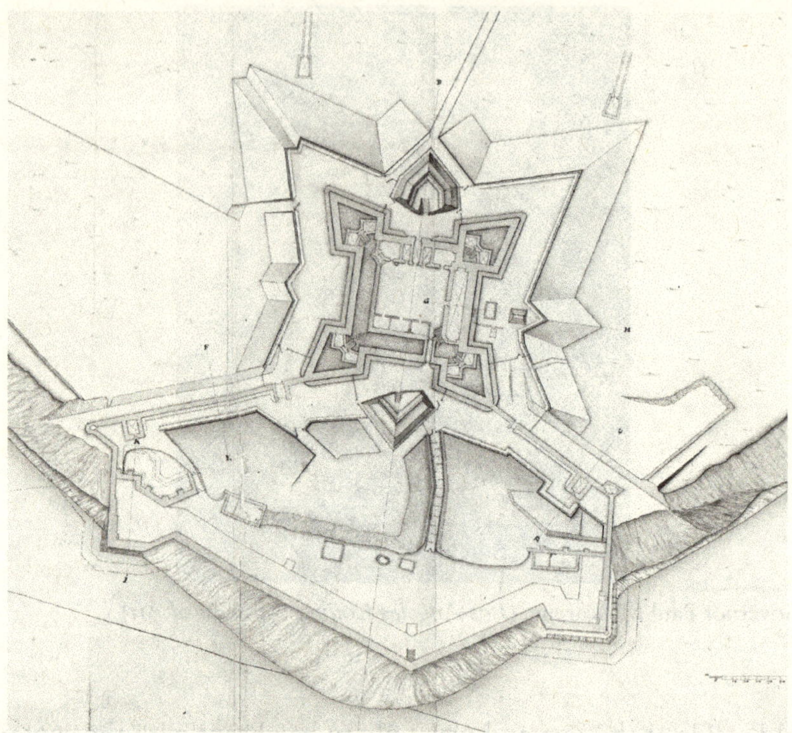

Castle William on Castle Island. This 1705 plan shows the northern facing sea battery and the two bastions at the corners of this platform, which close to the water required constant maintenance. It also shows provisions left for creating an eastern facing battery, which Belcher and the Massachusetts Assembly completed in the late 1730s. (*Norman B. Leventhal Map Collection, Boston Public Library*)

> but the greatest part of what guns are now there, are old and honeycomb 'd, the iron work (as well as the wood) of the carriages much decay'd, and I think at this time there are but ten barrels of powder belonging to this fortification, and most other gunners' stores are wanting, with mortars, shells, and small arms.[13]

The governor then informed Newcastle that it would also be necessary to not only improve the defenses of Boston but also those of Salem, Plymouth, Marblehead, and Gloucester. Although it would come at a great expense "without them the King's Government and subjects here will lye constantly expos'd to the insults of their enemies."[14]

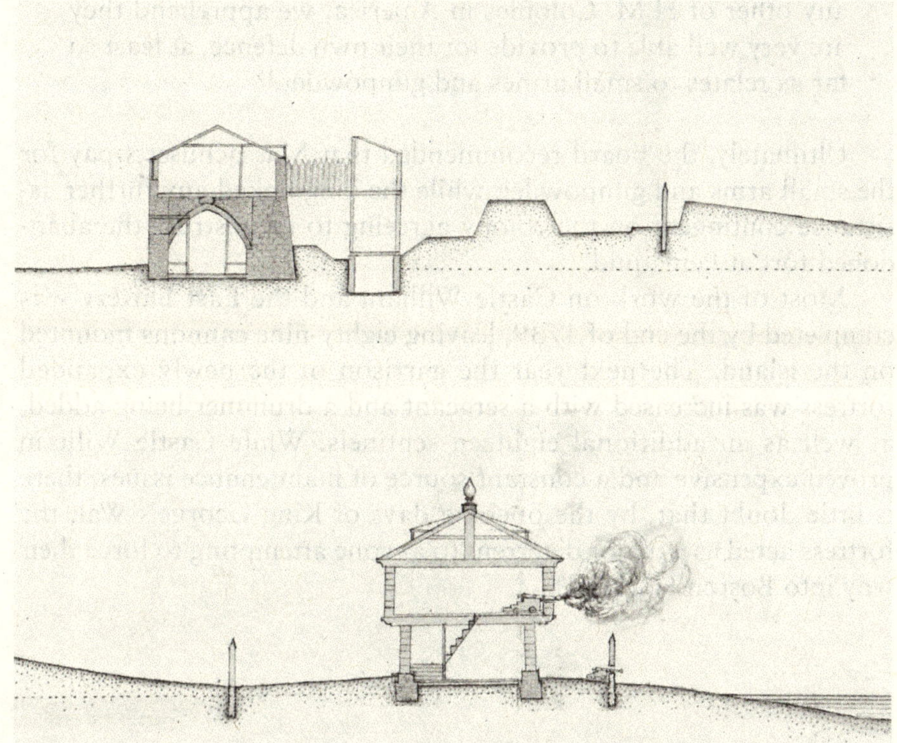

Top: A profile of one of Castle William's walls, with the fort's parade ground on the left and the glacis on the far right. (*Norman B. Leventhal Map Collection, Boston Public Library*)
Bottom: A cross-section of the blockhouse erected near the wharf on the southwestern side of Castle Island. (*Norman B. Leventhal Map Collection, Boston Public Library*)

Belcher's request to improve the defenses of Boston was taken up by the Board of Trade who passed their comments on to the king's Privy Council. When it came to heavy ordnance, the board understood why the colony would appeal to the king for assistance, but the appeal for small arms and munitions left them questioning.

> We must further take leave to observe to your Lordships that the circumstances of the people of New England are very different at present from what they were in 1704; they were then actualy at war with the French and in distress but they are now grown more populous and opulent; and being in possession of an extensive trade, much more considerable than

> any other of H.M. Colonies in America, we apprehend they are very well able to provide for their own defence, at least so far as relates to small armes and gunpowder.[15]

Ultimately, the board recommended that Massachusetts pay for the small arms and gunpowder, while the king linked any further assistance contingent on the colony agreeing to reconstruct the abandoned fort at Pemaquid.

Most of the work on Castle William and the East Battery was completed by the end of 1739, leaving eighty-nine cannons mounted on the island. The next year the garrison of the newly expanded fortress was increased with a sergeant and a drummer being added, as well as an additional eighteen sentinels. While Castle William proved expensive and a constant source of maintenance issues, there is little doubt that, by the opening days of King George's War, the fortress acted as a major deterrent to anyone attempting to force their way into Boston Harbor.[16]

Nine

KING GEORGE'S WAR AND THE SIEGE OF LOUISBOURG

In the summer of 1743 Britain militarily entered the ongoing War of Austrian Succession on the side of Empress Maria Theresa of Austria. Even so, it was not until March 1744 that an official declaration of war between France and Britain took place. In North America, the war, which was referred to as King George's War, combined with the current Anglo-Spanish struggle of the War of Jenkin's Ear in North America and the Caribbean to recreate the scenario of Queen Anne's War: the British colonies and their Native allies against a Franco-Spanish alliance and their Native allies.

One of the first individuals to receive this news was the Governor of Louisbourg, Jean-Baptiste-Louis Le Prévost Duquesnel. On May 3, 1744, the master of a merchant vessel sent from France handed the governor a pair of letters. The first announced the official declaration of war, while the second was from the minister of the marine, Jean-Frédéric Phélypeaux, Comte de Maurepas. The minister informed Duquesnel that a pair of French warships would arrive soon as would several provision ships. In the meantime, he was authorized to issue letters of marque. An attack on the long-disputed English post of Canso was also authorized, and the king expected that the governor would encourage the Micmac and Maliseet to launch attacks against the English.[1]

An attack was not foremost in Duquesnel's mind. The seasonal fishing fleet had not come out from France, meaning that the town was short on provisions and men. A handful of vessels arrived with some supplies, but within a few weeks the port was on the verge of famine. Fortunately, relief would come from Quebec, averting a disaster. With the sudden influx of supplies Duquesnel felt strong enough to attack Canso, which most thought would offer little resistance. The expedition would consist of 139 French and Swiss soldiers of the garrison and 218 sailors. Fourteen fishing vessels, a French privateer, the schooner *Success*, and a sloop were assembled to carry these troops. The flotilla would be under the watchful eye of the 50-gun French warship *Caribou*, launched at Quebec only a few weeks before.

By May 24 the French force was before Canso. The fort consisted of a wooden blockhouse and a number of dilapidated barracks and storehouses. The forgotten garrison of 120 men of the 40th Regiment were supported by a small sloop under the command of Lieutenant George Ryall, who was assigned to protect the fishing fleet. The garrison's commander, Captain Patrick Heron, was shocked when Captain Francois Du Vivier of the French marines demanded the fort and the town's surrender. Heron, like the rest of the English colonists, was unaware of the declaration of war. Caught completely by surprise and with a French 50-gun warship anchored before him, he capitulated. It was agreed that the women and children would be sent to Boston, while the men would be imprisoned at Louisbourg for a year.[2]

Governor William Shirley of Massachusetts would not receive official word of the conflict for another two weeks, but anticipating the war, Shirley had already begun to act after receiving a letter from Governor Mascarene at Annapolis Royal. Mascarene asked for Shirley to immediately dispatch two hundred men to bolster the defenses of Annapolis Royal. The Massachusetts Assembly balked at the expense but did agree to raise two companies of sixty men each, although most were unarmed in a foolish cost-saving measure.

Rumors of a large French and Indian war party gathering in the countryside dominated the summer as the garrison of Annapolis Royal, eventually reinforced by 170 Massachusetts militia, including a detachment of rangers, toiled away at their earth and wooden

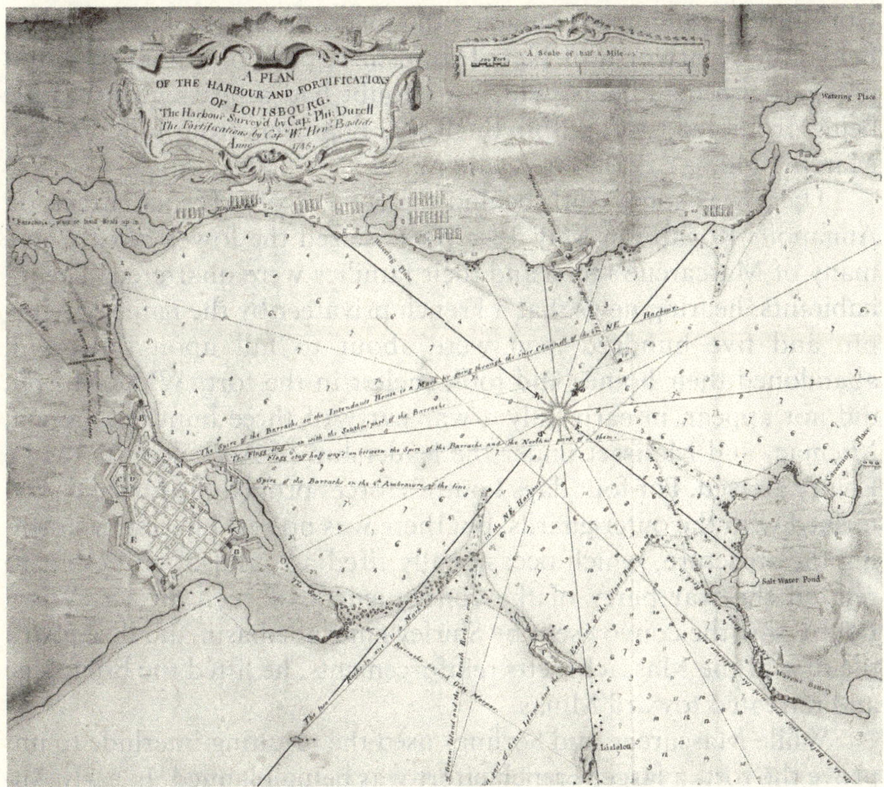

A 1745 map of Louisbourg by John-Henri Bastide. (*Norman B. Leventhal Map Collection, Boston Public Library*)

works. One of these reinforcements was Captain Bastide. With work on the new fort stalled, in the summer of 1743 Bastide was ordered to examine the coastal fortifications of New Hampshire and Massachusetts. Starting with the former he inspected Fort William and Mary at Newcastle. He conducted a survey of the cannons within the fortification, and although a large number were found unserviceable, there were more than enough on hand to meet the needs of the fort. The engineer found the river and harborside defenses of the fort adequate, and with some minor changes the landside defenses could be brought up to the same level. Bastide continued on to Massachusetts where he visited Castle William in Boston Harbor and drew up the necessary changes to mount an additional battery of cannons on the island. At Marblehead, Cape Ann, and Falmouth he surveyed the ground and drew out plans for new gun batteries at each location. The engineer's work brought him into contact with Governor Shirley and Governor Benjamin Wentworth of New Hampshire, both of whom were impressed with his talents, which no doubt had a bearing on Bastide being promoted twice within the Royal Engineers from June 1742 to March 1744.[3]

There was some truth behind the rumors of a French attack on Annapolis Royal. On May 18 a panic seized the lower town where many of Mascarene's men and their families were quartered. The inhabitants, hearing news that a French privateer by the name of Morpin and five hundred men were about to fall upon the town, abandoned their homes and took shelter in the fort. While Morpin did not appear, in early July a war party of three hundred French, Micmac, and Maliseet under the leadership of Abbe Jean-Louis Le Loutre arrived. For four days Loutre's forces probed the fort and skirmished with the outer guards, but there was no real interest in storming the structure, which occasionally fired a round of grapeshot to remind the war party of the consequences of such an act. When Loutre saw the convoy sent by Shirley enter the basin and disembark the first of the Massachusetts reinforcements, he lifted the brief siege and retreated toward Minas.

While Mascarene and Sorlings used the resulting interlude to improve the fort, a larger French effort was being planned. In early August Du Vivier landed at Green Bay in eastern Nova Scotia with a company of regular troops and a few hundred militia. From here he marched to Minas where he rendezvoused with Loutre and his forces. Looking to resecure the area for France, on August 27 Du Vivier issued a decree to the French inhabitants of Nova Scotia. "The inhabitants of Mines comprising the parishes of Grand Pre, River Canard, Piziquid and Cobequid, are ordered to acknowledge the obedience they owe to the King of France," the dictum began. It called for military support from this populace in the form of horses, men, provisions, and powder horns. To make matters worse for the Acadians, those who did not comply with the oath of fidelity to the French king would be viewed as British and have their homes visited by French and Indian war parties. Du Vivier did not spend long following up on these orders. Duquesnel had given him until September 15 to seize the British fort. He was only to attempt this if he could surprise the garrison. If this could not be done, but after a reconnaissance of the structure he believed that the fort could be taken, Duquesnel would send several vessels to assist him. Otherwise, Du Vivier was to leave a few handpicked French and Indian detachments in the countryside and return to Louisbourg.[4]

By early September, Du Vivier was encamped a mile from Fort Anne at Annapolis Royal. For the next few days, he sent patrols forward to gauge the strength of the British fort. On September 14 he reported to Duquesnel that he should send the warships. The French governor responded that he was sending the 64-gun *Ardent* and the 50-gun *Caribou*, with sizable reinforcements. With the fort before him invested, and reinforcements on the way, Du Vivier focused on making scaling ladders and preparing for an attack. Then, on October 4, he was ordered to fall back to Minas by a recently arrived captain who had seniority. This foolish order would have serious consequences for the French. The promised French flotilla appeared near Annapolis Royal three weeks later, but when Du Vivier's troops could not be located, it returned to Louisbourg, ending one of the best opportunities the French would ever have for retaking Annapolis Royal. While nothing was ever certain when it came to colonial sieges, the botched campaign would haunt the French given that, had it been executed correctly, the odds were high that the decaying Fort Anne would have been forced to surrender. This in turn would have brought the loyalty of a sizable portion of the French populace and French control over all of Nova Scotia. More importantly it would have disrupted Governor Shirley's plans to make a bold strike against the French.

In the summer and fall of 1744 a prisoner exchange took place between Duquesnel and Governor Shirley. The French commander did not have the resources to feed these captives, consisting mostly of the garrison of Canso, some of their families, as well as crews from captured privateers. Shirley was anxious to speak with the returning captives, who amounted to 340 over the course of the summer and early fall. Many were women and children who professed no knowledge of the fortress, yet even here Shirley was able to extract useful information regarding the garrison and French inhabitants they had encountered. The returning soldiers offered more direct military data regarding the nature of the fortifications, their positioning, the number of cannons, and the men at each. Taken as a whole they painted a surprising picture of the state of Louisbourg. Enough so that Shirley began to piece together the skeleton of a risky plan.[5]

In particular, two of these men, Captain Joshua Loring, whose privateer had been captured and carried into Louisbourg by a French warship, and Ensign John Bradstreet, who had been captured at Canso, cast doubts upon the reputation of the French stronghold. Both men were talented, young officers who would go on to make names for themselves in the last French and Indian War, and at the moment, were slowly gaining the governor's trust. While the works themselves were solid, they informed Shirley, those that backed them were not. Everything was lacking, from food to ammunition. The city relied on convoys from France for almost everything, and with the fishing fleet having not arrived it had only made matters worse. There were too few men to man all the fortifications, a general lack of artillery skill, and a major morale problem among them. After a mutiny not long before, it had been agreed that the garrison would be sent back to France next fall.

Armed with this knowledge, Shirley and a small group of supporters, which included Loring, Bradstreet, and William Vaughan, began to formulate an attack on the French fortress. Two elements quickly came to the forefront. First, the attack had to come in the spring of 1745, before the supply fleets arrived from France. This left little time to organize and put together the resources required for such an operation. Second, they needed the Royal Navy. Troops and artillery Shirley could raise in New England, but warships he could not. Perhaps a handful of small frigates and a number of armed schooners and sloops could be outfitted in New England ports, but without Royal Navy support a single French man-o-war could lift the blockade and end any attempt on the stronghold in a complete disaster.

After some debate and primarily through the actions of Vaughn, who focused on the economic benefits that would come with the destruction of the French fishing trade, the Massachusetts Assembly approved of the project, voting the money for three thousand men and their transportation. They formally asked Shirley to seek the participation of the New England colonies New York and Pennsylvania and to write Admiral Peter Warren in the West Indies to request Royal Navy assistance. While the recruits and supply agents went to work assembling the forces, Shirley turned toward the matter of Admiral Warren. The governor did not have official assurance that Royal Navy support would be forthcoming, but in late fall the secretary of state, the Duke of Newcastle, promised Shirley that he would order Warren to his assistance in the spring to support any effort he wished to undertake. Given the current circumstances in Great Britian and Europe, the duke was in no position to release any other British army re-

Governor William Shirley, left, and Admiral Peter Warren, right. (*William Johnson Papers, v. 1; National Maritime Museum, Greenwich*)

sources for the venture. However, he understood the critical timing of the operation, and if Shirley wished to press forward with colonial troops, Warren's squadron would support these efforts.

While Shirley believed via this correspondence that Warren would have been issued orders to assist in his campaign, the problem was that Warren had yet to receive these directives when Shirley's letter reached him on February 22, 1745. Warren shook his head at the request. He had no orders to leave station with his squadron, and although he was told to cooperate with the colonial governors regarding naval defenses along the coast, this went beyond that. After meeting with his captains, it was agreed to dispatch the *Launceston* to Boston and the *Mermaid* to New York. With the recent loss of the *Weymouth* it was the best he could do at the moment.

It would be several weeks before Shirley received Warren's response. In the meantime, formations of men drilled in open areas as the transports began taking on provisions and the siege artillery. The latter consisted of eight 24-pound and twelve 9-pound cannons, two 12-inch mortars, one 11-inch mortar, and one 9-inch mortar. New York would send an additional ten 18-pound guns, but this was all that could be had on such short notice without seriously weakening the seaboard defenses of either colony.

While this activity moved to a conclusion Shirley dispatched his colonial fleet to Louisbourg in mid-March. The flotilla was led by the newly completed 22-gun frigate *Massachusetts*, which would act as Commodore Edward Tyng's flagship. Alongside this was the contracted 24-gun frigate *Molineux*, the 14-gun snow *Prince of Orange*, and the 12-gun *Boston Packet*. A pair of privateers were commissioned from Rhode Island as well. The first, the *Fame*, was a 250-ton, 24-gun frigate while the second, the *Caesar*, was a smaller 14-gun snow. A pair of 10- and 6-gun Massachusetts sloops, the *Resolute* and the *Bonette*, would also move forward to scout the rendezvous point at Canso. Icy weather and the staggered departures brought Tyng's flotilla before Louisbourg in piecemeal fashion, but by March 20 the colonial vessels began to patrol off the harbor. The *Resolute* and the *Bonette* cruising along the coast of Nova Scotia reached Canso on March 25. The site was abandoned, and there were no indications of the enemy nearby.[6]

With the colonial fleet deployed along the southwest coast of Cape Breton, the troops began filing onto their transports. On March 21 Shirley was informed that the New Hampshire contingent had set sail for Canso in eleven transports under the protection of the 10-gun sloop *Abigail*. A few days later, on March 24, a much grander version of this event took place at Boston. At 4:00 p.m. the first detachment, some 2,800 men, departed in fifty-one vessels under the watchful eye of a few armed sloops and Captain Rous in the 24-gun frigate *Shirley*.

While the second detachment, which was scheduled to depart on the twenty-eighth, tended to its final preparations, Shirley received Admiral Warren's disappointing response. It was hardly the level of commitment the governor had hoped for, and although even one or two Royal Navy warships might well make the difference, it added an unexpected risk that cast a cloud over the entire venture. A few days after the second contingent set sail this anxiety would suddenly dissipate when Shirley was handed another letter from Warren on March 30. Newcastle had made good his promise to the governor and sent orders for Warren to proceed to New England with his squadron. When Warren received these orders a few weeks after Shirley's initial request, he sent Shirley a dispatch and ordered his vessels out to sea.[7]

The army landed at Canso and encamped amidst the freezing rains and overcast skies for three weeks until, on April 22, signal flags sent alarms throughout New England forces as a large warship was seen approaching. If it were French, the transports would be captured and the expedition brought to a hasty end. There was a scramble to arms when suddenly the flags switched to blue, meaning all clear. It was the 40-gun H.M.S. *Eltham* with news that Admiral Warren in the 60-gun *Superb* and the 40-gun frigates *Launceston* and *Mermaid* would arrive tomorrow. Fearing for the colonial force, Warren had intercepted a local vessel headed for Boston, taken its pilot, and sailed straight for Canso. Spirits soared as many who had grumbled over the last month questioning the hastily organized expedition were suddenly eager to press forward now that they possessed naval superiority.

Warren arrived the next day, and after consulting with the expedition's commander General William Pepperrell, it was agreed that Warren would proceed to Louisbourg and with a handful of colonial warships already on station blockade the port. Once the wind shifted and cleared the ice along the shores, Pepperrell would follow with the army and conduct landing operations along the northern portion of Gabarus Bay about two miles from the French fortress.

On April 29 the winds cooperated, and Pepperrell's army set sail. Over a hundred vessels arranged in four divisions proceeded to Gabarus Bay under the watchful eye of three armed Massachusetts vessels. Pepperrell's fleet pressed forward and by sunset found themselves half a dozen miles from the landing site. As it was too late to do anything, orders were passed that the army would land tomorrow morning.

At dawn cannons on the city's ramparts sounded the alarm, which was followed by the ringing of church bells throughout Louisbourg. Governor Louis Du Chambon raced to the ramparts just in time to watch Pepperrell's fleet enter Gabarus Bay. The governor, who had temporarily assumed command when Governor Duquesnel died in the fall of 1744, was stunned by what he saw. When rumors had reached him earlier of activity at Canso, he had ordered the French commander at Port Toulouse to send out a scouting party. The four-man detachment found immediate success, capturing four Englishmen near the post. Unfortunately, the captives soon turned the tables and captured the detachment. There was also news from ships recently entering the harbor speaking of an English naval presence off the coast, with one of the arrivals having even exchanged several broadsides with an enemy warship before running into the harbor. With no news from Port Toulouse of English activities at Canso, Du Chambon viewed these last reports as the work of English privateers, which was hardly unexpected, and as such, he did little to put the town in a state of readiness, even though this was precisely the time of year to expect an attack.

Du Chambon hesitated and then sent a detachment of seventy-five men under Port Captain Pierre Morpain to observe the enemy landing, and if possible, contest it. Morpain attempted the latter, but by now there were hundreds of New Englanders ashore. Numbers quickly tolled, and after a sharp engagement the French detachment retreated back to Louisbourg carrying their wounded, Morpain to be counted among them. When he spoke with the rattled survivors Du Chambon realized it was too late to oppose the enemy landing. Reports claimed there were over one hundred vessels in the bay and two to three thousand men ashore near Flat Rock. Given these numbers, the governor also ruled out a sally by the garrison. At the moment the best that could be done was to call out the militia, man the ramparts, and warn the Royal and Island Batteries of the enemy landings.

With the threat posed by Morpain's detachment removed the English advanced guard pushed forward and established a skirmish line along a string of wooded hills seven hundred yards to the southwest of the town. Behind them some two thousand men went ashore, and a camp was established at Flat Point. A few shots from nervous sentries interrupted the night, but at daylight Pepperrell and the rest of his men went ashore. The artillery and provisions followed, but without proper harbor facilities everything had to be brought across the beach from open boats. The strong surf hampered these operations and often forced men into freezing waist-deep water to accomplish their task. Some days the weather made it impossible to conduct this work, meaning that it would be several weeks before all the supplies and munitions were ashore.[8]

That evening Du Chambon listened to the reports from nervous scouts as the occasional musket shot echoed over the landscape. What was far more alarming was a message he received from Captain Chassin de Thierry, the commander of the Royal Battery. With the landward defenses of the Royal Battery under repair, in Thierry's opinion the position was untenable against a land assault. He recommended that the garrison be withdrawn and the structure blown up. The governor summoned a council of war where the chief engineer agreed with Thierry's opinion, although he did not find it necessary to destroy the battery given the powder it would take and its already weather-damaged condition. There were a few dissenters, but with the council of war in favor of abandoning the Royal Battery, Du

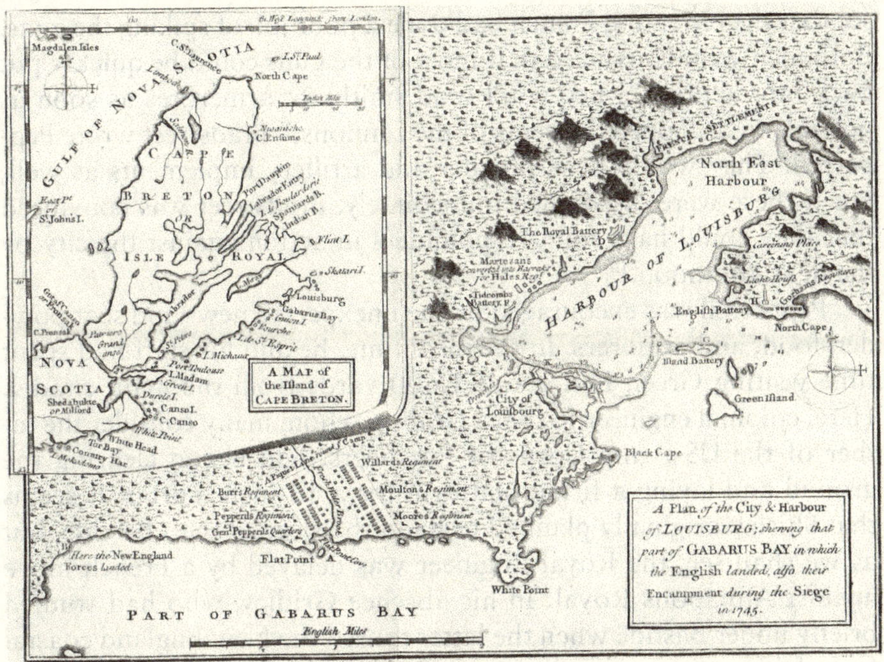

Pepperrell's landing at Gabarus Bay. (*Gentleman's Magazine*, 1758)

Chambon ordered Thierry to spike the guns and carry away whatever food and ammunition he could. By the afternoon of May 1 this had been accomplished and the post abandoned. Thus, without a shot being fired, Du Chambon had already lost a key piece of the harbor's defenses. "It would be difficult to give any reason for such an extraordinary action," one French journalist wrote of the event.[9]

It would not take long for the English to capitalize on this action. Early the next morning a scouting detachment took possession of the abandoned structure, and by noon Pepperrell's second in command, General Samuel Waldo, arrived with three companies from his regiment and Lieutenant Colonel John Bradstreet with Pepperrell's regiment. As the occasional mortar round fell near the stone structure, Waldo and Bradstreet examined the army's first conquest. The two men agreed that the structure was in poor condition, and after examining the cannons left behind, they discovered twenty-eight 42-pound guns and a pair of 18-pounders. All the guns had been spiked, but their carriages were intact and there was an ample supply of shot still in the magazines. Upon closer inspection the pair were delighted to see that the retreating French had done a poor job of spiking the guns. Both men were convinced that most of the guns could be quickly put back into action. "I beg you'l send smiths & armerores as soon as possible to drill open the vents of the cannons," Bradstreet wrote Pepperrell. They would need powder and artillery implements as well, but if these were dispatched immediately, Bradstreet was convinced that they could have four 42-pounders in action against the city by the next afternoon.[10]

Pepperrell was encouraged by the unexpected news and sent powder, food, and armorers. In the meantime, he and his staff had spent time visiting Green Hill about 1,600 yards from the main citadel. Here, colonial engineer Richard Gridley, whom many consider the father of the US Army Corps of Engineers, had begun clearing the ground and laying a firing platform for a 13-inch mortar. It seems that Shirley originally planned to hand the siege over to Bastide, but as we shall see, the Royal Engineer was delayed by a French move against Annapolis Royal. In his absence Gridley, who had studied briefly under Bastide when the latter toured the New England coastal forts, laid out an approach to force the Dauphin's Bastion, which protected the town's main gate. The siege mortar at Green Hill was the first step. Following a line of east-west running hills from there, the plan was to erect the First Battery of cannons at the eastern end of this high ground, some 1,100 yards from the King's and Dauphin's Bastions. Using the cover fire from these guns and Green Hill the trenches would be advanced until breaching batteries could be raised a few hundred yards from the main gate.

The next day, while ground was being broken on the First Battery, teams of men and confiscated cattle hauled the five-ton 13-inch mortar and its ammunition to the top of Green Hill. In the distance Waldo, who had raised an old British ensign from a fishing boat over the Royal Battery, had managed to repair one of the 42-pound cannons and by mid-morning was firing upon the city, to the cheers of the besiegers. By evening Waldo's men had repaired a second 42-pounder, which was soon adding its fire to the first. Both the Island Battery some 4,800 yards away and the city's guns, slightly closer, fired on the Royal Battery with round shot and mortar rounds throughout the day, inflicting some damage on the stone citadel but not enough to impede the English bombardment.

On May 5 Pepperrell held a council of war. With the occasional thump of the 13-inch mortar on Green Hill and Waldo's battery of

General William Pepperrell, left, and Brigadier General Samuel Waldo, right. (*National Maritime Museum, Greenwich; Bowdoin College Museum of Art*)

four cannons firing at the city in the distance, the general started the meeting by presenting Admiral Warren's plan to seize the Island Battery. The operation called for a small boat attack launched under the cover of darkness. The members discussed the matter but delayed any decision. Instead, most of the discussion centered on siege details. The trenches had been started at the end of the hill line to the east of Green Hill. Here, some nine hundred yards from the Royal Bastion, it was agreed to erect the First Battery, which would consist of eight 24-pound cannons. It was also agreed that these guns should be put into place and commence firing on the fortress as soon as possible. From here the trenchworks would be advanced to within a few hundred yards of the Dauphin Gate and a Second Battery erected, consisting of a pair of 42-pound and a pair of 18-pound cannons captured at the Royal Battery. These in turn would be supported by a battery of Coehorns located a short distance to the rear as well as the 9-inch and 11-inch mortars at Green Hill, which were currently out of range.

Both sides greeted each other the next morning with a brisk exchange of cannon fire until around 11 a.m. when the New England guns fell silent. With a drummer beating out a parley a British envoy, Captain James Agnue approached the town under a flag of truce and delivered Pepperrell's and Warren's surrender demand to Du Chambon. The French commander's response was that he "could not listen to any such proposition until after a decisive attack." When the British envoy asked if that was his final response the governor informed him that "my only other answer would come from the mouths of the cannons."[11]

With any hope of seizing Louisbourg in a quick fashion having vanished, matters focused on tightening the siege and blockade. As for the first part of this equation, work was pushed forward on the First Battery with a pair of regiments guarding this effort. The eight 24-pound cannons, supplemented by a number of Coehorn mortars, were dragged into place and soon began targeting the town and Royal Bastion. Work on the main sap continued under harassing fire and the occasional blast of grapeshot, eventually terminating in a branch running parallel to the Dauphin Gate a few hundred yards away. Here the Second Battery was started, and after a communications trench and parallel was dug a few hundred yards to the rear, the mortar battery was erected.

At the Royal Battery, Waldo's regiment now had five cannons in action and was firing into the town with more regularity. Here the issue was one of powder. It would prove a problem throughout the siege, one that was only magnified by the makeshift colonial commissary and supply system. It was also aggravated by the larger powder charge needed for the 42-pound naval guns. For those who manned the captured guns under constant fire from the Island Battery and the city, there was another concern. "The short supply of rum, the severall Captains tell me, is of prejudice to the people," Waldo wrote Pepperrell. Combined with these two problems was a desperate need for trained gunners. On more than one occasion the novice New England gunners accidentally fired their pieces with a double-charge of powder, which burst the gun, wounding those about it. "We are in great want of good gunners that have a disposition to be sober in the daytime," Waldo informed the general after two of his best gun commanders were injured in such incidents.[12]

With the bombardment of the fortress and the construction of the breaching batteries underway, attention shifted to two other elements of the siege. Thus far Warren and his makeshift fleet of colonial warships had struggled to maintain the blockade of the harbor. Weather, particularly fog, greatly limited the effectiveness of the fleet, so too did the number of vessels available. Alongside the four warships in his squadron, Warren had another seven colonial warships and a few small schooners for shallow water work and dispatch service. The

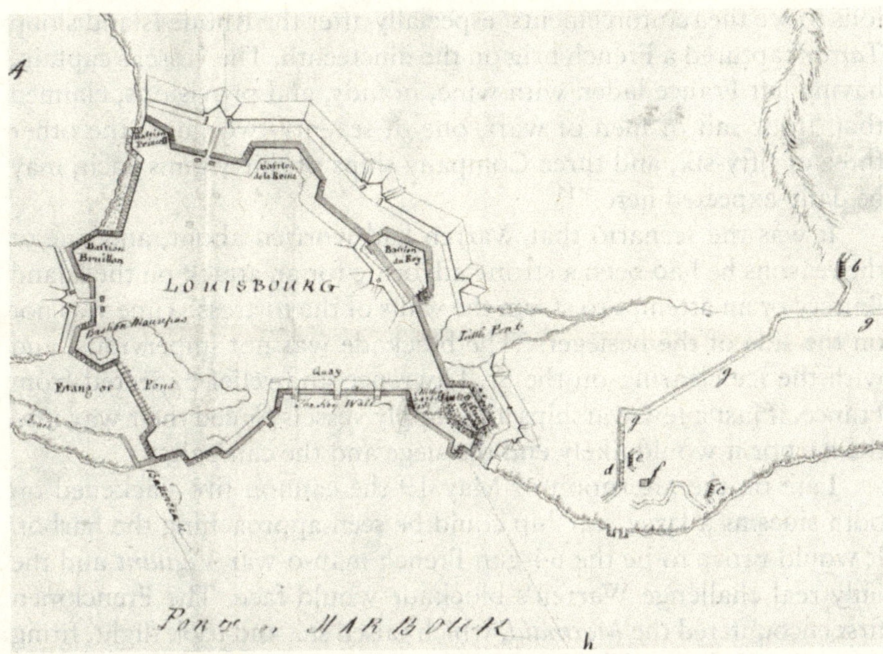

A sketch of the siege of Louisbourg by Royal Engineer John-Henry Bastide. b: battery of eight 22-pounders; c/e: Mortar battery of ten Coehorns, one 9-inch, and one 11-inch mortar; d: Five gun breaching battery; f: Powder magazine; g: main siege trench. (*Norman B. Leventhal Map Collection, Boston Public Library*)

problem was that a number of these ships were employed in escort duty or patrolling the smaller harbors along the coast for French blockade runners, while yet others would be off station resupplying. This left Warren with perhaps half a dozen vessels to enforce the blockade, and although he had made a few captures, he realized how porous the screen was and recommended that small colonial guard ships patrol near the entrance to the harbor at night to deter smaller enemy vessels from slipping into the harbor.

Good news came when the 30-gun privateer *Bien Aime* arrived from Boston, but the schooner Warren had sent to St. John's, Newfoundland, had returned with news that neither the fishing fleet nor the squadron that escorted them had arrived. Warren had hoped to borrow several of the warships from the escorts, but it would have to wait. A few days later, on May 16, news reached the commodore that the 60-gun H.M.S. *Princess Mary* and the 40-gun H.M.S. *Hector* had arrived at Boston and would join him in a few days. Warren was anxious to see the reinforcements, especially after the Rhode Island sloop *Tartar* captured a French brig on the nineteenth. The vessel's captain, having left France laden with wine, brandy, and provisions, claimed that "four sail of men of warr, one of seventy-two guns, the other three of fifty-six, and three Company ships of thirty guns each, may be daily expected here."[13]

It was the scenario that Warren had worried about, and one of the reasons he had been a strong advocate for an attack on the Island Battery or an attempt to storm the walls of the fortress. Time was not on the side of the besiegers. The blockade was not impervious, and with the ice clearing on the St. Lawrence and relief expected from France, if just a few warships and supply vessels forced their way into the harbor it would likely end the siege and the campaign.

Late on the afternoon of May 19 the cannon fire slackened on both sides as a large warship could be seen approaching the harbor. It would prove to be the 64-gun French man-o-war *Vigilant* and the only real challenge Warren's blockade would face. The Frenchmen first encountered the *Mermaid*, which raised sail and took flight, firing its guns in defiance. The *Vigilant* followed looking to take the British frigate as a prize, until a lookout called out three sails. The commander of the *Vigilant*, realizing that the tables had been turned, reversed his course, but it was too late. By 8:00 p.m. the *Superb*, *Shirley*, *Eltham*, and *Mermaid* were firing on the French warship, which would not surrender until its rigging was so damaged that it had to be towed back to Gabarus Bay the next morning. All breathed a sigh of relief when they heard the news. Reports were that the French vessel was carrying four months of provisions for the garrison, three hundred reinforcements, a thousand barrels of powder, twenty brass cannons, and rigging for a 70-gun ship being built at Quebec.[14]

The 42-pound guns of the Second Battery and the bombs from the mortar battery behind it had opened fire and were slowly dismantling the Dauphin Gate. The defenders attempted to seal the fractures with dirt and sandbags at night, but doing so was dangerous work as the mortars frequently fired over the evening to discourage such activities. Combined with the bombardment by the guns in the First Battery and Waldo's cannons at the Royal Battery, the town was being demolished by explosive rounds, fire, and solid shot that tore through the wood and stone buildings. The defenders seldom fired back, conserving their powder and shot, but at the same time they showed no indication that they were close to surrender.

One plan to break the stalemate was the earlier plan that called for a small boat attack on the Island Battery. With the Royal Battery in British hands, the Island Battery was the key to breaking the fortress's defenses and opening the harbor to Warren's warships. Numerous attempts were made to launch this volunteer expedition, in fact six, but each was aborted for one reason or another. After the last of these failures Warren had seen enough and met with his captains aboard the *Superb* later that day. Here a council of war laid out an amphibious operation that called for running the guns of the Island Battery and landing troops in Louisbourg Harbor while the fleet and army bombarded the town and the Island Battery. Warren and his captains all agreed to the plan, which would be led by the admiral's squadron. What was required was 1,600 troops to be loaded onto these warships, the captured *Vigilant*, and a number of armed colonial vessels in order to execute the landing. When Pepperrell and his officers reviewed the plan the next day they had a number of issues. It was simply too many men, and it would leave the land forces investing the town vulnerable to a sally. Besides, the *Vigilant* was not ready for such an operation. The plan was by no means shelved, just slightly modified with the numbers going into the harbor reduced, and a feint against the Dauphin Gate was now included. It now just became a matter of organization, supplies, and weather.[15]

Part of the hesitation on the part of Pepperrell's officers was fostered by a desire to see the small boat attack on the Island Battery go forward. After all, if this venture were successful, it would make the commodore's plans moot. It was not until the evening of May 26 that another attempt was made to conduct this operation. This time close to four hundred volunteers armed with muskets, pistols, and hand grenades pushed off in small boats from the Royal Battery around midnight despite what Warren would later call the roughest surf he had seen since his arrival. Some became hopelessly lost in the darkness and fog, but the bulk reached the French-held island a little before 1:00 a.m. and began landing in a haphazard fashion along the north shore of the island. Visibility was poor, but when the vessels came within thirty yards of the beach they were greeted by the discharge of several cannons firing langrage, a mixture of bolts, nuts, nails, and small pieces of chain. Designed to damage sails, it rippled the nearby waters and splattered against the wooden vessels and their inhabitants. More importantly, it quickly dissuaded almost half the attacking craft from landing, although Waldo, who had seen the attackers as they assembled at that Royal Battery, wrote Pepperrell the next day that, "I am sensible from what I saw at the beginning of the attack that the greater part thereof never intended to land." The rest pushed forward in the face of several hundred French muskets that erupted from the ramparts. It was a difficult landing with the high surf toppling several boats and leaving many of those who made it to shore wet, along with their powder. Others disembarked with a "Huzzah" and pressed forward with ladders to scale the wall.

The French commander, Captain Charles Joseph d'Aillebout, had been prepared for an attack and the 250 French marines and militia in the garrison were quickly at their stations, but the staggered English landings had certainly helped him. The musketry, as well as some of the fort's cannons and a dozen swivel guns, soon stalled the British advance. A few men under the expedition's commander, Captain Edward Brooks, managed to place a dozen ladders against the wall and appeared on the ramparts but were soon cut down by the garrison. For the rest, it was clear that they had underestimated the French defenses. Facing a concentrated fire, they found themselves pinned down on the beach and embroiled in a brisk firefight. After not being able to advance, a few of the attackers took to the handful of boats that had not been damaged by the surf or French fire. For the rest, 120 or so, with no way off the beach and the freezing waters of the harbor out of the question, it was just a matter of time. They traded fire with the defenders in hopes that the vessels would return to evacuate them, but when no relief arrived, they surrendered at dawn.

Daylight also brought a better picture of the disaster, which would be the worst day of the siege for the New England army. Wrecked boats lined the shore or moved aimlessly with the tide filled with stilled occupants. So too did many of the slain attackers who now drifted near the shore. Others were lying clustered in spots along the beach, but most, including a number of wounded, were now loaded into boats and transferred to the town under the eyes of the besiegers. In all, 119 men were taken prisoner, while another seventy were either killed, wounded, or drowned.[16]

It was a blow to morale that was made worse in early June when Pepperrell reported that there were 1,500 sick and wounded in his camps, and the supply of powder and shot for the cannons was almost exhausted. "Our powder has been some days since expended," the general wrote Shirley on June 2. Commodore Warren had already lent the army 187 barrels and could be of no further help. Taken together it created a situation where Pepperrell had been "oblig'd very much to keep silent our artillery."[17]

For Du Chambon and his men, it almost did not matter. The heavy guns of Pepperrell's 2nd Battery pummeled the Dauphin Gate, while the mortars behind it made it impossible to patch the damage or remount the damaged cannons. Waldo's guns at the Royal Battery had taken a toll as well, making it impossible to "stay behind the wall of the pier which had been riddled through and through." The flank of the Royal Bastion had been devastated by the 24-pound guns in Pepperrell's First Battery, and as for the town, which saw both solid shot and explosive rounds from the English mortars, Du Chambon reported that, "All the houses in the town were demolished, riddled with holes, and not fit for habitation." There was little that could be done. With his powder running low and only a handful of bombs left for the mortars the governor had rationed his return fire such that only a handful of cannons were fired throughout the day. Fortunately, the enemy guns had slowed as well, but the French commander realized this was but a lull. The enemy were masters of the waves and could resupply from Portsmouth, Boston, Providence, or New York at any point, while without relief he and his garrison had perhaps a week of powder left in their magazines.[18]

Matters would soon turn worse for Du Chambon. Early in the siege Pepperrell and his council of war had agreed to mount a battery of cannons near the lighthouse across the channel from the Island Battery. The idea had been placed on hold until all the other siege batteries were in place. With this having been accomplished, efforts were revived in this direction and a regiment was sent to secure the location. In doing this a large cache of French cannons was found in shallow waters near the proposed battery. Many had deteriorated, and others were too small to be of use, but among those discovered in serviceable condition were half a dozen eighteen-pound cannons.

While Pepperrell's troops would not be confused for professional soldiers, as pioneers they were worth two professional soldiers in a siege. An earth redoubt was raised in front of the lighthouse about 1,200 yards from the barracks at the Island Battery. The sound of hammer and saw rang out as firing platforms were laid out and carriages constructed. When this was accomplished, work crews dragged the captured 18-pound cannons to the location and then mounted the two-ton guns on their recently fashioned carriages. Over three hundred men toiled at this work as the guns of the Island Battery attempted to disrupt their activities with the occasional cannon ball or bursting mortar round.

On the morning of June 10, Captain Michel de Gannes de Falaise, who had relieved d'Aillebout as commander of the Island Battery, realized that his limited efforts had not dissuaded the enemy when a pair of 18-pound cannons opened fire on the island. Over the course of the next few days four more 18-pound guns would be added to the Lighthouse Battery, although powder shortages still limited their fire. These frustrations would soon be set aside as two events quickly altered current operations. First was the arrival of the H.M.S. *Chester*, *Canterbury*, *Sunderland*, and *Lark* over the next few days. Second was the arrival of a convoy carrying the crew for the recently repaired *Vigilant* and a supply of powder and shot from Governor Shirley.

On the morning of June 15, a large mortar placed in the Lighthouse Battery announced the day by dropping 13-inch explosive rounds onto the parade ground of the Island Battery. Now well provisioned, the 18-pound cannons followed with solid shot that punched holes in the interior buildings and skipped down the length of the fortification, making it impossible to man the ramparts and service the cannons. After a few hours there was an explosion as a bomb found one of the fort's magazines. The barracks and a few interior buildings soon caught fire, obscuring the location in rolling black smoke. Pepperrell's batteries before the town also opened fire, as did the Royal Battery, and with the French counterfire added to this chorus the entire harbor vibrated with cannon fire.

Against this background Pepperrell met with his officers at a council of war. The influx of warships, manpower, and powder meant that Warren's original plan to run past the Island Battery and conduct a landing on the waterside of the fortress could go forward. The colonial troops not participating in the landing or the bombardment would launch an attack on the Dauphin Gate. Although several large breaches close to fifty feet wide had been opened in the walls of the bastion, it would be a harrowing 250-yard dash under the cover fire of their own guns to reach the walls of the fortress. Fortunately, it was to be a diversionary attack. If Warren was able to enter the harbor, there would not even be a need to land troops. With half a dozen 50- and 60-gun warships at his disposal he could easily bombard the town and turn the harborside defenses of the fortress into ruins. The French would certainly see this and surrender. All involved agreed with Warren, and the attack was scheduled for the next morning.

It proved a restless night for those on the land and those aboard Warren's rolling ships. For all, tomorrow held far more uncertainty than most days. However, it was not the sound of gunfire and cannons that greeted the Anglo-American force the next morning but that of French drums beating out a parley. A loud cheer was the response from land and sea. A flag of truce was sent out by Du Chambon to discuss surrender terms. The governor really had little choice. One witness claimed that French internal discussions centering on the surrender of the fortresses abounded in panic and fear, but in reality, with even more enemy warships blockading the port, the Island Battery flanked and badly damaged, and down to their last forty-seven barrels of powder, surrender was a wise move. Envoys from both sides met and, after some negotiations, the French flag was replaced the next morning with the Union Jack.[19]

The scale of Pepperrell's and Warren's victory was stunning. The fortress, the town, its garrison, and inhabitants, along with over 135 pieces of artillery, thousands of small arms, and a dozen captured French vessels, including the 64-gun *Vigilant,* were now in British hands. Like Port Royal, Nova Scotia, two generations before, the great maritime threat had been eliminated. No wonder when reports reached the shores of New England church bells rang for hours announcing the news.

Ten

THE FALL OF FRENCH ACADIA

Louisbourg would be repaired and garrisoned by British troops for the remainder of the war. The French would send a fleet the following year in an attempt to retake Louisbourg and Nova Scotia, but, harassed by British warships, scattered by bad weather, and decimated by illness, the operation accomplished little before the shattered remains crawled back to France. With Louisbourg and Nova Scotia now firmly in British hands it appeared that the contest between the coastal forts in the region had come to an end. New England had finally solved its maritime security issues and opened greater opportunities with the expulsion of the French fishing fleet. However, such was not to be the case, as under the Treaty of Aix-la-Capelle in 1748, which ended King George's War, all territories were to be restored to their pre-war state, meaning that Louisbourg would be returned to the French. Thus, it would take one more war and one more siege to make the fortress's capture permanent.

It was a frail peace that both sides knew would not last. Officially, it would last for eight years, but in North America the peace would come to an end much sooner. In May of 1754 a young Virginia colonel named George Washington clashed with French forces in the

Ohio Valley. Washington and his men were defeated and sent scurrying back over the Allegany Mountains with word that the Ohio belonged to France. The British disputed these claims, and the French responded with disputes over British claims to portions of Nova Scotia. America had now become the focus of the two powers. Both sides were looking to strengthen their positions in preparation for the conflict they knew was to come, and both sides saw America as a place to start. Soon other elements worked their way into the problem, such as matters involving French aggression in Nova Scotia, questions as to the French fort at Niagara, issues as to the western and northern boundaries between the two colonies, and finally the erection of Fort St. Frederic on Lake Champlain, which the English claimed was built on Iroquois land. For the moment, however, the matter was still colonial in scope and, as such, was held at arm's length from the general peace in Europe. This was to change with the decision to appoint General Edward Braddock military commander in North America and send him, along with two regiments of British regulars, to enforce the Crown's claims in North America. What had started as an isolated colonial incident in the Ohio Valley was about to become an assault on the limits of New France and the genesis of the Seven Years' War.

Perhaps no one in North America was more pleased with news of the upcoming British military efforts than Governor Shirley. In early December 1754 the governor and Sir William Pepperrell were both directed to raise regiments of a thousand men each and begin the necessary logistical preparations in expectation of Braddock's arrival the following spring. Although he would not be privy to the scope and actual details of the campaign for several months, it did not take much of an imagination on the governor's part, given the summer's recent events, and the fact that Braddock was destined for Virginia to see what was unfolding. Besides, the nature of the targets made little difference. What counted was that the crown was finally prepared to deal with the French as Shirley had been advocating for years.[1]

When King George's War came to an end, Shirley was chosen to represent British interests at the Paris peace commission, establishing, among other things, colonial boundary disputes. His stay with the commission did little to change his attitude toward the French. Stalled talks, exchanges of memorandums, and bickering over the language to be used only convinced him that the two sides were too far apart to ever reach a negotiated settlement. Recalled after a series of disputes with his colleagues, Shirley spent the next year in London work-

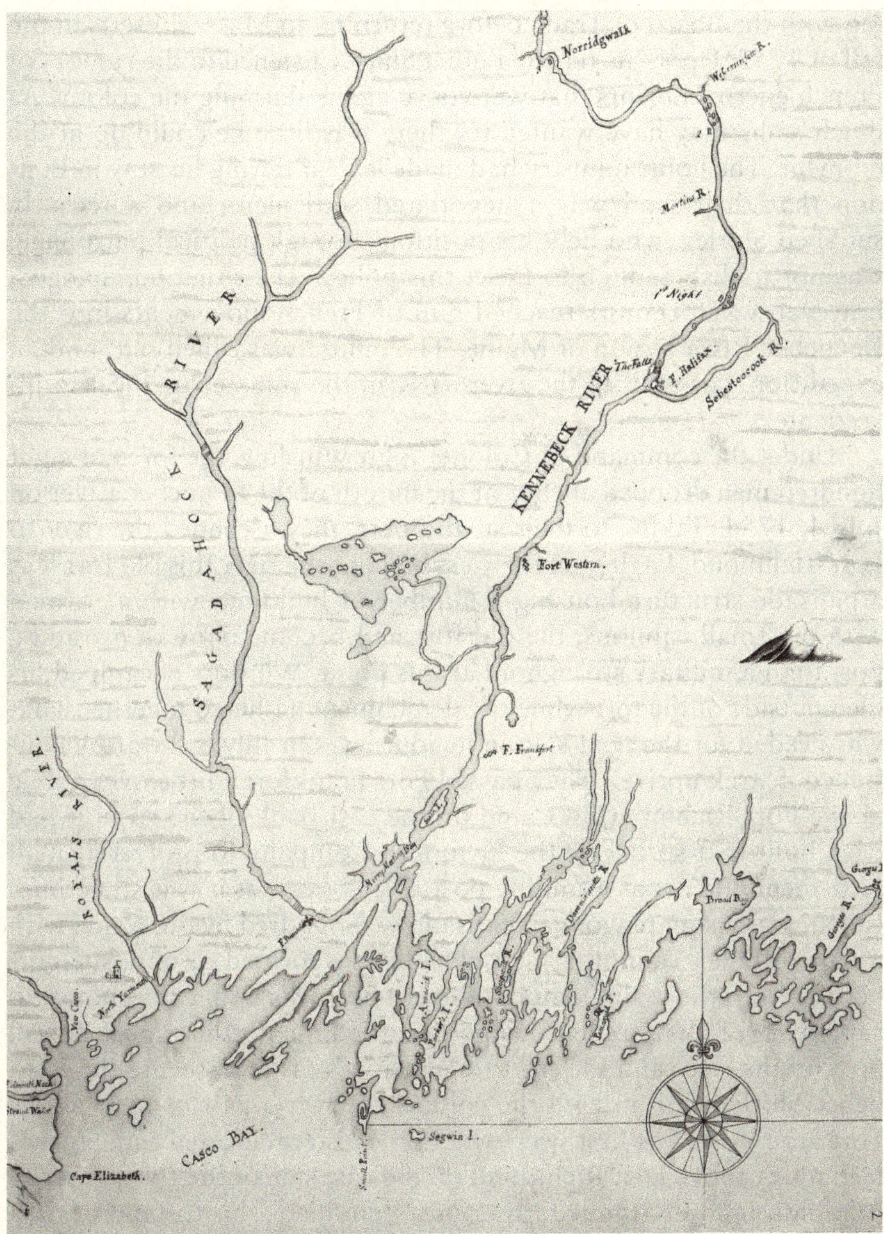

A 1761 map of the Kennebec River from the coast to Norridgewock. (*Norman B. Leventhal Map Collection, Boston Public Library*)

ing with the Board of Trade before returning to Massachusetts in the fall of 1753. Upon his return a quiet Shirley listened to the rumors of French encroachments that were once again alarming the colony. As much as he may have wanted to, there was little he could do at the moment. The home ministry had made it clear during his stay in London that their goal was a negotiated settlement, and a recently snubbed Shirley, who held his position through political patronage, was not foolish enough to upset this policy. The situation changed, however, when rumors reached him of French movements into the Kennebec River region of Maine. The militia was called out, and an expedition was sent up the river early in the summer of 1754 to investigate.[2]

Under the command of Colonel John Winslow, the force of eight hundred men dropped anchor at the mouth of the Kennebec River on July 4, 1754. Taking to their small boats, they ascended the river to Fort Richmond. Laying on the west bank of the river this old fort was a palisade structure housing a number of buildings within. Armed with ten small cannons, the old fort had become more of a trading post than a military stronghold at this point. Winslow encamped his men outside of the fort while the detachment gathered together what was needed for the next step in its journey. On July 8 the army continued its trek upriver. They passed Fort Frankfort a little over a mile above Fort Richmond. Located on the east bank of the river, it had been built that spring by the Plymouth Company to protect a small settlement and act as a trading post. Frank Fort, as it was sometimes called, was a square wooden palisade two hundred feet to a side with a pair of taller, cannon-armed blockhouses located at opposite corners. Within the main compound were barracks and a storehouse to support the Indian trade. This post marked the northernmost British post on the river and the start of Winslow's task. To secure the Kennebec Shirley had ordered the colonel to erect a pair of forts above Fort Frankfort. The first was to be Fort Western, located some seventeen miles above Fort Richmond on the east side of the river. A series of rapids and falls a mile farther upstream made this the end of navigation for any craft that could not be dragged out of the water and carried around this obstacle.

On July 12 the expedition started work on Fort Western, clearing the land for the distance of two musket shots from the shore before raising the wooden structure, which was a slightly smaller version of Fort Frankfort. Work was also started on an outer palisade that would

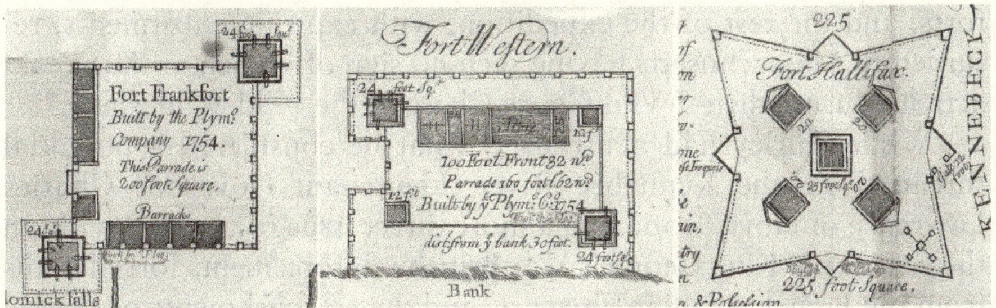

The Kennebec River Forts Frankfort, Western, and Halifax. (*Norman B. Leventhal Map Collection, Boston Public Library*)

further protect the structure. Leaving two hundred men at Fort Western to defend and continue work on the post, Winslow pressed forward on July 21. The second fort the governor wanted was near Ticonic Falls, eighteen miles farther upriver. Carrying eight cannons and a pair of mortars, for the next five days Winslow's men arrayed in dozens of small boats and canoes struggled against the river. Winslow wrote that it "was five days of the hardest Duty that ever I saw any Troops employ'd on, we were Continually in the Water from Morning till Night getting our Boats over Rocks, Sand & Falls many places of which there was scarse half the Water they drew." The task consumed the entire detachment, including Winslow, who informed a friend that "I dont Remember any of these Days, but that I was some hours of each in the Water and once in a while put to Swimming."[3]

By the twenty-fifth Winslow and his men went ashore on a point of land formed by the junction of the Kennebec and Sebasticook Rivers. The next day the artillery arrived and a site was selected on the peninsula for Fort Halifax. The fort was an eight-sided-star-shaped palisade with redans built into the center section of each wall, which spanned approximately 225 feet to a side. Blockhouses and storehouses made of interconnecting timbers laid horizontally one upon another occupied the interior of the structure, and provisions were made for the ten small cannons and mortars that backed the garrison. While work continued on Forts Western and Halifax, Winslow sent a large war party around Ticonic Falls to scout farther upriver. This detachment returned fifteen days later with nothing of any substance to report. In late September garrisons were appointed for the forts, and the rest of the expedition, with expiring enlistments, returned to Massachusetts having seen no sign of French or Wabanaki activity during their "Wild Goose Chase in the Wild Wilderness."[4]

While Shirley had neutralized what he considered a potential threat along the Kennebec River, Lieutenant Governor Charles Lawrence of Nova Scotia had a more direct issue to contend with. In the years after King George's War British reinforcements forced oaths from the French Acadian citizenry, and the establishments of several towns, such as Halifax, had gone far in securing the colony. Even so, small French and Indian war parties still lurked along some of the interior roadways, with most of this activity concentrated to the north side of the Bay of Fundy. In particular, Chignecto Neck, a narrow strip of land between Green Bay and Chignecto Bay that connected Nova Scotia to the mainland, became the nexus of this endeavor. Since the Treaty of Aix-la-Capelle had returned all territories to their prewar status, this meant that the Treaty of Utrecht, which ended Queen Anne's War, was in effect. This treaty spelled out British possession of Acadia (Nova Scotia) as defined by its ancient limits.

The French would claim that everything south of the Missaguash River was the ancient limits defined in the treaty. To carry through with this approach the recently arrived governor of New France, Jacques-Pierre de Taffanel de La Jonquière, the Marquis de La Jonquière, dispatched Captain Louis de La Corne, the Chevalier de La Corne, to the area with seventy marines. La Corne was to coordinate with Father Le Loutre, the local missionary, to win over the Acadian populace and oppose any English expansion. In order to defend the northern side of the Missaguash, La Corne forcibly removed the Acadian settlements on the south bank and then burned several of their villages so they could not be of use to the British. Resettled, the 350 displaced families to the north gave La Corne a force of well over a thousand marines, militia, and Micmac and Maliseet allies to call upon.

After several French and Indian raids into the colony from across the Missaguash River, in April 1750 Governor Edward Cornwallis dispatched the future lieutenant governor, Major Charles Lawrence, and four hundred men to establish control over Chignecto Neck. When Lawrence and his flotilla arrived at the head of the bay on May 1, he spied La Corne and close to a thousand French and Micmac arrayed along the north side of the Missaguash. Outnumbered and looking to avoid an engagement, Lawrence spoke with La Corne, who

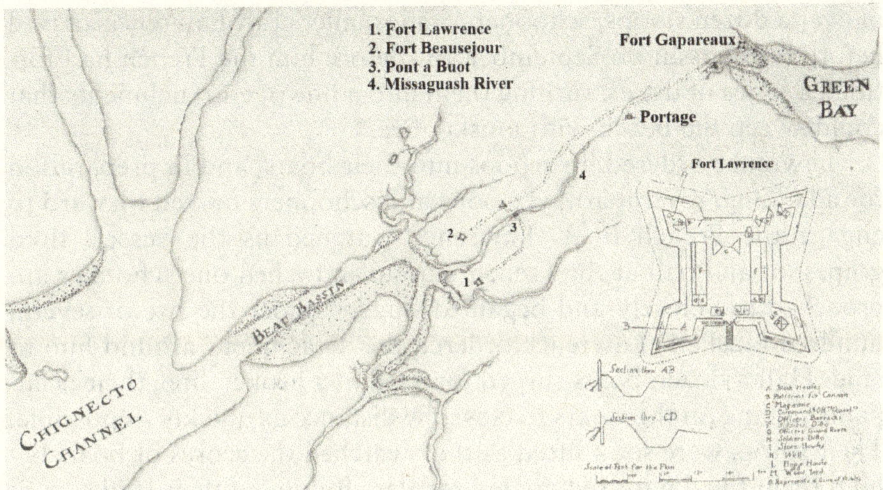

A map of Chignecto Neck from Baye Francoise (Chignecto Bay) across the isthmus to Baye Verte (Green Bay) in the west. Note how the Missaguash waterway, which traverses most of the isthmus, makes it an ideal defensive barrier. Fort Beauséjour can be seen on a height near Chignecto Bay with Fort Lawrence located across the river. With British naval control over the Bay of Fundy and the Gulf of Maine, the wooden Fort Gaspareaux at Green Bay would act as a supply point for Fort Beauséjour and the French forces located north of the river. (*Norman B. Leventhal Map Collection, Boston Public Library*)

informed him that his orders were to defend the north bank of the river as the border between British Nova Scotia and French Acadia. He then suggested that Lawrence land at the town of Beaubassin, which had been abandoned when its denizens crossed over to the northside of the river. Lawrence, looking to scout the south shore for a location to erect a fort, agreed and commenced landing operations. The town, however, was put to the torch by a retreating French and Indian war party. Outnumbered, and wrapped in a pall of smoke and drifting embers from over a hundred burning homes, Lawrence ordered his men back into their boats and returned to Halifax.[5]

That summer Cornwallis was reinforced by four hundred men from Lascelles's regiment (soon to be the 47th Regiment), a pair of companies from Newfoundland, and additional recruits for Warburton's regiment (45th) already on station. With the sudden influx of manpower the governor dispatched recently promoted Lieutenant Colonel Lawrence with a force of nearly a thousand regulars and militia to erect a fort on the south side of the Missaguash River. Arrayed in over a dozen sloops, schooners, and smaller craft Lawrence arrived before Beaubassin on September 15. Before him the French had fortified a series of dykes, turning them into a line of entrenchments that could sweep the beach with musket fire.

Lawrence ordered his troops into their boats, and in preparation for a landing, several armed sloops and schooners moved forward to engage the French lines. Lawrence watched as the vessels fired grapeshot and ball at the French works, and when one schooner approached too closely and began to stagger under the fire of several hundred muskets, Lawrence ordered the detachment around him to land. Half a dozen boats surged forward in a broken line, their occupants pulling on their oars to close the distance as quickly as possible. Their spirits were soon lifted as they watched the scores of boats behind them filled with red-coated regulars following their lead.

What appeared as errant shots now became more focused as the first boats beached and their occupants went over the sides with a shout. Lawrence and a little over a hundred men were now ashore. Quickly forming their ranks, the lieutenant colonel ordered a bayonet charge on the entrenchments before them. The French irregulars made covering the distance costly, leaving a trail of almost a score of dead or wounded in its wake, but the charge brought Lawrence and his troops to the edge of the trenches. The enemy had decided to abandon their defense and were busy trying to escape when the British troops, who had not fired a shot, poured a volley into the retreating defenders at point-blank range and then leapt into the trenches, quickly clearing them with their bayonets.[6]

With the rest of his army only moments behind him and the French in full retreat, Lawrence soon established control over the south bank of the river. Now it became a question of where to place a fort. After scouting the area, it was decided to place Fort Lawrence at the end of a shallow ridge about a quarter of a mile from the river. Logistics and the season dictated the nature of the fort. The structure was built of wood, employing four bastions linked by double palisade walls. This last feature allowed for a firing platform along the length of the curtain walls, while the bastions would mount the stronghold's cannons and act as magazines and bomb-proof shelters for the garrison. A ditch was dug around the base of the fort and the dirt piled on the other side to create a covered way. Interior buildings followed, and given their proximity to the French, a garrison of 450 men was planned for.

While Lawrence was able to raise and garrison his fort before winter set in, he could not help but notice that the next spring the French were busy constructing a fort of their own across the river. In fact, the decision had been made to build two forts and reinforce a third. The first and strongest, Fort Beauséjour, was located on a hill near the head of Chignecto Bay and a little over a mile from the Missaguash River. Laid out and built by French engineer Gaspard-Joseph Chaussegros de Léry and artillery officer Ensign Louis-Thomas Jacau de Fiedmont, the structure was star shaped with bastions at each point. A stone base was placed along the fort's outline, and earth from the ditch was used to erect fifteen-foot-tall walls on top of this platform. The walls for the bastions were much thicker than the curtain walls. This allowed for a rampart to be cut out of the earth and wooden firing platforms laid for the fort's cannons. Wood-lined embrasures were then carved out of the earth to create parapets to allow the cannons to fire. The curtain walls had a much smaller rampart and were reserved primarily for musketry or swivel guns.

The interior buildings were raised close to the walls and bombproof shelters dug out of the bastion walls. Reinforced with timbers and covered with half a dozen feet of earth, one of these would act as the fort's magazine and the others as refuge for the garrison, although the British engineer who would capture the fort noted that these shelters were "neither dry nor bomb-proof." The counter-scarp of the ditch had a palisade to slow down any infantry attack, but the fort did not have a glacis because its hilltop location served this function. Two-dozen swivel guns were mounted along the ramparts while the heavier cannons, 8-pounders, were placed in the stronghold's bastions. There was also a 9-inch mortar in the parade ground. The garrison officially consisted of a company of marines, about sixty men and their officers, but given the tense situation there were typically militia and Micmac in the fort, perhaps doubling this number. Just as importantly, more men could be called upon from the village that had grown up near the post.

Although sod was placed on the earth walls in an attempt to delay the ravages of rain and snow, earth forts in such climates required a great deal of maintenance to prevent them from falling into ruin. On the positive side, earth forts such as Beauséjour were far more resilient in the face of artillery fire and were easily repaired. Combined with the fort's elevated position and open field of fire for over nine hundred yards it would require a concerted effort on the part of the enemy to capture it.

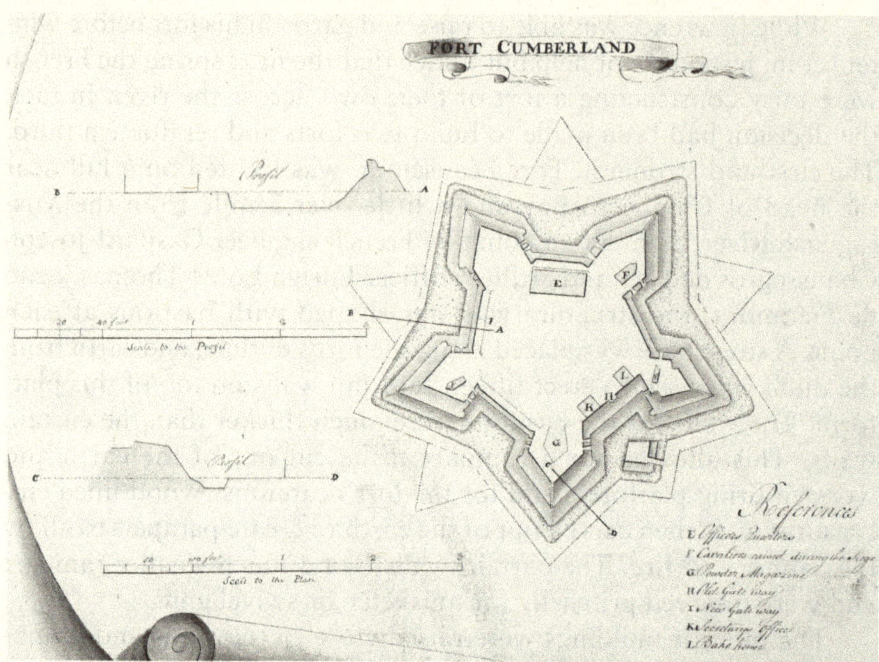

Fort Cumberland (Fort Beauséjour) in 1756. Note the profile A-B showing the cross-section of a curtain wall, and the profile C-D showing the walls of the bastions. (*Norman B. Leventhal Map Collection, Boston Public Library*)

Built at the same time as Fort Beauséjour, Fort Gaspareaux on Green Bay was a classical wooden structure. The four bastions were made of horizontal timbers and the interconnecting curtain walls made in a double-rowed wooden palisade. It was not a large structure but still mounted half a dozen small cannons. The fact that a sixteen-man garrison lived in huts outside the structure, because the barracks had yet to be completed, speaks to the state of the post, which acted more as a supply depot and communications post than a real fortification. To the west, work on the ruins of old Fort Jean at the outlet of the St. John River started in 1749 when the French commander in this area, Lieutenant Charles Deschamps de Boishébert, received orders to secure the harbor. Rebuilt along the same trace as the old fort, the resulting structure was renamed Fort Menagouche. It was a four-bastioned earth fort with wooden firing platforms placed on the bastions and along the curtain walls. Wooden barracks and storehouses lined the curtain walls, and the gate on the landside approach to the

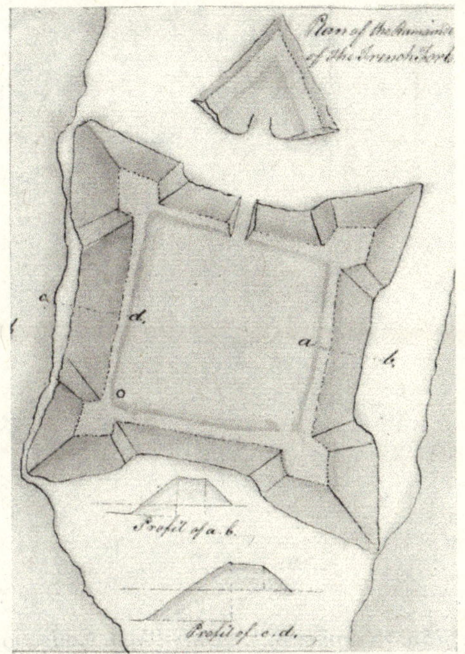

The earth ruins of Fort Menagouche, September 1758. Anything wooden was burned when the post was evacuated after the fall of Fort Beauséjour in 1755, but there was no time nor the resources to disrupt the earth walls of the structure. The British would use this trace to establish Fort Frederick three years later. (*Norman B. Leventhal Map Collection, Boston Public Library*)

fort was protected by an earth redan, which could easily support a number of swivel guns or small cannons. The fort would perform the same function as Fort Gaspareaux, and together with Fort Beauséjour, established another communications link to Louisbourg from Quebec.[7]

The net effect of these French and British strongholds in the Chignecto Peninsula was to create several years of small-scale raids and counter-raids along this disputed border. On the British side the answer to ending these attacks seemed clear. Enforce royal claims by reducing both Fort Beauséjour and its supply depot, Fort Gaspareaux. Such a move, however, would likely spark a general conflict in North America, something that neither the government in London nor Paris were interested in pursuing at the moment.

This would change with rumors of French activity in Maine and news of Virginia Colonel George Washington's capture and expulsion from the Ohio Valley in the summer of 1754. As in King George's War, Governor Shirley was quick to react. He penned a letter to Sec-

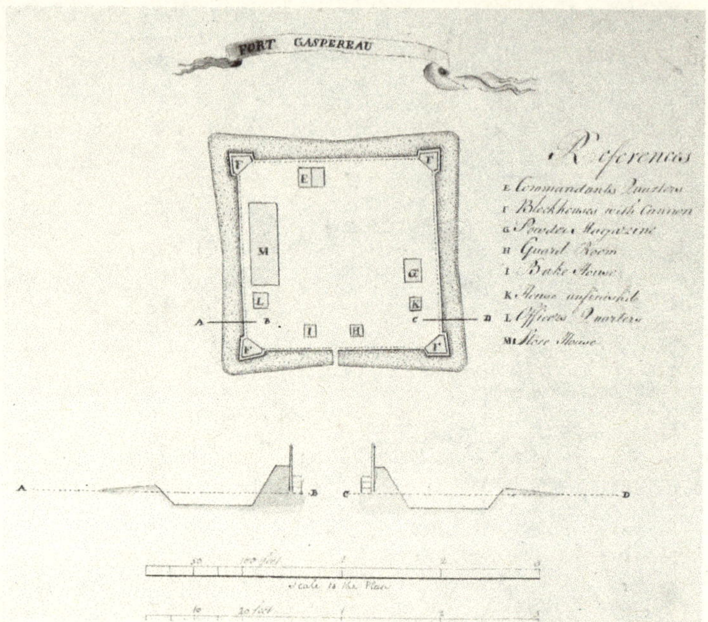

Fort Gaspareaux in 1756. (*Norman B. Leventhal Map Collection, Boston Public Library*)

retary of State Sir Thomas Robinson in which he outlined a scheme to secure his majesty's eastern colonies from French and Indian aggression. Besides the current efforts on the Kennebec River, the plan called for the removal of the disputed French forts in Acadia and the construction of an English fort "less than a point-blank shot from Fort St. Frederick," on Lake Champlain.[8]

The governor contacted Lieutenant Governor Lawrence, who had long been a proponent of reducing Fort Beauséjour, and began planning a joint venture to strike at the French post in the spring. Shirley would soon find out that the government's response to French expansion into the Ohio Valley was to send General Edward Braddock, two regiments of regulars, and a detachment of Royal Artillery to Virginia with the aim of seizing Fort Duquesne in the spring of 1755. London viewed this action as a measured response to a frontier border dispute and suspected that the final outcome would be to accelerate ongoing negotiations concerning the limits of the French and British colonies. There proved to be two problems in executing this limited response. The first was the departure of six regiments of French regulars for Quebec and Louisbourg in the spring of 1755. These reinforcements

Lt. Colonel Robert Monckton. (*New York Public Library*)

would clearly pose a major threat to Braddock's expedition, and as such, attempts were made by the Royal Navy to intercept this fleet, but the vast majority arrived safely.

The second and larger problem faced in carrying through with the original scope of operations was Braddock and the broad powers granted to him under his orders. When the general arrived at Alexandria in April 1755 he found that a pair of colonial expeditions were in the process of being formed. The first, under Lieutenant Colonel Robert Monckton of the 47th Regiment, would strike at French Fort Beauséjour in Nova Scotia while the second, commanded by colonial General William Johnson, would move against Fort St. Frederic on Lake Champlain. Since both of these attacks would draw French resources away from his campaign, and required nothing on his part to execute, Braddock ordered both to go forward. In fact, to further stretch the French defenders, a fourth attack was added. Governor Shirley, the prime motivator behind Johnson's and Monckton's expeditions, would lead several regiments to Oswego, and after building the ships and bateaux needed to move his army, would lay siege to Fort Niagara. If this important supply post fell, it would greatly weaken the French forts in the Ohio Valley, including Fort Duquesne. Thus, what London had hoped to be a limited response that would not trigger a general conflict in North America had transformed to a four-pronged assault on New France.[9]

Monckton's expedition would prove to be the most successful of the four ventures. In February, after consulting with the Massachusetts Assembly and Lieutenant Governor James de Lancy of New York, Shirley confirmed that the colony would raise two thousand men and contribute four 24-pound siege guns to the effort. New York would supplement this battery with ten 18-pound cannons, while additional cannons and munitions could be supplied from Halifax. Lieutenant Colonel John Winslow of Massachusetts, who had spent the previous summer on the Kennebec River, would command one battalion of a thousand men, while Captain George Scott of the 40th Regiment would command the second battalion. Monckton would be in overall command and would call upon the regular troops in garrison at Fort Lawrence to assist with the effort. The recruitment and buildup was done with as much secrecy as possible. French citizens in Boston were held and foreign vessels in port stopped from departing for several months.

Even with these precautions, the process moved far slower than hoped, and it was not until May 26 that Monckton's forces assembled at Annapolis Royal. Here the colonel met Captain-Lieutenant John Brewse of the Royal Engineers and the artillery stores sent from Halifax. With everything in place, the convoy set sail for Chignecto on June 1 under the escort of three 20-gun frigates. The boats went ashore the next evening, and the army encamped around Fort Lawrence for the next few days as bad weather slowed the landing of the siege train and supplies.

At 6 a.m. on the morning of June 4 the two thousand New England troops, supported by 250 regulars from the fort and a field battery of four 6-pounders, began their march toward Pont a Buot, the only practical river crossing in the area. When Monckton's troops arrived a little before noon, they saw a French blockhouse and a series of entrenchments lining the opposite bank. The field guns began to deploy as Monckton ordered the column to advance on the French works. As it was low tide the river was not as much of an obstacle as the high bank and enemy emplacements on the other side. A pair of French cannons and a number of swivel guns fired grapeshot at the approaching formation, but from their elevated position most sailed

A map of Fort Beauséjour (Fort Cumberland) and Fort Lawrence near the outlet of the Missaguash River. (*Norman B. Leventhal Map Collection, Boston Public Library*)

over the heads of Monckton's troops. Within moments a series of shouts and yells came from the enemy lines followed by a volley of not less than six hundred muskets, according to one witness. The fire must have been at extreme range, as only a handful of troops were struck. Part of the advancing column began to fire back, but their officers yelled at them to hold their fire and maintain their ranks. By now the battery of British 6-pounders had come into action, repeatedly striking the blockhouse with clouds of grapeshot that chipped away at the structure and dug up the earth around the entrenchments. With the unbroken formations of enemy troops still approaching and their cannons quickly neutralized by the larger British field guns, the French commander ordered the blockhouse put to the torch and retreated back toward Fort Beauséjour.[10]

The battle had resulted in a little over a dozen casualties on both sides. "This I think to be ye most Remarkble thing I Ever Saw," one British soldier would write of the engagement. "Yet we Should Receive So much of thare Fire & Nothing to Cover us from it & yet no more Killd & wounded." Now established on the north bank, effectively cutting the road between Fort Beauséjour and Fort Gaspareaux, the army turned left and marched until they were within two miles of the former fort. Here they made camp as columns of smoke emanated from the village near Fort Beauséjour, which had been purposely set ablaze by the defenders. For the next week Monckton's troops scouted the French position and fortified their encampment as the siege guns and supplies were dragged forward.

On the night of June 8, a detachment under Winslow moved forward, and after a brief skirmish, secured a piece of ground about nine hundred yards to the northeast of the fort. With the fort now invested and most of the necessary supplies brought forward, Captain Brewse began formal siege operations. Over the next few days, a pair of firing parallels were dug as half a dozen cannons from Fort Beauséjour fired grapeshot and ball at the pioneers toiling away with pick and shovel. The fort's mortar also began lobbing bombs at the saps, but the handful of casualties that resulted from this did not slow the work. On the morning of the fourteenth, dawn was announced by three British 8-inch mortars, which dropped exploding rounds onto the fort's ramparts and into the parade ground.[11]

For Captain Louis Duchambon de Verger, who had taken command of the fort from La Corne several years before, the British mortars had placed him in a difficult position. Several hundred militia had responded to his call and were stationed in hastily dug trenches outside the fort, but their loyalty was beginning to waver as the enemy surrounded the stronghold. On the twelfth, Verger launched a sally on the British right in an attempt to drive them from their trenchworks, but it quickly bogged down and was abandoned. While heavy rains late that evening and the following day slowed British efforts, the hollow thump of heavy mortars echoed across the landscape late on the afternoon of June 15 as a handful of 13-inch bombs exploded in the fort, spraying the parade ground and interior buildings with shrapnel before sunset brought an end to the bombardment.

At this point there was little for the garrison to do but place a handful of men on the ramparts to service the cannons and send the rest into the bomb-proof shelters to weather the upcoming bombardment. It now just became a question of whether or not a French relief force would appear to drive the British from their fieldworks and lift the siege. At daybreak on June 16 the barrage resumed as a column of dust and exploding geysers of dirt clutched the stronghold. Any hope of holding out until a relief column arrived was dismissed mid-morning when a 13-inch mortar round pierced the roof of one of the bomb-proof shelters and exploded inside, killing the occupants, a number of whom were the garrison's officers.

With most of the militia having already deserted, and his fort incapable of protecting the garrison, Verger lowered the French flag at 10:00 a.m. and, after a brief parley, surrendered Fort Beauséjour. Fort Gaspareaux at the other end of Chignecto Neck would surrender without a shot being fired a few days later when a detachment under Winslow appeared before it. Thus, within the span of a few weeks, and at the cost of only a handful of casualties, the French position in Acadia had completely unraveled and, for all practical purposes, had been lost for good.[12]

Eleven

A RETURN TO LOUISBOURG

With the fall of Fort Beauséjour and Fort Gaspareaux the last French position of strength in the Canadian Maritimes was Fortress Louisbourg on Cape Breton Island. The return of the fortress after King George's War meant another large campaign was required to secure this location before pushing forward to Quebec. The first attempt at this occurred in early 1757. The previous fall General John Campbell, the Earl of Loudoun, who had replaced Governor Shirley as commander in chief in North America, wrote Whitehall that an attack on Quebec should be the focus of the next year's campaign. The reason was simple; seize Quebec, and the rest of the French colony would fall with it.

William Pitt, who had become prime minister of Britian, did not disagree, but he was also not going to leave an active Louisbourg in the rear of an expedition up the St. Lawrence River. In early May 1757, when Pitt's directives finally reached Loudoun, who had been waiting in New York City for London's approval of his plan, he found that Louisbourg was to be the focus of this year's campaign and, if time permitted, was to be followed by an attack on Quebec. After detaching forces necessary to secure the frontier, Loudoun was directed to assemble his forces and transport them to Halifax. Here he would rendezvous with Admiral Francis Holburne and some eight thousand reinforcements sent from England. Although the orders differed from Loudoun's suggested plan, it was an approach that "in a great measure," he wrote Pitt, "coincides with the preparations I have made."[1]

Leaving his third in command, Brigadier General Daniel Webb, in charge of the New York frontier with 7,500 men, Loudoun ordered his six regular regiments and Rogers' Ranging companies onto transports in New York Harbor and departed for Halifax on June 20. Once at the Nova Scotian port Loudoun did not have to wait long for Admiral Holburne's fleet and the transports from England carrying the 5,200 regulars and the artillery train. By mid-July sixteen regiments of regulars, almost fifteen thousand men, were encamped near the new town. In the harbor sat seventeen ships-of-the-line, another sixteen smaller warships, and 150 transports adding another ten thousand sailors and marines to the total. It was a force that dwarfed Shirley's expedition against the French fortress just a dozen years before and one certainly capable of not only seizing Louisbourg again but striking at Quebec if the season still permitted.

Unlike Shirley's effort during King George's War, this time there would be no element of surprise. Suspecting that the British would make an attempt on the port, the French navy directed three different squadrons to converge on the location, and by June 20 eighteen ships-of-the-line along with a score of smaller warships and privateers rested at anchor in the harbor. In fact, the influx of manpower and supplies had sparked the question of whether or not the French should go on the offensive. While such an action by Admiral Emmanuel-Auguste de Cahideuc, the Count Dubois de la Motte, would have certainly disrupted Loudoun's campaign and might have even intercepted the general's poorly guarded fleet on its way to Halifax, it was decided to act in a defensive manner. The French admiral dispatched several ships-of-the-line and a few frigates to escort a convoy to Quebec that was carrying two battalions of the Berry Regiment and then focused on helping to improve the defenses of the fortress.

After having sent several small vessels forward to examine Louisbourg Harbor and take any prisoners they could, Loudoun became alarmed by the reports reaching him. One scout reported ten ships-of-the-line and four frigates in the harbor, and the crew of a captured fishing schooner stated that there were ten ships-of-the-line and fourteen frigates at anchor but that five of the ships-of-the-line and a pair of frigates had sailed for Quebec. Bad weather had thwarted several attempts to confirm these reports, leading Loudoun to hold a council of war on July 23 to discuss this information and agree on a general plan of attack.[2]

While there was first debate as to a landing site, a number of participants pointed out that, if the French fleet was as large as reported, it would be foolish to attack without reinforcements. Others still held confidence that the army could be landed, at least if the weather held, but Captain George Scott of the 40th Regiment, who had served in Nova Scotia for several years, pointed out to Loudoun that it was already too late to launch an attack. Working under the proviso that the weather was good and the French did nothing, Scott estimated that it would take five weeks to get the army, its supplies, and its siege guns ashore at Louisbourg. Meaning that, even under ideal circumstances, it would be the first week of September before a siege could commence. Should the weather take a turn for the worse or the French put up a stiff resistance before falling back on their defenses, it might well be October before the ground was broken on the siege trenches. This was clearly too late in the year to keep an army in the field on Cape Breton Island, especially as the siege might last months.

Loudoun was inclined to agree with Scott, but with such a force assembled he also believed that an attempt had to be made. On August 2 he ordered his troops onto the transports and was preparing to depart when a captured French schooner was brought into port. The vessel was carrying official dispatches which spoke to twenty-two French ships-of-the-line being at Louisbourg and that the garrison of four thousand men had set up new gun batteries at the possible landing sites. The captured ship's crew confirmed the reports and were even able to provide the names of many of the French warships.

The news settled the matter for Loudoun who wrote London on August 5 with his decision to abandon the campaign. Weather and delays in assembling the forces, coupled with the arrival of a French squadron powerful enough to threaten Nova Scotia and coastal New England, had left him with little choice but to pursue the prudent path. While a number of the council of war disagreed with the decision, in something of a confirmation as to the wisdom of this path a few days after the decision, Sir Charles Hardy, sailing with his squadron near the French port, was able to discern several large encampments through a break in the fog, along with seventeen French ships-of-the-line and numerous frigates riding in the harbor. The operation, had it gone forward, he wrote Loudoun shortly thereafter, "in my opinion would have ended with the ruin of our Army." There was also the matter of such a large French fleet operating in American waters. If the attack failed or the weather worsened and crippled Holburne's fleet, they would be left free to create havoc up and down the eastern seaboard.[3]

Loudoun realized that, no matter how correct his decision, it would create an uproar, and in this he was not mistaken. When news reached London, the ministry was divided on how to proceed. Several, like the Earl of Halifax, thought that Loudoun's actions were "not only irreproachable but highly judicious," and Secretary of State Henry Fox, for one, believed that the general had "done right and acted sensibly." Others were of a different mind. Both Newcastle and Admiral Anson believed that Loudoun should have taken the risk and pushed on to Louisbourg. The lord high chancellor, the Earl of Hardwick, shrugged at the report and pointed out that he had never been in favor of Loudoun's appointment, and after consulting with several officers that were present, concluded that the guiding philosophy behind the expedition had been "nothing is to be undertaken where there is risk or danger."[4]

Pitt, who held Loudoun's command in his hands, was his most outspoken critic. "Nothing is done. Nothing is attempted," he complained. "We have lost all the waters. There is not a boat on the lakes. Every door is open to France." Coupled with the news of Fort William Henry's loss, the first minister's initial reaction was to recall Loudoun in September, but when no suitable replacement could be found, he delayed the decision. Loudoun did nothing to help his cause during this brief reprieve. On August 16, shortly after calling off the attack on Louisburg, Loudoun wrote Pitt. In the letter he railed against Pitt's policy of directing operations from London, leaving the person in charge to conduct the affair "with a halter about his neck."[5]

Pitt had seen enough of Loudoun and recalled him, appointing his second in command, Major General James Abercromby, as the new commander in chief in North America. The prime minister then laid out the ambitious details for the campaign of 1758, which called for three attacks on New France. To the west a contingent of seven thousand provincials and regulars under the command of Brigadier General John Forbes would besiege Fort Duquesne in the Ohio Valley while Abercromby would personally lead six thousand regulars and twenty thousand colonial troops against Fort Carillon and Fort St.

Frederic in the Champlain Valley. Lastly, to the east, fourteen thousand men and a sizable fleet would be assembled at Halifax by late April with the aim of besieging Louisbourg at the first possible opportunity.[6]

Pitt had selected Colonel Jeffery Amherst, who was stationed in Germany, to lead this last effort with the new rank of major general. The forty-one-year-old Amherst had a rapid rise through the ranks of the British army. Amherst was not born to a prominent English family. His father was a well-known lawyer practicing in Kent, and whether through his efforts or by simple proximity, at the age of twelve Amherst became a page in the nearby house of Lord Dorset, a gentleman soon to be appointed lord lieutenant of Ireland. In 1735 his service to Dorset no doubt obtained him a cornet's position in Major General John Ligonier's cavalry regiment, then stationed in Ireland. It was a fortunate arrangement, for Ligonier, one of the best British soldiers of the day and destined to become Lord Ligonier and captain general of the British army, took an instant liking to Amherst, who he frequently referred to as his "dear pupil." With Dorset and Ligonier's patronage, Amherst quickly obtained rank. Upon the outbreak of the War of Austrian Succession, Amherst served on Ligonier's staff and saw action at the Battles of Dettingen in 1743 and Fontenoy in 1745. Later that year he was appointed a captain in the 1st Foot Guards, a prestigious position that carried the rank of lieutenant colonel in the regular army. In 1747 he was given a position on Cumberland's staff when the latter was appointed commander of allied forces on the Continent. Amherst served in this role throughout the remainder of the conflict, participating in a number of sieges and the Battle of Laffeldt in 1747. Upon the outbreak of the Seven Years' War in 1756, he was assigned the task of commissary to the eight thousand Hessian troops taken into British pay. He returned to England later that year at which time he was appointed colonel of the 15th Regiment of Foot. Leaving his new regiment to its lieutenant colonel, Amherst returned to the Continent the following year, and with his Hessian contingent, was part of Cumberland's defeat at the Battle of Hastenbeck. As a consequence of the defeat, Cumberland resigned his post as captain general of the British army in October of 1757. The new captain general was none other than Amherst's old mentor, John Ligonier.

Thus, when the question of a commander for the Louisbourg expedition appeared, Ligonier recommended Amherst. The idea of

John Campbell, the Earl of Loudon, left, Major General Jeffery Amherst, center, and Admiral Edward Boscawen, right. (*National Galleries of Scotland; National Archives of Canada; National Portrait Gallery, London*)

Amherst, a junior colonel who had never served in a command capacity, proved problematic. Both Pitt and the Duke of Newcastle had questions as to the selection, but both trusted the judgment of Ligonier, and both wished to remain on good terms with the new captain general. As such, they separately petitioned the king for the appointment of Amherst to the rank of major general in North America through both normal and not so normal channels. The efforts paid off, and in late 1757 Amherst received his new command.[7]

Amherst was supported by a force of thirteen regiments, a sizable detachment of Royal Artillery, and a corps of rangers, some twelve thousand men in all. To lead these troops Amherst was fortunate to have three good brigadiers under his command: James Wolfe, Charles Lawrence, and Edward Whitmore. The first, Wolfe, entered the army at the age of sixteen as an ensign in the 12th Foot in 1741. He would serve throughout the War of Austrian Succession, fighting at the Battle of Dettingen before being sent to Scotland to suppress the Jacobite uprising led by Bonnie Prince Charlie. Wolfe would be at the Battle of Falkirk in 1745 and the Battle of Culloden Moor in 1746. After a brief stint in the highlands chasing down Jacobite rebels, Wolfe returned to Flanders the following year and was wounded at the Battle of Laffeldt in July. When the conflict came to an end Wolfe was a major in the 20th Regiment stationed at Stirling Castle in Scotland, and in 1751 he was made lieutenant colonel of this regiment. With the opening of the Seven Years' War in Europe, Wolfe served as quartermaster general for General John Mordaunt's expedition against the port of Rochefort in September 1757. While the expedition was a failure the young officer's conduct had impressed many and would result in a promotion to colonel and shortly thereafter an assignment to Amherst's expedition.[8]

Of Amherst's brigadiers Lawrence was the one most familiar with the area. After having served in Flanders during the early part of the War of Austrian Succession and rising to the rank of captain in the 45th Regiment, he was transferred to Louisbourg in 1747. Spending the next two years in garrison duty with the return of the fortress to France in 1749 Lawrence was transferred to Halifax. From here he was first promoted to major and then to lieutenant colonel of the 40th, all while becoming a mainstay on the volatile Chignecto frontier. In 1754 he was made lieutenant governor of Nova Scotia and the following year coordinated with Governor Shirley to successfully remove the French threat at Chignecto Neck. Lawrence was still acting in his capacity of lieutenant governor when he was promoted to brigadier general and assigned to Amherst's command.

The last of Amherst's brigadiers, Edward Whitmore, was the oldest among them. As an ensign Whitmore had participated in Admiral Hanoveran Walker's ill-fated expedition against Quebec in 1711. He would serve as an infantry captain at the failed siege of Cartegena in 1741, and along with Wolfe, at the Battle of Culloden Moor. The following year he was made lieutenant colonel of the 22nd Regiment. In 1757 Whitmore's regiment was sent to Nova Scotia to take part in Loudoun's attempt to capture Louisbourg. Staying in Nova Scotia after the campaign was abandoned, later that year he received orders promoting him to colonel of the 22nd and brigadier general for Amherst's upcoming Louisbourg expedition.[9]

Amherst was also fortunate to find Admiral Edward Boscawen had been assigned to oversee the naval affairs. As a Royal Navy lieutenant in command of the 20-gun *Shoreham*, Boscawen would find himself embroiled in the Caribbean portion of the War of Jenkin's Ear. He participated in the siege of Porto Bello and Cartagena, being rewarded for his daring with the command of the 60-gun *Prince Frederick*. Boscawen returned to Britian in the spring of 1742 and as a captain commanded a squadron during the opening years of the War of Austrian Succession. In 1747 he was promoted to rear admiral and placed in command of an expedition against the French stronghold of Pondicherry in India. Although this campaign did not succeed, Boscawen's efforts were recognized, and he was given a position on the Admiralty Board. In the opening days of the last French and Indian War Boscawen was tasked with intercepting French reinforcements destined for Canada. While this mission did not prove to be successful, Boscawen returned to England and served with the Channel Fleet before being appointed to command the naval forces at the siege of Louisbourg.[10]

After assembling in Halifax, by early June 1758, a fleet of over two hundred British warships and transports lay near Gabarus Bay, a half a dozen miles southwest of Louisbourg. The north shore of this bay had been used by the New England troops that captured the fortress in 1745, and Amherst had selected this location as well, as it would quickly put him in position to invest the town. Scouting the shore from a small boat on the evening of June 2 Amherst, Wolfe, and Lawrence discovered that the French had fortified the shoreline from Black Cape to Flat Point with a string of wooden redans and gun batteries. A large number of French irregulars patrolled the shoreline, especially to the west, while the cannons and strongpoints were manned by marines from Louisbourg.

For the defenders much of the work done to the defenses of Louisbourg had been at Garbarus Bay. Unless an enemy army wished to make a march and extend their supply lines for several miles this was the only logical landing place. It was also one with several defensive advantages. The first was the nature of the bay, whose waters were subject to the tricky weather patterns around Cape Breton. While this limited enemy landing opportunities, the high ground near the handful of practical landing areas was the key to the defenses. The majority of the work was done between Flat Point and White Point where redoubts and several blockhouses armed with cannons that could sweep the nearby beach with grapeshot had been erected. To support these works a pair of encampments had been established to the east of Flat Point. To the west of Flat Point the French had established retrenchments and a camp at Kennington Cove (La Coromandiere), but between Kennington Cove and Flat Point the defenses relied on patrols, as the rocky nature of the beach would discourage any landing. The real problem was not so much the defenses but the manpower committed to effectively utilize these. In order to repel the British at the beaches it would require a force considered too large to risk, but even so, there were close to a thousand men and a score of cannons defending the coast from Kennington Bay to Cape Black.

Amherst's original plan called for a naval bombardment followed by three simultaneous landings between White Point and Flat Point.

The north coast of Gabarus Bay from Kennington Cove (Ance de la Cormorandiere, marked 'A' on the map) to White Point, showing French defensive works erected along the shoreline. The point labeled 'E' is where Wolfe would actually land. (*Norman B. Leventhal Map Collection, Boston Public Library*)

Weather, however, intervened. For almost a week storms, fog, and heavy surf ruled out any attempt. It did not stop the dueling between the British frigates and the French defenders along the shore. The warships would occasionally pass close enough to the enemy batteries that the marines aloft could use their muskets. The French guns responded and found their mark, leaving the HMS *Kensington* with almost a dozen casualties after a day of action. The defenders even used one of their 8-inch mortars to fire several shots at the anchored fleet on the morning of the fifth. Captain John Montressor of the Royal Engineers watched the shells arch toward the vessels. Montressor noted that they "did no execution, though they fell very nigh some of the Ordnance store-ships that were at anchor near the shore." Filled with cannons and gunpowder, the ships wisely moved a little farther away. On June 7 the weather broke, and while the surf was not ideal, it was not intolerable. The original arrangement for three attacks had been modified. After a brief bombardment by Royal Navy frigates both Lawrence and Whitmore were to land at White Point and Fresh Water Cove, while Wolfe with four companies of grenadiers, six hundred light infantry, and a battalion of Fraser's Highlanders would attempt to land at Kennington Cove to the west.[11]

At four in the morning Wolfe's men took to their boats and rowed toward Kennington Cove. The surf was more difficult than anticipated, and so too were the defenses. Although the Royal Navy had scouted the shoreline and fired upon points of interest, the French had not returned fire to give away their positions. Had they remained this disciplined and let the enemy detachment land on the narrow beach before opening fire, it is likely that they would have decimated the landing force. Fortunately for Wolfe, the enemy cannons opened fire on his boats while they were still a few hundred yards from shore.

Flashes appeared along the shoreline in the twilight, and almost instantaneously columns of water erupted near the flotilla and the murky forms of cannon balls suddenly materialized out of the shadows skipping past like a rock on the surface of the water. The sharp retort of swivel guns followed, throwing clouds of grapeshot at the attackers. As the vessels advanced closer musket flashes filled in between the flare of cannons and lit up the shore. In the rising light Wolfe could see that the French had thrown up an abatis along the length of the beach. Combined with the volume of fire coming from the defenders it would be suicidal to attempt a landing.

The general signaled the flotilla to turn right with the intent of landing at any place where it appeared feasible. Another detachment of a hundred light infantry veered to the left looking to land at the end of the enemy's line. The maneuver exposed the length of the vessels to ball and grapeshot, but according to one witness, the strong surf, which had postponed so many landing attempts, suddenly became an ally. "When the boats were lifted up by the violence of the swell to a considerable height, the enemy's shot, which would probably have done execution, had we been upon even water, passed under us; and in like manner some flew over us, in our quick transition from high to low," he later wrote. "This is the only reason that I can assign for our not losing more men by the enemy's fire."[12]

When Wolfe's vessels reached the northeastern portion of the French line, a small rocky cove was spotted. Noting that there was no abatis along the shore to impede their progress, the general ordered his men to pull for the cove. Not waiting to ground, Wolfe jumped over the side in the waist-deep surf and charged for the shore. The example animated his troops who did likewise. When enough men were ashore, Wolfe led an attack on a nearby battery. The gun crews bolted, which, when combined with news that a British force had landed at the other end of the line, created a zipper effect along the length of the French defenses.

Lawrence and his men landed at Freshwater Cove, and Whitmore followed, landing below White Point, but by now the entire French army was in retreat. With Wolfe penetrating the defenses at Kennington Cove and more enemy coming ashore to the east, there was fear among the defenders that they would be cut off from the town. Given that a large portion of the garrison was at Gabarus Bay, their capture would doom Louisbourg. Wolfe realized this and quickly advanced on the fortress, but the French, many of whom tossed away their arms, were too fast. The general and his men pursued them almost to the gates of the fortress before French cannons halted their advance.

The bold landing had cost the British 105 killed, wounded, or missing, but it had completely shattered any notion that the French would halt the enemy at the beach. The British had captured seventeen cannons ranging from 24-pounders to 6-pounders, as well as fourteen swivel guns and a pair of mortars. They had also taken seventy-four prisoners, including a pair of French grenadier captains who were now speaking with Amherst and his staff. As Amherst's army came ashore and began making camp, Captain Henry Gordon, a future general of the Royal Engineers, examined Wolfe's landing site and was stunned with what he found.

> The obstacles the Troops had to Surmount in landing was an Enemy Posted to the greatest advantage, their intrenchments being 15 feet above High Water mark, the approaches to which was rendered impracticable by large Trees being laid very thick together upon the Beach, all round the Cove, their Branches laying towards the Sea, the distance of 20 yards in some places, and 30 in others between their lines, and the Waters edge. Then the Surge was extremely violent, most of our Boats being staved, and the Rocks coming out so far that the greatest part of the Army landed to their middle in Water, many were much hurt, others crushed to Pieces being carried away by the Surge, and the Boats driving over them with the return of it.

> Had the Enemy permitted the Troops of the Left attack to have landed in the Cove, They must certainly have put it out of our power to have troubled them afterwards, as by reserving their Fire till then in all probability they would have put us in confusion, and we afterwards must have been at their mercy.[13]

While news of the landing and Wolfe's role in it added to his growing reputation, the general was more surprised by their success than anyone. He wrote his friend Rickson, "Amongst ourselves, be it said, that our attempt to land where we did was rash and injudicious, our success unexpected (by me) and undeserved. There was no prodigious exertion of courage in the affair; an officer and thirty men would have made it impossible to get ashore where we did." Others did not view it in this light and pointed to the aggressive actions and quick thinking of Wolfe.[14]

Amherst's main camp was set up near Flat Point, but the weather deteriorated over the next few days, halting the off-loading of supplies and artillery. On the twelfth the lashing rains did not stop Wolfe, and a detachment of a little over 1,200 men set off for the lighthouse. Once he had secured this point, cannons and tools would be landed at the village of Lorembec, a mile east of the structure. Wolfe would then raise a battery of guns to bombard the Island Battery and the French warships in the harbor. In the meantime, Amherst, his engineers Colonel John-Henri Bastide and Major Patrick McKellar, along with Colonel George Williamson of the Royal Artillery had agreed to approach the fortress via Green Hill. The hope had been to erect batteries along the north shore of the west bay, where Colonel Titcomb had positioned guns in 1745 to attack the French shipping in the harbor, but the position was considered too vulnerable and the lack of roads caused the idea to be abandoned.

On the evening of the nineteenth Wolfe's recently completed battery opened fire on the Island Battery. These guns exchanged shots with the Island Battery and the warships for the next few days, but by dusk on the twenty-fifth the brigadier reported that the island's guns had been silenced. More cannons, 32 and 24-pounders, were landed to allow Wolfe to raise a pair of batteries farther up the peninsula to better bombard the French warships. The latter, along with the city's cannons, fired grapeshot, ball, and bombs at the advancing British trenches near Green Hill. Along with small war parties that

Amherst's siege trenches and batteries to the west of Louisbourg. (*Norman B. Leventhal Map Collection, Boston Public Library*)

struck in the early-morning hours, these efforts caused a handful of casualties, but it was the nature of the ground and the weather that were the real impediments.[15]

With the silencing of the Island Battery there was fear in the French camp that the British Navy might force its way into the harbor, which, given the size of Boscawen's force, would end in disaster for the defenders. Given the stakes, it was agreed to sink the warships *Apollo*, *La Fidelle*, *La Pierre*, and *La Biche* on the night of June 30 to obstruct the main channel. The remaining five ships-of-the-line anchored closer to the city while the 36-gun frigate *L'Arethuse* would establish a reputation for harassing the British trenchworks.

While the British besiegers near the town were occupied in dragging forward twenty 24-pounders, half a dozen 12-pounders, and seven mortars into four positions to bombard the town, Wolfe's batteries were involved in daily duals with the Royal Battery and especially the French warships. Wolfe's contribution to the siege was quickly coming to the forefront. The brigadier found himself involved in half a dozen skirmishes and could be frequently seen in the advanced trenches as bombs burst nearby. He was so active that, according to one observer, "There is no Certainty where to find him, but wherever he goes, he carries with him a Mortar in one Pocket and a 24 pounder in the other."[16]

On the afternoon of July 21 Major McKellar, who had taken over the siege when Bastide was hobbled after being struck in the foot by a spent musket ball, informed Amherst that the main batteries were ready. Ammunition was now being forwarded, and the guns would open fire at daylight. The two men and several of the general's staff began discussing other matters when a thunderous explosion attracted the attention of everyone in the area. A mushroom-shaped cloud clutched the French 64-gun *Célèbres*. A well-aimed shot had struck the vessel's powder magazine, creating a cloud of flaming debris that rained down upon a pair of warships anchored nearby. Moments later the *Célèbres* was engulfed in flames as a secondary explosion threw out more burning matter, igniting the nearby 74-gun *Entreprenant* and the 64-gun *Capricieux*. Efforts were made to try and save the latter craft but were soon abandoned, leaving all who could see to watch as the three French warships burned to the waterline over the course of the afternoon.

Amherst celebrated this unexpected success by opening fire on the fortress the next morning with a pair of batteries consisting of thirteen 24-pounders and seven mortars. Combined with the shot coming from Wolfe's cannons, it demolished sections of the town setting several buildings ablaze, including the citadel barracks. "Burning the town is spoiling out own nests," Amherst noted, "but it will probably be the shortest way of taking it." The French fired grapeshot in the form of "old Iron Nails" and bits of jagged metal at the enemy batteries, but it failed to slow their fire. Mackellar's men worked on two more firing parallels, and the next day both opened fire on the fortress, focusing their efforts on the citadel and the Dauphin Bastion.[17]

That evening Boscawen launched a small boat attack on the two remaining French ships-of-the-line, the 74-gun *Prudent* and the 64-

A view of the siege of Louisbourg from the Light House on the east side of the main channel. (*Published by Thomas Jefferys, London, 1762*)

gun *Bienfaisant*. Six hundred men arrayed in small boats under navy captains John LaForey and George Balfour quietly paddled out into the harbor after sunset and in the early morning hours of the twenty-sixth appeared out of the darkness beside the French ships. Caught by surprise, the ship's watch and a few others on deck put up a brief fight, but after a burst of gunfire and a thunderous "huzzah" the attackers were on board with much of the ship's complement still below deck. Both vessels surrendered and the *Bienfaisant* was towed to the safety of northeast harbor, but the *Prudent* went aground early in this process, and unable to free the vessel, LaForey ordered it put to the torch.

While the defenders of Louisbourg had managed to delay Amherst, it had now become an impossible situation. With the Island Battery having been silenced and the remainder of the French fleet now captured or destroyed, there was no way to prevent Boscawen's fleet from clearing any obstacles and entering the harbor to conduct a landing or bombard the weak harborside defenses of the town into dust. That morning French drums beat out a parlay, which brought all activity to a standstill, and the following morning the garrison officially surrendered.[18]

While the surrender of the fortress had resulted in a vast cache of artillery and military stores, it had come at the price of 524 British casualties and a similar number of French military casualties. If the civilian population is included, 411 had been killed in the siege with another 1,790 of the 5,637 captured, listed as sick, or wounded.

The scale of the operation is pointed to by the fact that the British expended over twenty-three thousand rounds of shot, shell, and incendiary in the siege. It showed. The smoldering city was in ruins and would have to be rebuilt to house a British garrison, and the French vessels sunk in the main channel would have to be raised, but likely could be repaired and put into service. The Island Battery would have to be repaired as well. More importantly, just as it had in 1745, the capture of Louisbourg had once again opened the way for an attack on Quebec. There was still time to move against the French colonial capital, and both Wolfe and Amherst wished to proceed, but reports had come from General James Abercromby of his defeat at Ticonderoga and his need for reinforcements. Thus, the plan was set aside, and it would be an expedition under Wolfe that would capture the French capital the next year.

The British maintained and garrisoned Louisbourg for the remainder of the conflict, and many wondered if, like the last conflict, the fortress would be returned to France upon the eventual peace treaty. While such a possibility existed, in February 1760 Pitt would guarantee that the French would inherit nothing from such an action by ordering,

> that the said Fortress, together with all the works, and Defences of the Harbour, be most effectually and most entirely demolished; And I am in consequence thereof, to signify to you His Majesty's Pleasure, that you do as expediously as the Season will permit, take the most timely and effectual Care, that all the Fortifications of the Town of Louisburg, together with all the Works, and Defences whatever, belonging either to the said Place, or to the Port, and Harbour, thereof, be forthwith totally demolished, and razed, and all the Materials so thoroughly destroyed, as that no use mav, hereafter, be ever made of the same.[19]

Before Pitts's orders arrived, however, there was another expedition and fort raised in the region. In September 1758, a few months

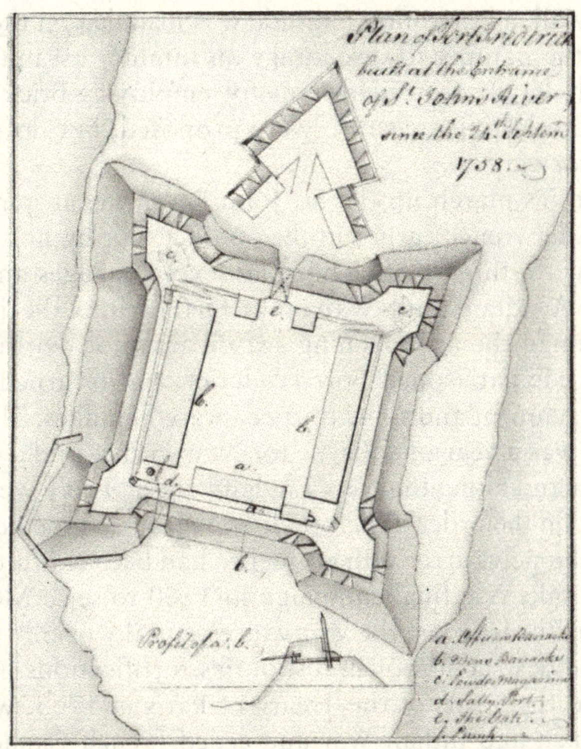

Fort Frederick in September 1758. Much of the work in restoring the old fort went quickly with the large amount of manpower available, and by the onset of winter the fort was in a defensible condition and ready to accept a garrison. (*Norman B. Leventhal Map Collection, Boston Public Library*)

after the fall of Louisbourg, Brigadier General Robert Monckton would lead over a thousand regulars and New England Rangers up the St. John River to destroy the one hundred or so Acadian settlements there. There had been no attempt by the French to rebuild Fort Menagouche, which had been abandoned since 1755, but rumors of French and Indian war parties forming on the waterway had led to warships being dispatched to the location on several occasions. With a surplus of manpower and command of the local waters, Monckton embarked on securing the river and its outlet.

The first stop on this expedition was the site of Fort Menagouche. The interior and firing platforms had been burned, and the earth walls battered by the elements, but there was no reason that the original fort could not be kept and upgraded. The interior buildings and platforms were replaced, and to temporarily deal with the lack of a vertical outer wall, a horizontal palisade was installed on the face of the walls near the parapet to discourage an infantry assault. The result was Fort Frederick. Considerations for employing brick or stone to create a more lasting structure were proposed, but do not seem to have gone forward.

Monckton's march up the St. John River was inspired by comments from Lawrence earlier in the conflict, but by now this region was no longer a threat. After burning several villages and chasing a number of Acadians and Wabanaki farther into the interior, the colonel claimed the approaching season was not worth the risk of continuing. He garrisoned Fort Frederick and returned to Halifax with his detachment and some thirty captured families. The following year, 1759, was a year of collapse for New France and a quiet one in Nova Scotia and along the New England coast. There were still raids but nothing on the order of before. It was clear that the tide was turning, and when news arrived that Quebec had been captured, all knew it. It would take one final campaign in 1760 to seize Montreal, but along the northeast coast the war was essentially over.[20]

With the destruction of Louisbourg's fortifications in the spring of 1760 and the terms of the Treaty of Paris in 1763, which ended the last French and Indian War and ceded French Canada to Great Britian, the forts of the New England and Nova Scotia coast fell silent. Many of the smaller posts were abandoned and left to fall into ruin while the larger ones became munitions storehouses, staffed with only a handful of men to act more as custodians than a garrison. This would only last a little over a decade until the American Revolution once again brought their true purpose to the forefront and ushered in another age for some of these strongholds.

Epilogue

SENTINELS BY THE SEA

It is perhaps remarkable that in this seventy-five-year story of the French and British fortifications along the New England and Nova Scotia coasts so much of what was done was reactive versus proactive. Even in the cases of generational works such as Castle William, Louisbourg, and Fort William and Mary, lessons learned from previous conflicts were seldom acted upon until the mistake was made again in what all participants realized was a long campaign for control of the region. The real culprit was money: lack of it on the side of the French and an unwillingness to part with it on the side of New England and Britain.

British naval power, supplemented by New England privateers and colonial warships, would spell doom for the French fortifications of Acadia and Cape Breton. It would lead to the French inability to support Port Royal and the smaller French strongholds in the region. It also meant that the French could not maintain a consistent supply chain with their Wabanaki allies, further weakening their position in the region, and it was a component in why the French were never able to win back the bulk of the French Acadian settlers that found themselves under British rule.

It is interesting to note that French naval activity in this area during King William's War, particularly concerning the activities of Captain Pierre Iberville and Captain Simon Bonaventure, along with exaggerated rumors of their next targets, helped France and their Wabanaki allies hold New England to a standstill. True, Port Royal was captured along with its dismounted cannons, but the fort was in such poor condition that it was being replaced, which is why the guns were dismounted. As such, there was little for the English to destroy, and showing no interest in occupying the location, they withdrew shortly thereafter. The change in French naval philosophy toward commerce raiding was apparent in the next three French and Indian Wars in New England and Nova Scotia and would lead to the supply issues mentioned earlier. In 1746, during King George's War, a large French fleet did attempt to recapture Port Royal and Louisbourg, but disaster befell the expedition and none of these goals were accomplished. Yet even though this attempt proved a costly failure, the application of French naval resources brought such concern to New England that it saved French control over the Champlain Valley and in turn Montreal, the gateway to the west.

The inability of the French navy and privateers to actually fulfill New England's fear by using Port Royal as an operating base could be attributed to the decrepit fort that would guard their anchorage. There was certainly no lack of targets in the area, and while British frigates patrolled the waters along with a few colonial warships, a few French frigates, or a few large privateers, would prove a fair match for these, and should they win an engagement with the enemy warships, panic would ripple through the coastal New England communities and maritime industries. This inability to exploit Port Royal likely saved the French post for a few years, and its commander, Captain Subercase, along with British indecision, would save the post twice before Nicholson appeared in 1710 with a large force of colonials, British marines, and Royal Navy warships to quickly seize the fort and the town.

The Treaty of Utrecht, which ended Queen Anne's War, would leave New France in a difficult position. Acadia according to its ancient limits was now British. There were arguments about what this really meant, but after a long war this was put aside for a time. The French had also lost the fishing colony of Placentia on Newfoundland's Avalon Peninsula, not to military action but at the bargaining table. The loss of these two positions forced the French government

State/Province	Location	Fort/Forts	Comments
Massachusetts	Boston	Hill Fort (Fort Andros)	Site demolished and hill leveled 1865
		North/South Batteries	Today Battery Wharf and Rowe's Wharf
		Castle William, Castle Island (Ft. Independence)	Ft. Independence state park and exhibit
	Salem	Queen's Fort	Winter Island Marine Park, Ruins of later forts.
	Marblehead	Old Battery	Today Ft. Sewell Park. Ruins of later forts.
New Hampshire	Newcastle	Ft. William and Mary	Today Ft. Constitution State Park. Ruins of 1808 fort built over the original colonial fort.
Maine	Falmouth	Ft. Casco	No remains
	Castine	Ft. Pentagoet	Earth mounds only remains
	Pemaquid	Ft. Charles/William Henry	Tower reconstructed in 1908, ruins of fort and museum.
	Portsmouth	Ft. Loyal	No remains - plaque
	Biddeford	Ft. Saco	No remains - marker
	Thomaston	St. George's Fort	No remains - plaque
	Richmond	Fort Richmond	No remains - marker
	Dresden	Fort Frankfort/Ft. Shirley	Now the site of the Pownalborough Courthouse
	Augusta	Fort Western	Old wooden fort and museum
	Winslow	Fort Halifax	One old blockhouse remains on the site.
Rhode Island	Newport	Fort Anne/Ft. George/Ft. Wolcott (Goat Island)	Plaque
New Brunswick	Fredericton	Ft. St. Joseph/Ft. Nashwaak	Canadian Historic Site - ruins of fort/exhibit
	Saint John	Ft. St. Jean/Ft. Menagouche/Ft. Frederick	Canadian Historic Site - plaque
	Aulac	Ft. Beauséjour/Ft. Cumberland	Canadian Historic Site - ruins of fort/exhibit
Nova Scotia	Annapolis Royal	Fort Royal/Fort Anne	Canadian Historic Site - ruins of fort/exhibit
	Louisbourg	Fortress Louisbourg	Canadian Historic Site - ruins of fort/exhibit
	Canso	Grassy Island Fort	Canadian Historic Site - ruins/trace of fort
	Ft. Lawrence	Ft. Lawrence	Canadian Historic Site - plaque
	Baie Verte	Ft. Gaspareaux	Canadian Historic Site - marker

List of the major forts mentioned in this text and their current status.

to build the naval fortress of Louisbourg on Cape Breton Island as a last option to control the Gulf of St. Lawrence and access to Quebec via the St. Lawrence River. While the French literally built what New England feared most, the British colonies did little to improve their position on Nova Scotia or their defenses along the Maine and New England coast during this time.

At the beginning of King George's War, the French forces in Acadia and Louisbourg missed the last true opportunity to expel the British from Acadia and place the war on New England's doorstep. Once this window closed, Governor William Shirley embarked on a risky plan to seize Louisbourg that, to the surprise of many, succeeded and sealed the fate of the French fortifications in the region. However, the Treaty of Aix-la-Chapelle in 1748, which ended King George's War in North America, returned Louisbourg to the French. The latter would only occupy the fortress for a decade before the last French and Indian War brought a siege by British forces in 1758 that captured the fortress and would later demolish the works.

Today there are only a handful of reminders of these old fortifications and the important role they played in the early conflicts in North America. Fortunately, a superlative example exists at Fortress Louisbourg National Historic Site on Cape Breton Island. The reconstruction of this fortress and a section of the village within is easily the largest project of its type in North America, and it is open to the public. Other examples also exist. The tower of Fort William Henry at Pemaquid was reconstructed in 1909, and along with the trace of the rest of the fort, can be visited today. As can the ruins of Fort William and Mary and its many renovations, in New Castle, New Hampshire. In a similar fashion Fort Independence on Castle Island outside of Boston is as close as one can get to Castle William, which was destroyed by the retreating British in 1776 and rebuilt into a star-shaped fort later called Fort Independence. Elsewhere smaller examples, which have not born the tests of time as well, can be found marked by plaques, signs, and monuments, which when taken together with the ruins that still stand form a network of markers denoting the final resting places of these former sentinels by the sea.

GLOSSARY

Banquet: A firing platform.

Bastion: A small blockhouse structure, typically diamond in shape, located at the junctions of the fort's walls. While platforms on the bastions were used for the fort's cannons, the primary purpose of the structure was to provide flanking fire against any troops attempting to storm the adjacent curtain walls.

Bateau: Small wooden shallow-draft boats, similar to whale boats, which could either be rowed or powered under a simple square sail arrangement. In some cases, these vessels would also be armed with small cannons on their bow and/or stern.

Bomb: An exploding mortar round.

Bomb-proof: A shelter with overhead cover built to withstand the impact of an exploding mortar round.

Breastwork: A field fortification made of earth and timber.

Cannons: The cannons used during this period were muzzle-loading guns, classified simply by the weight of metal they used, with perhaps the caveat long or short, which pertains to the barrel length and exit velocity. They were manufactured in two materials: brass and iron. Brass guns were lighter and better withstood the metal fatigue that came with repeated firing, but because of the construction costs they were typically limited to six-pound cannons or smaller. These qualities made brass guns popular on small naval vessels, where weight was at issue, and among field artillery units. Iron cannons were heavier but cheaper to produce and came in all sizes from diminutive three-pound guns to thirty-two- and forty-eight-pound behemoths that were reserved for the strongest fortresses and ships-of-the-line. Weight was always a consideration with larger cannons. For instance, a twenty-four-pound cannon, which would be considered a siege gun, weighed two and a half tons. So too did two hundred rounds of ammunition for the gun, not to mention the powder for this ammunition, which could easily exceed another ton. It would also require a dozen men to operate this cannon. Another artillery piece that was employed on naval vessels of all types were swivel guns. These were cannons below two or three pounds that were small enough to be employed on a socket-style mount along the ship's deck rails or along the wall of a fort. Small, light, and easily operated by a pair of men, these guns were favored by the smaller ships that plied the inland waterways of North America.

Ammunition for cannons of this time came in three basic types. Round shot or simply "ball" was by far the most common type employed and was typically used against vessels or fortifications. As the name implies, these solid projectiles used greater powder loads, which in turn would create higher exit velocities and more kinetic damage to the target. Round shot or solid shot, as it was sometimes called, was occasionally heated in an attempt to start fires within an enemy stronghold or on an enemy vessel, and under such circumstances it was known as hot-shot. Chain-shot and bar-shot were designed to damage the rigging of enemy vessels, making them almost exclusively reserved for naval use. The last type of ammunition was grapeshot. This was typically a bag of musket balls, the former being quickly shredded by the forward flight of its contents. This ammunition was used in a close-range anti-personnel manner. Of course, a number of items could be used in lieu of musket balls. Langrage, for instance, was cut-up pieces of leftover iron objects, nails, and broken screws.

The direct fire applications of cannons were supplemented by mortars and howitzers. These squat wide-mouthed guns were designed to lob an explosive projectile, aptly referred to as a "bomb," over a wall or other obstruction. These destructive instruments, which came in sizes ranging from a few inches in bore to siege guns thirteen inches in diameter, could create devastation within the interior of a fort and were one of a besieger's best weapons. Howitzers were a compromise between cannons and mortars. They were large-bore, low exit velocity guns that could be employed in an indirect fire manner using bombs like mortars but if required could also be used in a direct fire manner.

The primary ammunition associated with mortars and howitzers is the spherical cased, fused explosive round known as a bomb. Another ammunition type was the carcass. This was an early incendiary round. Initially, these were open iron-framed oblong rounds holding a leather pouch within their confines filled with a flammable mixture. Because of their construction these rounds had to be fired from low exit velocity guns such as mortars and howitzers. Later the leather pouch approach would be replaced by a hollow iron sphere, which had several openings for the burning liquid to escape from. Both types had to be loaded into the gun, lit through a fuse, and then fired.

Another artillery piece that was primarily employed by fortifications was the wall gun. These swivel-mounted heavy muskets were often positioned along sections of the fort's wall to provide more accurate long-range fire, especially against the sappers and pioneers busy digging siege trenches. Easily transportable these guns could be quickly moved around the fort's perimeter to either concentrate their fire or take advantage of an opportune firing angle.

Eighteenth-century artillery types and ranges:

CANNON TYPE	POINT-BLANK RANGE (yards)	EFFECTIVE RANGE (yards)	MAXIMUM RANGE (yards)
3-pounder	400	400-600	2,000
6-pounder	650	500-600	3,300
9-pounder	700	900	3,500
12-pounder	730	800–1,000	3,650
18-pounder	600	800–1,000	3,100
24-pounder	650	700-900	3,250
32-pounder	630	1,000–1,300	3,100
42-pounder	580	1,000–1,300	2,900
5 ½ Howitzer	300	500-700	1,350
8-inch mortar	250	800–1,000	2,550
13-inch mortar	300	900–1,400	2,800

CASEMATE: A bomb-proof shelter designed to either protect the garrison or the fort's magazine from artillery fire.

CHEVAL DE FRISE: This defensive structure is a row of sharpened stakes driven into the ground and angled toward the attacker. Often trees were used in place of stakes with their branches sharpened to points. This field fortification was originally used to repel cavalry charges, but it was also used to slow an infantry attack.

COVERED WAY: This is a platform cut into the ditch side of the glacis to allow for troop movement and protected small arms fire.

CURTAIN WALL: An interconnecting wall between two bastions.

Demilune: A demilune is a smaller crescent-shaped fortification typically placed in front of a curtain wall. Such structures are small forts unto themselves and are frequently connected to the nearby wall via a drawbridge.

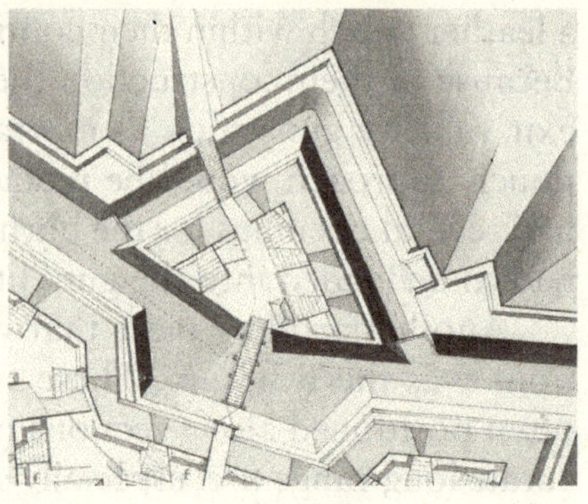

A portion of a 1735 French plan showing a demilune. Note the drawbridge which provides access to this structure from one of the fort's walls. The use of demilunes made it much harder to target large portions of the fort's walls. (*Norman B. Leventhal Map Collection, Boston Public Library*)

Dry ditch: A technique used to cross a swamp or marshy land when a traditional trench is impractical. In such cases, a causeway is built and then shielded with gabions and a timber roof.

Embrasures: Openings cut into the parapet to allow for either musket or cannon fire.

en barbette or barbette: A cannon mounted such that it can fire over the parapet. While such an arrangement does not offer as much protection for the gun or its crew, it does allow the gun to be trained over a much greater field of fire.

Fascine: A fascine is a bundle of small branches or pieces of wood. These were used to support earthworks and in particular to brace the walls of a siege trench when crossing wet ground or to fill in a ditch to allow for crossing.

Gabion: A barrel filled with earth. Gabions were typically used as temporary field fortifications or as temporary repairs to damaged or incomplete fortifications.

Glacis: Sloping ground placed in front of the fort's walls to reduce the amount of wall that can be seen and targeted by enemy cannon fire. Shots that are too short deflect off the glacis and over the fort's wall.

Grapeshot: Bags of musket balls fired out of cannon. This type of shot was used to repel an infantry attack.

Grenade: The idea of a thrown explosive, or a hand grenade as it would become known, had become popular in seventeenth-century armies. In fact, the term grenadier traces its name to this idea. While a commonplace idea today, the use of early grenades on the battlefield, which had to be lit just moments before their use, proved impractical. For the defenders of fortifications, however, the grenade was an ideal weapon. It could be safely tossed over the ramparts to clear the base of the fort's walls of attackers or used against an enemy that had advanced into the ditch before the fort. Most forts stocked an ample supply of these devices, which certainly created yet another obstacle for anyone looking to take the stronghold by storm.

MORTAR: An artillery piece designed to fire exploding rounds (bombs) in an arching trajectory so they will clear the fort's walls.

PALISADE: A wooden wall made of trees placed vertically in a filled ditch and then bound together.

PARALLEL: A perpendicular, or near perpendicular, extension of the main sap designed to employ a battery of guns from which the besieged fort can be bombarded.

PLACE OF ARMS (or PARADE GROUND): This is the open interior portion of the fort where the garrison can be assembled.

RAVELIN: A redan.

REDAN: A V-shaped fortification where the point is aligned with the direction of an enemy attack. Redans were typically employed as outworks or field fortifications as well as in fort walls to provide flanking fire down the length of the wall.

REDOUBT: A self-contained fortification with a ditch about its perimeter and earth and timber walls.

SAP: A trench.

SAP ROLLER: A large cylinder, typically made of bound branches, which is placed in front of the sap being dug to provide shelter for the work crews. The device is then rolled forward as the trench advances.

STORM (to take by): Meaning an infantry attack on the fortifications. Such measures were either combined with the element of surprise or viewed as last resorts given the chance of success and the large number of casualties that would come from the effort.

TRACE: The outline of a fortification.

FORT TYPES AND CONSTRUCTION

THE FORTS IN THIS TEXT fall into two categories: structures designed to withstand artillery and structures that are not. One commonality between these categories was that the stronghold had to be designed to repel an infantry attack against its walls. This was partly accomplished by the fort's layout. Most forts encountered during this period, regardless of their construction, were square or rectangular with two or four bastions to provide flanking fire along the fort's curtain walls. Five-bastioned structures, or star forts as they were called, were also used to accomplish this task. Another desirable feature to discourage an infantry assault was a vertical barrier, such as a ditch, that would force the enemy to employ ladders to scale the walls.

While both types of forts had to defend themselves from being taken by storm, the basic difference between structures designed to withstand artillery and structures that are not was construction. The three basic building materials available to erect a fort along the New England or Nova Scotia coast were wood, earth, and stone. The latter two would be required to raise a fort capable of withstanding an artillery barrage. That and a sizable amount of money and manpower. Thus, the fortifications in this text generally fall into three groups: wooden forts, wood and earth forts, and stone forts, each of which came with its own inherent set of strengths and weaknesses.

WOODEN FORTS

With an abundant supply of timber available, the most common type of fort encountered in North America was the wooden palisade fort. The general approach to this type of fort was to dig a trench along

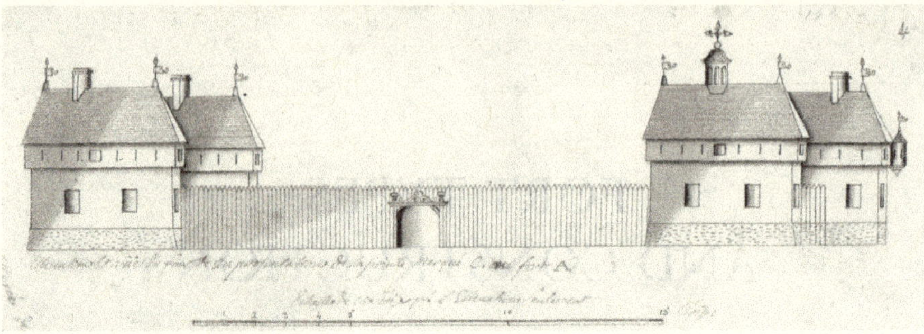

Fort La Presentation on the St. Lawrence River is an example of a wood and stone fort. The masonry blockhouses are connected by wooden curtain walls. (*Norman B. Leventhal Map Collection, Boston Public Library*)

the outline of the fort, place the vertical posts in this trench, and then backfill with a burnt earth, lime, and water mixture, which acted as a crude form of concrete. The posts would then be lashed together and connected at the corners by bastions or blockhouses. At this point the builders had several options. Firing ports could be cut in the wall to allow for cannon fire and/or musketry, and if the walls were tall enough, a platform could be built to allow the garrison to fire over the top of the wall.

Another option in this regard was to build the barracks and other internal structures up against a wall. Not only would it make the structure less susceptible to direct cannon fire, but the roof of the structure could be used as a firing platform for cannons and musketeers. A more common arrangement in such forts was to mount the structure's cannons in corner bastions that flanked the walls. Usually, this would be at all four corners, but in some cases only one or two bastions were used. A room was constructed in the bastion, the roof of which was used as a platform for the fort's cannons. Typically reinforced to withstand this function, these rooms were often used as magazines, storehouses, and bomb-proof shelters for the garrison. Another option seen was a blockhouse arrangement in place of the bastions. This was useful, as each acted as a watchtower and could even mount a few small cannons or swivel guns.

While relatively straightforward in their construction, and designed primarily to repel raiders and not withstand an artillery siege, these types of forts were economical but temporary solutions. Fire, whether unintentional or employed by an attacker, was the greatest

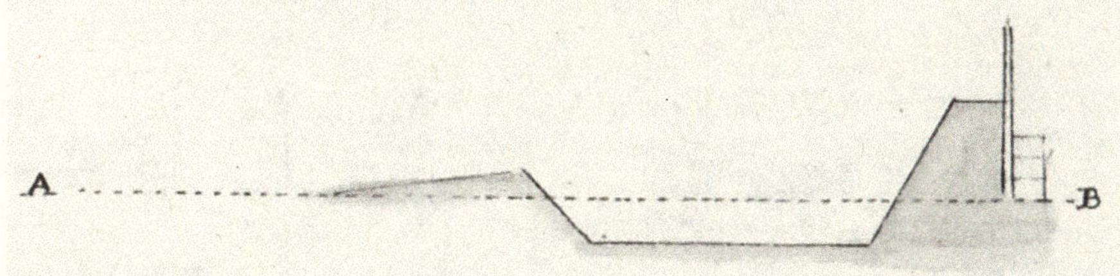

A cross-section of the curtain walls of Fort Gaspareux. Note that in this case the earth from the ditch has not only been used to create a small glacis, but has been piled against the palisade wall to provide better protection against cannon fire. Another approach was to pile the dirt from the ditch against the interior side of the wooden wall, and fashion the ramparts and firing platforms from this earth. (*Norman B. Leventhal Map Collection, Boston Public Library*)

enemy of these types of forts. In addition, rain and seasonal changes would quickly attack the wood, meaning that large garrisons were required, not necessarily to defend the fortification but to maintain it. As such, many were eventually abandoned or torn down and rebuilt for financial reasons.

WOOD AND EARTH FORTS

The most basic form of this fort was created by fashioning the walls out of mounds of dirt, typically from digging a ditch about the trace of the fort. Firing platforms for cannons and musketeers could be carved out of the walls at the same time. This was an easily erected and very powerful fort when it came to resisting artillery. The dirt walls quickly absorbed the impact of even the largest cannon rounds of the day, and if the walls were a dozen-feet thick or more, there was really little damage that could be done to the structure that could not be quickly repaired. There were, however, two major problems. The first was that this type of fort would decay even faster than a wooden fort, particularly in areas of heavy rainfall, while the second was that the walls could not be made vertical but instead had a slope to their ascent. Given that this did not impose the desired obstacle to an infantry attack, a larger garrison would be required and a reliance on outworks to help cover this weakness.

One way to address the major maintenance issues with earth forts was to either cover the walls with sod or face them with wood in order to help slow their decay. While this certainly helped, it hardly prevented the dirt from seeping away. Even with these measures, given

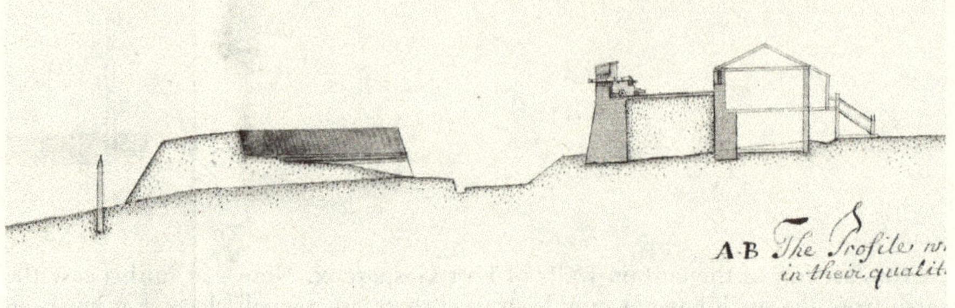

A northeast to southeast cross-section of Castle William on Castle Island. To the left, a palisade, backed by a wood-lined earth redan, fronts the ditch to the fort. Note how the cannons in the fort can fire over the redan. (*Norman B. Leventhal Map Collection, Boston Public Library*)

the harsh weather along the New England and Nova Scotia coasts, such a solution was unsatisfactory. A better approach was to reverse the process. A pair of wooden parallel walls were constructed along the outline of the fort and then attached to one another through internal bracing. The intervening space was then filled in with dirt and a platform or rampart built on top of this. The bastions, typically employing the fort's artillery, were built in the same fashion. Sometimes called a sandbox fort, with walls ten to over twenty feet thick, these forts could stand before heavy artillery and now possessed the desirable vertical walls. They also did a better job of containing the earth, which gave the structure its strength. However, there were still maintenance issues and the financial commitments that came with them, which were a major deterrent to any long-term service.

STONE AND STONE-CLAD FORTS

The answer to the maintenance and overall financial commitment toward a major coastal stronghold was a stone-clad or stone fort. A stone-clad fort was an earth or the sandbox fort described earlier, ensconced in a covering of stone. It is not that the stone brought additional strength to the structure, the walls were already a dozen feet or more of earth, but more importantly, it weatherproofed the structure. Although water leaks were always a constant source of problems, they were manageable. Such a fort not only had a longer serviceable life but required a smaller garrison to maintain. Essentially, these forts had all the strength of a sandbox fort with only a fraction of the maintenance headaches.

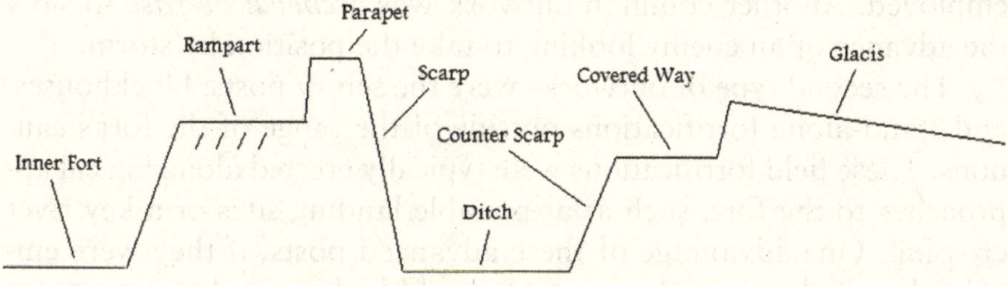

Cross Section of a Fort's Outer Works

Stone forts were traditional masonry structures using quarried stone and mortar. Such structures, if built correctly, could boast excellent weather resistance and walls over ten feet thick. They also offered another advantage, fire immunity. This was particularly true if the interior buildings were also constructed of stone. The real issue with either stone-clad forts or stone forts was the initial cost, allocating the manpower resources, and the time to erect the works. In some cases, such as Castle William, Fort William and Mary, and Fortress Louisbourg, the locations were of strategic importance, and as such, were built in stone with long-term maintenance in mind. In other cases, a compromise was struck. That is, a fort that employed masonry construction for a section of the structure and wood or earth for the remaining parts of the stronghold.

OUTWORKS

In many ways the strength of a fort was subject to the extent of its outworks. The deployment of these supporting fortifications could significantly change the strength of the main fort. Outworks came in two types: works immediately adjacent to the fort and advanced posts or outposts. The most common of the first type was a ditch. A deep and wide ditch made the curtain walls tall enough that attacking infantry would be forced to use ladders to scale the walls. The earth from the ditch, if not used in the construction of the walls, could be piled on the counter-scarp side of the ditch. Here the earth would be fashioned such that a glacis and covered way, often crowned with a palisade fence, could be formed. Outworks in the form of demilunes or redans were commonly placed before walls that might be subject to bombardment or storm, and detached redoubts for cannons to cover a specific approach to the fort or create a crossfire were also employed. Another common outwork was a *cheval de frise* to slow the advance of an enemy looking to take the position by storm.

The second type of outworks were the sentry posts, blockhouses, and stand-alone fortifications outside of the range of the fort's cannons. These field fortifications were typically erected along logical approaches to the fort, such as at possible landing sites or a key river crossing. One advantage of these advanced posts, if they were employed, was that from here patrols could be launched to act as part of the garrison's early warning measures.

NOTES

Abbreviations

NY Col. Doc.	O'Callaghan, *Documents Relative to the Colonial History of the State of New York.*
NEHGR	*New England Historical and Genealogical Register*
MHSC	*Massachusetts Historical Society Collections*
DCB	*Dictionary of Canadian Biography Online*
Cal. A&WI	*Calendar American & West Indies Papers*
RFL	*Researching the Fortress of Louisbourg National Historic Site of Canada*
CWS	*The Correspondence of William Shirley*

CHAPTER ONE: THE FIRST FORTS

1. Whitmore, *Andros Tracts*, III, 71–75; *Cal.A&WI*, IX, 465, XII, 350–351. There was an old wooden blockhouse on Fort Hill that was abandoned in 1665 when Major General John Leverett built the South Battery. Housing thirteen cannons the general referred to it as "the compleatest work in America" when he finished. (Drenth & Riley, *First Col. Soldiers* II/1, 128–129.)

2. Perley, *History of Salem*, II, 237–240, 388, III, 169; *Cal.A&WI*, XII, 402, 422, 472, 474, 607–608. "Sackers (6-pounders) or long guns will be best for arming it (the Hill Fort), but we have not enough here, and no field pieces," Andros wrote London on November 28. "I beg for a supply of ammunition and small arms, and some hand mortar pieces like those at Tangier. . .We have none here but a few old matchlocks, and we shall want some soon if the French persist in their invasion." (Ibid., *Cal.A&WI*, XII, 474.)

3. Perley, *History of Salem*, III, 169; Roads, *Marblehead*, 23, 27; *Cal.A&WI*, XI, 38–39, 312; Potter, *Military History of New Hampshire*, 10–12.

4. *NH Prov. Papers*, II, 46–47; Charlevoix, IV, 15–16; Wheeler, "Fort Pentagoet," *Proceedings Maine Hist. Soc.*, 2nd Ser., IV, 113–123. During the raid on Castin's trading house, Andros noted that Fort Pentagoet was unoccupied and in ruins. (Ibid.)

5. Drake, *Border Wars of New England*, 10–11; *Doc. Hist. Maine*, VI, 429–430.

6. Goold, *Portland in the Past*, 131–133; *NY Col. Doc.*, III, 248–249; Hull, *Siege of Fort Loyall*, 10–12.

7. Whitmore, *Andros Tracts*, III, 31–36; *Doc. Hist. Maine*, X, 47–50; Thornton, *Ancient Pemaquid*, 65, 127.

CHAPTER TWO: KING WILLIAM'S WAR

1. Johnston, *History of Bristol and Bremen*, 163–170; Charlevoix, IV, 39–42; *Collection de Manuscrits . . . Relatifs Nouvelle-France*, I, 477–481. Of the 156 men assigned to the fort desertion and recalls had reduced their numbers to a little over thirty at the time of Castin's attack. (Johnston, *History of Bristol and Bremen*, 163.)

2. *Cal.A&WI*, XIII, 114–115; *Ten Years at Pemaquid*, 144–153; Charlevoix, IV, 42–44.

3. *Doc. Hist Maine*, IX, 66; *Giles Memorial*, 108–111.

4. *Cal.A&WI*, XIII, 111, 120.

5. *NY Col. Doc.* IX, 471–473; Hull, *Siege of Fort Loyall*, 61–72.

6. Charlevoix, IV, 133–137; *Cal. A &WI*, XIII, 272; Hull, *Siege of Fort Loyall*, 72–79; Palfrey, *History of New England*, 47–48.

7. Ibid., V, 59–63. Fears of a French fleet operating out of Port Royal would escalate to a point that one Bostonian wrote his colleague, "We are in great danger, if four or five French ships should attack us sharply we should probably be reduced under another Government." (*Cal A&WI*, XIII, 213.)

8. Phipps, Sir William, DCB, III. Phips lists his squadron as: *Six Friends* (42 guns), *Porcupine* (16), *Mary* (8), *Union* (4), *Mary Anne* (2), and a pair of ketches, the *Lark* and the *Bachelor*. Total compliment: 286. (*A Journal of the Proceedings of the Late Expedition to Port Royal*, 15)..

9. *Cal. A &WI*, XIII, 275–276. *NY Col. Doc.*, IX, 474–475, 921. Captain Southack of the *Porcupine* claimed that there were eighty-four French prisoners in all (*Doc Hist Maine*, V, 127). The French engineer, de Saccardy, who was dispatched to erect a new fort at Port Royal was taken prisoner by New Englander privateers in the Bay of Fundy not long after Phipps's departure. Fortunately for him, a French privateer overtook his New England captives and freed him a few days later. (*NY Col. Doc.*, IX, 474–475; *Villebon Memoirs*, 22–24). One of Southack's crew on this voyage was none other than future privateer/pirate Captain William Kidd.

10. *Doc Hist Maine*, V, 64.

11. Belknap, 134–135.

CHAPTER THREE: THE RISE AND FALL OF PEMAQUID

1. Drake, *Border Wars of New England*, 70–72; *Cal. A &WI*, XIV, 475– 477.

2. *Cal. A &WI*, XIII, 529–530, 546, 550, 572–575.

3. Church, *King Phillip's War*, 173–182; *Cal. A &WI*, XIII, 700, 721. Fear that supporting Fort William Henry might prove difficult was born out in late November 1692 when a twenty-ton supply vessel was captured by a Kennebec war party in sight of the fort. (*Villebon Journal*, 46.)

4. *Ancient Pemaquid*, 150–151; *Doc. Hist. Maine*, X, 47–48. After his examination of the fort Romer concluded that the structure had "been extremely ill built and not defensible . . . there was no order or proportion observed in building it, and its Walls were made of clay mixed with Sand brought from the Sea shore instead of Lime." (Ibid., 47) Governor Villebon gave another opinion, saying of the fort "that within it they are quite safe from the Indians, unless they be taken by surprise." (*Villebon Journal*, 67.)

5. *NY Col. Doc.*, IX, 510–512.

6. *Ibid.*, 404–408, 510–511. *Mass. Acts and Resolves*, I, 42–43.

7. *NY Col. Doc.*, IX, 574–576.

8. *Collection de Manuscrits . . . Relatifs Nouvelle-France*, II, 200; *Villebon Journal*,

81; Bonaventure, after speaking with an English prisoner, claimed that the *Sorlings* lost three killed and thirty wounded in the engagement.
9. *N.Y. Col. Doc.*, IX, 574–576, 590; *Villebon's Journal*, 83–85.
10. Pierre Le Moyne D'Iberville, DCB, II.
11. *Collection de Manuscrits . . . Relatifs Nouvelle-France*, II, 216–218; *Father Baudoin's War*, 15; Charlevoix, V, 22–24.
12. *Father Baudoin's War*, 17; Miles, *Captains and Colonies*, 189–190; *Cal. A &WI*, XV, 132, 224. An account by Lieutenant Roger Wright estimated Iberville's flagship at 48 guns and the *Profond* at 40 guns. Wright also claimed that the *Sorlings* did not disengage until after the *Newport* had surrendered, at which point Captain Paxton drove the frigate ashore to prevent it from sinking. (Ibid.)
13. *Father Baudoin's War*, 17–20; *N.Y. Col. Doc.*, IX, 658.
14. Charlevoix, V, 24–26; *Cal. A &WI*, XV, 70–71, 142–144.
15. *Cal. A &WI*, XV,144; *Ancient Pemaquid*, 157–160. *Father Baudoin's War*, 21. Credit Iberville and the other French leaders for preventing a massacre.
16. Charlevoix, V, 27–28; Hutchinson, II, 94; *Cal. A &WI*, XV, 132.
17. Church, 148–150. Church noted that, after plundering and burning down the inhabitant's homes, "The French being sensible of the major's kindness to them, kiss'd his hand, & were very thankful to him for his favour to them in saving their lives." (Ibid., 150.)
18. Ibid., 90–92; Hutchinson, II, 98–99. Fort St. Joseph was a four-bastioned wooden palisade structure running almost 115 feet to a side. Also known as Fort Nashwaak or Fort Naxoat the location would be abandoned after King William's War.
19. *Villebon's Journal*, 92–94; *Cal. A &WI*, XV, 132, 218.

CHAPTER FOUR: THE KING'S ENGINEER

1. *NY Col Doc.*, IV, 244, 256; Lee, *Dictionary of National Biography*, XVII, 184–185; Dalton, *English Army Lists and Commission Registers, 1661–1714*, III, 234; Porter, *The History of the Corps of Royal Engineers*, I, 56, 61, 136. "Civil List Debt: Army Debt, Equitable Claims," in *Calendar of Treasury Books*, Volume XVII, 1702, 1190–1203.
2. *Cal A&WI*, XVII, 214.
3. *Cal A&WI*, XVII, 291.
4. *Cal A&WI*, XVII, 291; *Mass. Acts and Resolves*, VII, 680–681. Bellomont and Romer visited the fort together in mid-June. Unfortunately, the occasion was marred by an accident when a cannon that Romer requested be fired burst, killing one gunner and severely wounding another. (*Mass. Acts and Resolves*, VII, 618.)
5. *Documentary History of the State of Maine*, X, 45–46.
6. *Cal State Papers*, XVII, 412; Baxter, *Doc. Hist. Maine*, X, 46–52.
7. *Cal A&WI*, XIX, 289; *Mass. Acts and Resolves*, VII, 698–699.
8. *Mass. Acts and Resolves*, VII, 699.
9. *Mass. Acts and Resolves*, VII, 670, VIII, 721; *Diary of Samuel Sewell*, MHSC, 5th series, VI, 40.
10. *Cal A&WI*, XIX, 266, 314, 319–320, 434–435, 665.
11. *Cal A&WI*, XIX, 241, 266, 287, 314, 319, 404, 435, 463, 570, 577, 582, 584, 592, XX, 495, XXII, 310. Dealing with his own frustrations, Lieutenant Governor Nanfan wrote the Board of Trade on September 24, saying that he believed Romer was purposely extending his stay at Boston because he feared being sent back to the

Onondaga Country (*NY Col Doc*, IV, 915). A few weeks later, on October 2, the lieutenant governor wrote another letter to the board saying, "Col. Romer is a most unaccountable man, I have not been able to gett him hether as yett from Boston." (*Cal A&WI*, XIX, 556.)

12. Edward Hyde, Viscount Cornbury and later the 3rd Earl of Clarendon (1661–1723). Hyde was a former officer in the Royal Horse Guards and was one of the first commanders to desert James II's banner for that of William III.

13. *Cal A&WI*, XX, 558–559, 591.

14. *Mass. Acts and Resolves*, VII, 349, 372, 722, 723, VIII, 269, 290; *Cal A&WI*, XXI, 323, 565, 690–692, 774, 821, 823. Interestingly, the other Massachusetts commissioner assigned to Castle William, Thomas Brattle, turned his powers over to Romer a few months after Clarke's dismissal (*Mass. Acts and Resolves*, VIII, 290).

15. Boulton, *Documents and Records Relating to the Province of New Hampshire*, II, 445–446; *Cal A&WI*, XXII, 325, 454–455.

16. *Hist. of New London*, 256–257; *Cal. A &W.I.*, X, 576–577.

17. Talcott Papers, *Conn. Hist. Soc. Coll.*, V, 219–224, 430–431; *Hist. of New London*, 385–391.

18. Arnold, *Hist. Rhode Island*, II, 5–6, 24–25, 54, 69; *Rec of Colony of Rhode Island,* IV, 57, 298, 473; Talcott Papers, *Conn. Hist. Soc. Coll.*, IV, 228–229.

19. Arnold, *Hist. Rhode Island*, II, 93, 114–115, 125, 130, 156; *Rec of Colony of Rhode Island,* IV, 428–429, 477, 487, V, 9–12, 89, 117, 131–132; *Cal A&WI*, XLI, 412–413, XLII, 4–5.

20. *Cal A&WI*, XXII, 130, 228, 462.

21. *Winthrop Papers*, MHSC 6th series, III, 547–549.

22. *Winthrop Papers*, MHSC 6th series, III, 549.

23. *Winthrop Papers*, MHSC 6th series, III, 549–550. There is no doubt that Romer's letter came across as shrill, although when reading it one gets a sense that some of this may have been the result of his poor English. Ultimately, it is puzzling why Dudley did not accept Romer's offer. His basis seems to have been not wanting to usurp Redknap's authority nor being forced to employ two engineers, but given that a state of war existed between France and England, and a French fleet was known to have been operating in the area, one would have thought that completing the fort and securing New Hampshire's principal seaport would have taken priority over administrative matters.

24. *Cal A&WI,* XXII, 586.

25. *Cal A&WI*, XXIII, 327, XXIV, 22, 65, 82–83; Lee, *The Dictionary of National Biography*, XVII, 184–185. Not long after Romer's return to England the matter of the unfinished works at Fort William and Mary appeared before the Board of Trade. The Crown's agent for New Hampshire, George Vaughan, informed the board upon his arrival in the colony that nothing had been done to the fort since Romer's departure "save what is tumbling down and gone into decay." Vaughan's additional comments on the dismal state of the fortifications and the manner in which they were manned proved something of a vindication to Romer, and soon the board was asking his opinion on what was needed to secure this area, all of which Romer was more than happy to detail.

CHAPTER FIVE: QUEEN ANNE'S WAR

1. Drake, 159–161; Williamson, *Hist. Maine*, II, 43–44; *Cal. A &W.I.*, XXI, 689–690.

2. Tapley, *The Province Galley*, 5–6; Penhallow, 6–8; *Doc. Hist. Maine*, IX, 143–144, 150–152; *Cal. A &W.I.*, XXI, 689–690.
3. *Coll. Man. N.F.*, II, 405–406; *NY Col. Doc.*, IX, 756, 762; Charlevoix, V, 160–161.
4. *Cal A &W.I.*, XXII, 213–214, 274; *N.H. Prov. Papers*, II, 434–435; *Documents Relating to Towns in New Hampshire*, XII, 679–680; Church, *Journal*, 166–169. The names of the transports and their masters can be found in *Mass. Acts and Resolves*, VIII, 338–339.
5. Church, *Journal*, 181–189; *Mass. Acts and Resolves*, VIII, 314; *Coll. Man. N.F.*, II, 416–420; *Boston News-Letter*, Aug 7, 1704.
6. *New Hampshire Provincial Papers*, II, 463; *Doc. Hist. Maine*, IX, 218; *Mass Acts and Resolves*, VIII, 522–523, 532. In his report to the Massachusetts Legislature Redknap lists the cost of building a new seventy-by-seventy-foot fort at Winter Harbor as £1854 and estimated that it would take ninety-seven men four months to complete the task. When the Massachusetts Assembly saw the projected costs, the venture was put on hold. (Ibid.)
7. *New York Colonial Documents*, IV, 1185; *Boston Newsletter*, May 27, Aug 5, Oct 7, 1706; *Mass Acts and Resolves*, VIII, 551–552, 585–586; *Cal A&WI*, XXIII, 246–247.
8. *Mass Acts and Resolves*, VIII, 568; *Cal A&WI*, XXIII, 234, 247.
9. *Cal A&WI*, XXIII, 29–32.
10. *Mass Acts and Resolves*, VIII, 684, 694; *Cal A&WI*, XXIII, 678–679; Drenth & Riley, *First Col. Soldiers* II/1, 80–85.
11. Calnek, W.A., *History of the County of Annapolis*, 55; *Mass Acts and Resolves*, VIII, 715; *Cal A&WI*, XXIII, 438–439, 560, 587–588; "Barnard Journal," MHSC, 3rd series, V, 189–191.
12. *Cal A&WI*, XXIII, 777–778; "Barnard Journal," MHSC, 3rd series, V, 190–192.

CHAPTER SIX: THE SIEGES OF PORT ROYAL

1. *History of the County of Annapolis*, 4–55; *Cal A&WI*, XXIII, 777–778; *Coll. Man. N.F.*, II, 464–465, 467–468; "Barnard Journal," 191–192; René Baudry, "Auger de Subercase, Daniel D," in DCB, II.
2. "Winthrop Paper," MHSC, 6th series, III, 390–392; *Cal A&WI*, XXIII, 677–678, 777–778; *Mass Acts and Resolves*, 1703–1707, 725.
3. Ibid., *History of the County of Annapolis*, 56; *Cal A&WI*, XXIII, 677–678, 777–778. "Barnard Journal," 192–193.
4. "Winthrop Paper," MHSC, 6th series, III, 391; *Mass Acts and Resolves*, VIII, 725; *Cal A&WI*, XXIII, 777–780. *Coll. Man. N.F.*, II, 466–467, 468–469.
5. Calnek, W.A., *History of the County of Annapolis*, 56–57; *Mass Acts and Resolves*, VIII, 725; Penhallow, 42–43. In regard to Redknap's accusation that the colonial force lacked the military discipline and skill to conduct a siege, Governor Dudley had earlier expressed concerns about just such a matter. "I am sensible," he informed the Massachusetts Assembly not long after the expedition departed for Port Royal, "her Majesties Subjects of these Provinces have not seen such regular Service as the Wars of Europe or the present expedition may demand but I am well assured of their Courage." (Kimball, Everett, *Public Life of Joseph Dudley*, 121.)
6. *Coll. Man. N.F.*, II, 466, 469.
7. "Winthrop Papers," MHSC, 6th series, III, 388. *Mass Acts and Resolves*, VIII, 723–727; Drake, 233.

8. *Cal A&WI*, XXIII, 678–679.
9. *Cal A&WI*, XXIII, 678–679.
10. Kimball, *Life of Dudley*, 121–122. Donahue, *Mass. Soldiers in Queen Anne's War*, xi–xii; *Cal A&WI*, XXIII, 587–588; *Doc. Hist. Maine*, IX, 238–239.
11. *Mass Acts and Resolves*, 1703–1707, 728–731; *Doc. Hist. Maine*, IX, 235–238.
12. *Doc. Hist. Maine*, IX, 244–245; *Mass Acts and Resolves*, 1703–1707, 735–737; *N.H. Prov. Papers*, II, 506.
13. *Coll. Man. N.F.*, II, 470, 477–478; *Mass Acts and Resolves*, 1703–1707, 743–744; Hutchinson, *Hist. Mass.*, II, 167–171.
14. Charlevoix, V, 196–200; *Mass Acts and Resolves*, 1703–1707, 745–746; *Coll. Man. N.F.*, II, 478–481; "Barnard Journal," 193–196; Drake, 234–236.
15. *Coll. Man. N.F.*, II, 483; *Cal A&WI*, XXIII, 560.

CHAPTER SEVEN: THE CAPTURE OF PORT ROYAL

1. *Cal A&WI,* XXV, 25, 29–30; Kimball, *Dudley*, 125–126.
2. "Nicholson's Journal," *Coll. N.S Hist. Soc.*, I, 59–65; *Cal A&WI*, XXV, 12–13, 25, 84, 103–104, 126–129, 134–136; Donahue, *Mass. Troops in Queen Anne's War*, xvii–xviii; *Conn. Troops in Queen Anne's War*, 4–6, 13–14.
3. *Cal A&WI*, XXV, 183–184; "Nicholson's Journal," 64–66; Clowes, II, 526–527. A complete list and the organization of Nicholson's forces can be found in Drenth & Riley, *The First Colonial Soldiers*, II/1, 89–96.
4. *Coll. Man. N.F.*, II, 528–529; "Nicholson's Journal," 64–67; Wilson, "An Acadian Governor," *The International Review*, 486–487; Drake, 259–260.
5. "Nicholson's Journal," 67–79; Trumbull, *Hist. Conn*, I, 462.
6. "Nicholson's Journal," 79–89; *Coll. Man. N.F.*, II, 529–530.
7. *Cal A&WI*, XXV, 220–221, 226–227, 229–233; "Nicholson's Journal," 79–89; *Coll. Man. N.F.*, II, 529–530; *Conn. Troops in Queen Anne's War*, 17–21.
8. *NY Col. Doc.*, IX, 853–854.
9. Laramie, "Colonel Richard King: A Royal Engineer's View of the 1711 Canadian Expedition," *Fort Ticonderoga Museum Bulletin*, XVII, no. 4, 32–47. The expedition's bad luck continued upon reaching England. On October 15, a few days after arriving at Spithead, Walker's flagship HMS *Edgar* blew up at dock as the result of a magazine accident. Walker and the ship's captain were ashore at the time. Initially the matter was not investigated, but several years later it was taken up and as a result Walker was removed from the flag officer list. (Clowes, 528–529.)
10. *Cal A&WI*, XXVII, 229–231; Almon, *A Collection of Treaties*, I, 136–141, 171–176.

CHAPTER EIGHT: THE LONG PEACE

1. Lunn, "Agriculture and War in Canada," 123–136; McLennan, *Louisbourg*, 22–31; *Charlevoix*, V, 285–292; Pitcher, *Louisbourg's Labourer-Soldiers, 33*–34; Lanctot, *History of Canada*, II, 159–160.
2. Fry, "The Fortifications of Louisbourg," 20–21; Verville, Jean-Francois de, *DCB*, II; McLennan, *Louisbourg*, 50–52.
3. Penhallow, *Indian Wars*, 86; Sylvester, *Indian Wars of New England*, III, 192–193.
4. Williams, *History of Maine*, II, 125–128; Sylvester, *Indian Wars of New England*, III 227; *Mass. Archives*, Vol 72, 270; *Cal. A & WI Papers*, XXXIV, 429–432, 439. Penhallow noted that, in one instance, a large Wabanaki war party "surprized eight (vessels) with little or no opposition." (Penhallow, *Indian Wars*, 101.)

5. *Doc. Hist. Maine*, XXIII, 163–167; *Cal. A & WI Papers*, XXXIV, 429–432. Father Lauverjat, who accompanied this war party, claimed that the enemy blockhouse did catch on fire but that the garrison came out of the fort to extinguish the fire. The Natives, not expecting such an action, were not in a position to fire on this damage control party. (Ibid.)
6. "Devis de La Grande Batterie," Archives Nationales, Colonies, C11B, Vol. 6, ff. 298–308v; Krause, "Construction of the Royal Battery."
7. Krause, "Chronology of the Island Battery."
8. Downey, *Louisbourg: Key to a Continent*, 25–31; Bourinot, *Cape Breton*, 26–28; Krause, "Construction Chronology for the Royal Battery"; Ibid., "Domestic Building Construction at the Fortress of Louisbourg"; Fry, "The Fortifications of Louisbourg," 22–24. Fortunately for the reader interested in a more detailed account of the construction and life at Louisbourg, the fortress has been restored as a Canadian National Park. A comprehensive number of papers and documents concerning the location have been archived and placed online at Researching the Fortress of Louisbourg National Historic Site of Canada.
9. Johnston, "Louisbourg," 35–39; Wrong, *Lettre Habitant Louisbourg*, 30–32; Greer, "The Soldiers of Isle Royal, 1720–1745." One British ship that had anchored at the French port in 1735 reported that, "The grand battery mounts 44 guns of 48 pounders and the two towers 4 of the same nature. The island at the entrance of the harbour mounts 26 guns of 36 pounders. The Dauphin's battery at the town gate mounts 24 guns of 24 pounders. The Queen's Battery 16 guns of 18 pounders, and on the key are 6 guns of 18, there are likewise 12 guns to be mounted on the Fort." (*Cal. A&WI*, XLII,108–109.)
10. Dunn, "The Louisbourg Lighthouse."
11. *Cal. A&WI*, XXXIV, 34–37, XXXV, 197–199, 288, 300.
12. *New Hampshire Provincial Papers*, IV, 532–534, 647–648; *Cal A&WI*, XLIII, 150–15. Note that the governments of New Hampshire and Massachusetts were combined under Belcher's tenure (1730–1741) and were split when he left office.
13. *Cal A&WI*, XLI, 153.
14. *Cal A&WI*, XLI, 153–154.
15. *Cal A&WI*, XLI, 418–419.
16. *Mass. Acts and Resolves*, XII, 629, 697; *Cal A&WI*, XLI, 418–419.

CHAPTER NINE: KING GEORGE'S WAR AND THE SIEGE OF LOUISBOURG

1. Browning, *The War of Austrian Succession*, 137–161; McLennan, *Louisbourg*, 109; *Coll. Man. N.F.*, III, 196–201.
2. McLennan, *Louisbourg*, 110–112; *Coll. Man. N.F.*, III, 201–202; "Lettre d'un Habitant Louisbourg," in Wrong, *Louisbourg in 1745*, 17–18.
3. *NH Prov. Papers*, V, 223; *Journal of Mass. House*, vol. 20 (March 1743), 371.
4. McLennan, *Louisbourg*, 113–114; Murdoch, *History of Nova Scotia*, II, 29–32; *Pub. Doc. Nova Scotia*, 134–135.
5. Wood, *William Shirley*, 209–212, 231–232; *CWS*, I, 134–141, 144–147.
6. "Bidwell Journal," *NEHGR*, XXVII, no. 2, 159–160; *Memoirs of the Last War*, 37–40; Chapin, *New England Vessels Against Louisbourg*, 3–6.
7. *Memoirs of the Last War*, 40–42; Clowes, *Royal Navy*, III, 109–110.
8. *Pepperrell's Journal*, 10–12; "Lettre d'un Habitant Louisbourg," 38; "Du Chambon Journal," 205–206; McLennan, *Louisbourg*, 148–150; *D. Bradstreet's Diary*, 10–11; "Green's Journal," 148–149.

9. "Du Chambon Journal," 206–207; "Lettre d'un Habitant Louisbourg," 38–40.
10. *Pepperrell Papers*, 138–140; *The Importance of Cape Breton*, 129–131; "Cleaves' Journal," 118; "Du Chambon Journal," 207; "Giddings Journal", 298; *D. Bradstreet's Diary*, 11.
11. "Green's Journal," 151–152; *Pepperrell Papers*, 14–15; "Du Chambon Journal," 207–208.
12. *Pepperrell Papers*, 157–158, 166–168.
13. Chapin, *New England Vessels Against Louisbourg*, 16–17; Wood, *William Shirley*, 287; *Pepperrell Papers*, 187–188; *Gibson's Journal*, 17–18.
14. "Lettre d'un Habitant Louisbourg," 46–49; Chapin, *New England Vessels Against Louisbourg*, 17–19; McLennan, *Louisbourg*, 155–157; Hutchinson, *Hist. Mass.*, II, 417–418; Clowes, *Royal Navy*, III, 114–115.
15. *Pepperrell Papers*, 20–23, 213, 220–223; *D. Bradstreet's Diary*, 16.
16. "Du Chambon Journal," 213; *Pepperrell Papers*, 226, 231–233; "Curwen Journal," 14; *D. Bradstreet's Diary*, 16; "Green's Journal," 158–159; *Gibson Journal*, 21.
17. *CWS*, I, 222–225; *Pepperrell Papers*, 230–231, 238–245.
18. "Du Chambon Journal," 210–215.
19. *Gibson's Journal*, 22–26; Wolcott's Journal, 132–136; *Memoirs of the Last War*, 48–49; *Pepperrell's Journal*, 21–24; "Green's Journal," 161–165; *Pepperrell Papers*, 27, 270, 280–285, 290–291; "Du Chambon Journal," 214–219. A later survey of French armaments after the surrender of the fortress reported 384 barrels of gunpowder remaining. (McLennan, *Louisbourg*, 408.)

CHAPTER TEN: THE FALL OF FRENCH ACADIA

1. *CWS*, II, 97–101. The regiments to be raised were the 50th and 51st, the "Old Loiusbourg" garrison battalions that had been disbanded at the end of the last war.
2. *CWS*, II, 1754, 66–67, 80–82. "The Planning of the Beausejour Operation and the Approaches to War in 1755," *New England Quarterly*, 61 (1968), 558–559.
3. Pargellis, *Military Affairs in North America*, 54–56.
4. *Doc. Hist. Maine*, XII, 281–283, 320–332; Pargellis, *Military Affairs in North America*, 56–57; Williamson. *Hist. Maine*, II, 300–302.
5. Murdoch, *History of Nova Scotia*, II, 177–179; Webster, *The Building of Fort Lawrence*, 6, 17–20; *Collections Nova Scotia Hist. Soc.*, V, 56–57, XII, 26–27.
6. "Records of Chignecto," *Collections Nova Scotia Hist. Soc.*, XV, 13–14; Murdoch, *History of Nova Scotia*, II, 183–184, 187–188.
7. Webster, *The Building of Fort Lawrence*, 12–14; "Records of Chignecto," *Collections Nova Scotia Hist. Soc.*, XV, 11–15; Murdoch, *History of Nova Scotia*, II, 225, 245–246, 262–263, 321; Dixon, *Notes on Fort Monckton*, 1–3.
8. Ambler, *George Washington and the West*, 63–91; *CWS*, II, 62–68.
9. Clayton, "The Duke of Newcastle, the Earl of Halifax, and the American Origins of the Seven Years' War." *Historical Journal*, v. 24, no. 3 (1981), 571–603; Pargellis, *Military Affairs in North America*, 22–29, 45–47; Higonnet, Patrice Louis René. "The Origins of the Seven Years' War," *Journal of Modern History*, no. 40 (March 1968), 57–90; Riker, Thad, "The Politics behind Braddock's Expedition," *American Historical Review*, vol. 13, no. 4 (July 1908), 742–752.
10. *CWS*, II, 62–68, 133–138; Pargellis, *Military Affairs in North America*,146–147; "Winslow Journal," *Collections Nova Scotia Hist. Soc.*, I, 115–118, 144–147; "Records of Chignecto," *Collections Nova Scotia Hist. Soc.*, XV, 17–19; Webster,

Diary of John Thomas & Louis De Courville, 14–15, 45–47; Casgrain, Levis Papers, XI, "Relations et Journaux," 10–22; *Journal of Abijah Willard*, 19–20.

11. "Winslow Journal," *Collections Nova Scotia Hist. Soc.*, I, 147–156; Pargellis, *Military Affairs in North America*, 147–148; Webster, *Diary of John Thomas & Louis De Courville*, 15–17.

12. Mante, *Late War in North America*, 17–19; Casgrain, Levis Papers, XI, "Relations et Journaux," 23–38; *NY Col. Doc.*, X, 380–381; Webster, *Diary of John Thomas & Louis De Courville*, 47–50; "Winslow Journal," *Collections Nova Scotia Hist. Soc.*, I, 156–159. In February 1756 Verger and the commander of Fort Gaspareaux faced a court-martial for their conduct. The board, which held both marine and regular officers, quickly acquitted both. The Marquis de Montcalm, writing the French court, explained the decision. "In the case of Fort Beauséjour, regard was principally had to the fact that the Acadians have forced the Commandant to capitulate to save their lives. They had formerly taken the oath of allegiance to the English, who had threatened to have them hanged for violating it. In regard to Gaspareaux, a large stockaded enclosure, with only one officer and nineteen soldiers, it could not be considered a fort capable of sustaining a siege; accordingly the English burnt it and preserved only Beauséjour, which they placed in a better condition than it was in when we occupied it." (*NY Col. Doc.*, X, 671.)

CHAPTER ELEVEN: A RETURN TO LOUISBOURG

1. Kimball, *Pitt Correspondence*, I, 15, 53; Pargellis, *Lord Loudoun in North America*, 232.

2. Baugh, *Seven Years War*, 221–223; Pargellis, *Lord Loudoun in North America*, 236–240.

3. Gipson, *The Victorious Years*, 102–115; Pargellis, *Lord Loudoun in North America*, 238–243; Mante, *The History of the Late War in North America*, 97–108; Knox, *Journal*, I, 20–26.

4. Pargellis, *Lord Loudoun in North America*, 337–338.

5. Corbett, *England in the Seven Years' War*, I, 166–176; Pargellis, *Lord Loudoun in North America*, 251–252, 339.

6. Kimball, *Pitt Correspondence*, I, 134–140, 143–150, 151–153; Distribution of forces in North America for the Campaign of 1758, C.O. 5/50.

7. Mayo, *Jeffery Amherst*, 3–24, 55–61; C.P. Stacy, "Amherst, Jeffery, 1st Baron Amherst," DCB, IV.

8. Doughty, "Life of Wolfe," *The Siege of Quebec*, I, 5–19, 22–23, 28, 38, 76–86; "Gordon's Journal," *Collections Nova Scotia Hist. Soc.*, V, 97–102. Gordon details the forces involved and gives the siege artillery as, Cannon (brass) – 26 x 24 pdr., 18 x 12 pdr., 6 x 6 pdr., 1 x 3 pdr. Cannon (iron) – 8 x 32 pdr., 25 x 24 pdr., 4 x 6 pdr. Mortars (brass) - 2 x 13-inch, 2 x 10-inch, 7 x 8-inch, 10 x 5.5-inch, 30 x 4.25-inch. Mortars (iron) – 1 x 13-inch. Howitzers – 2 x 8-inch, 4 x 5.5-inch. Total: 88 cannon, 52 mortars, 6 howitzers. To support this siege train over 43,000 rounds of shot and shell had been provided.

9. D. Graham, "Charles Lawrence," DCB, III; Ford, *British Officers, 1754–1774*, 5, 105; Murdoch, *History of Nova Scotia*, II, 145, 177–181.

10. Lee, *The Dictionary of National Biography*, II, 877–881.

11. *Montressor's Journal*, 157–159; Webster, *Amherst's Journal*, 47–50; Doughty, "Life of Wolfe," *The Siege of Quebec*, I, 98–105; Knox, *Journal*, I, 164–169; "Gordon's Journal," *Collections Nova Scotia Hist. Soc.*, V, 110–114.

12. Doughty, "Life of Wolfe," *The Siege of Quebec*, I, 105–106; Webster, *Amherst's Journal*, 50–51.
13. "Gordon's Journal," *Collections Nova Scotia Hist. Soc.*, V, 115–116.
14. Gipson, *The Victorious Years*, 193–197; Downey, *Louisbourg*, 154–158; Doughty, "Life of Wolfe," *The Siege of Quebec*, I, 106–109; "Gordon's Journal," *Collections Nova Scotia Hist. Soc.*, V, 115–116.
15. Webster, *Amherst's Journal*, 51–57; *Montressor's Journal*, 159–163.
16. Doughty, "Life of Wolfe," *The Siege of Quebec*, I, 115–117.
17. McLennan, *Louisbourg*, 280–283; Webster, *Amherst's Journal*, 60–70; Downey, *Louisbourg*, 168–172; *Montressor's Journal*, 170–171; "Gordon's Journal," *Collections Nova Scotia Hist. Soc.*, V, 136–139.
18. Downey, *Louisbourg*, 177–178; McLennan, *Louisbourg*, 283–286; Gipson, *The Victorious Years*, 204–207.
19. "Gordon's Journal," *Collections Nova Scotia Hist. Soc.*, V, 140–149; McLennan *Louisbourg*, 287–290.
20. Knox, *Journal*, I, 202–207.

BIBLIOGRAPHY

MANUSCRIPT SOURCES

Canada. National Archives. (Ottawa)

Manuscript Division

MG1: Fonds des Colonies

Sèrie C11A, Canada et Dépendances (Lettres des Gouverneurs, Intendants, officers et autres)

Sèrie C11B, Correspondence generale

Sèrie F3 Collection Moreau de Saint-Méry

Massachusetts Archives (Boston)

Volumes, 29, 34, 51, 72

Great Britain, Public Record Office (London)

Colonial Office

C.O.5, America and West Indies, Correspondence, originals on microfilm.

PUBLISHED SOURCES

Acts and Resolves of the Province of Massachusetts Bay, vols. I-XIII. Boston: Wright and Potter, 1869–1905.

Akins, Thomas (ed.). *Selections from the Public Documents of Nova Scotia.* Halifax: Charles Annand, 1869.

Almon, John (ed.). *A Collection of all the treaties of peace, alliance, and commerce between Great Britian and other powers: from the revolution in 1688 to the present time* . . . 2 vols.; London: J. Almon, 1772.

Ambler, Charles. *George Washington and the West.* New York: Russell & Russell, 1936 (1971).

Anon. *The Importance of Cape Breton.* London: John and Paul Knapton, 1746.

Arnold, Samuel. *History of the State of Rhode Island*, 2 vols. New York: D. Appleton and Co., 1878.

Barnard, John. "Autobiography of Rev. John Barnard," *Collections of the Massachusetts Historical Society,* 3rd series, V. Boston: Mass. Historical Society, 1836, 177–243.

Bartlett, John Russell (ed.). *Records of the Colony of Rhode Island and Providence Plantations in New England.* 10 vols. Providence: A. C. Greene, 1856–65.

Baugh, Daniel. *The Global Seven Years War, 1754–1763.* London: Routledge Taylor and Francis Group, 2021.

Belknap, Jeremy. *The History of New Hampshire.* 3 vols. Dover: J. Mann and J.K. Remick, 1790–1812.

Bidwell, Adonijah. "Expedition to Cape Breton: Journal of the Rev. Adonijah Bidwell," *NEHGR*, XXVII, no. 2 (April 1873), 153–160.

Boston News-Letter

Bourinot, J.G. *Historical and Descriptive Account of the Island of Cape Breton.* Montreal: W. Foster Brown and Co., 1892.

Bouton, Nathaniel. *Documents and Records Relating to the Province of New Hampshire,* vols. I, II, III, IV, V*: 1686–1722.* Manchester: John B. Clarke State Printer, 1868.

Bradstreet, Dudley. *Diary kept by Lt. Dudley Bradstreet of Groton, Mass. at the Siege of Louisbourg.* Cambridge: John Wilson and Son, 1897.

Browning, Reed. *The War of Austrian Succession.* New York: St. Martin's Press, 1993.

Buckingham, Thomas. *Roll and Journal of Connecticut Service in Queen Anne's War.* New Haven: Tuttle, Morehouse, and Taylor, 1916.

Calnek, W.A. *History of the Country of Annapolis.* Toronto: William Briggs, 1897.

Cartland, John Henry. *Ten Years at Pemaquid.* Pemaquid: Private printing, 1899.

Casgrain, H.R. (ed.). *Collection des Manuscrits du Maréchal de Lévis.* 12 vols. Montreal and Quebec: C.O. Beauchemin & Fils and Demers & Frère, 1889–1895.

Caulkins, Frances. *History of New London, Connecticut.* New London: H.D. Utley, 1895.

Chapin, Howard. *New England Vessels Against Louisbourg.* Boston: New England Historical Society, 1923.

Charlevoix, Pierre-François-Xavier de. *History and General Description of New France.* 6 vols. Paris: 1744. (Trans. and ed.) John Gilmary Shea. New York: Francis P. Harper, 1900.

Church, Thomas. *The History of King Phillip's War.* Boston: Solomon Southwick, 1716.

Clayton, T.R. "The Duke of Newcastle, the Earl of Halifax, and the American Origins of the Seven Years' War," *Historical Journal*, vol. 24, no. 3 (1981), 571–603.

Cleaves, Benjamin. "Benjamin Cleaves's Journal of the Expedition to Louisbourg, 1745," *New-England Historical and Genealogical Register*, vol. 66 (1912), 113–124.

Clowes, William. *The Royal Navy: A History from the Earliest Times to the Present.* 6 vols. London: Sampson, Low, Marston, and Co., 1897–1902.

Collection de manuscrits contenant letters, mémoires, et autres documents historiques relatifs à la Nouvelle-France, recueillis aux Archives de la Province de Québec, ou copies à l'étranger. 4 vols. Québec, 1883–1885.

Collections of the Nova Scotia Historical Society. 20 vols. Halifax: Morning Herald, 1878–1921.

Corbett, Julian. *England in the Seven Years' War: A Study in Combined Strategy.* 2 vols. London: Longmans, Green, and Co., 1907.

Dalton, Charles. *English Army Lists and Commission Registers.* 6 vols. (1661–1714). London: Eyre & Spottiswoode, 1892–1904.

Dixon, Charles. *Notes of Fort Monckton.* Sackville: Chignecto Historical Society, 1892.

Documentary History of the State of Maine. 24 vols. Portland: Bailey and Noyes, 1869–1916.

Donahue, Mary. *Massachusetts Officers and Soldiers 1702–1722: Queen Anne's War to Dummer's War.* Boston: Society of Colonial Wars, 1980.

Doughty, "Life of Wolfe," *The Siege of Quebec and the Battle of the Plains of Abraham*, I. Quebec: Dussault and Proulx, 1901.

Downey, Fairfax. *Louisbourg: Key to a Continent.* Englewood, NJ: Prentice-Hall, 1965.

Drake, Samuel. *The Border Wars of New England.* New York: Charles Scribner's Sons, 1897.

Drenth, Wienand & Riley, Jonathon. *The First Colonial Soldiers.* 2 vols. Eindhoven: Drenth Publishing, 2014–2015.

"Du Chambon Journal," in Downey, Fairfax. *Louisbourg: Key to a Continent.* Englewood, NJ: Prentice-Hall (1965), 203–219.

Dunn, John. "The Louisbourg Lighthouse," *Fortress of Louisbourg Report MRS 32* (1971), *RFL.*

Ford, Worthington. *British Officers serving in America, 1754–1774.* Boston: Clapp and Sons, 1894.

Fry, Bruce W. "An Appearance of Strength: The Fortifications of Louisbourg," *Aspects of Louisbourg.* Sydney, Nova Scotia: University of Cape Breton Press (1995), 19–69.

Gentleman's Magazine

Gibson, James. *A Journal of the Siege of Louisbourg and Cape Breton in 1745.* Washington, DC: James Bowen Johnson, 1894.

Giddings, Daniel. "Journal Kept by Daniel Giddings of Ipswich during the Expedition Against Cape Breton in 1744–1745." *Historical Collections of the Essex Institute*, vol. 48, no. 4 (October 1912), 293–304.

Gipson, Lawrence Henry. *The British Empire Before the American Revolution, Volume VII: The Great War for the Empire, The Victorious Years, 1758–1760*. New York: Alfred A. Knopf, 1946.

Goold, William. *Portland in the Past with Historical Notes of Old Falmouth*. Portland: Thurston and Co., 1886.

Graham, Dominick. "The Planning of the Beauséjour Operation and the Approaches to War in 1755," *New England Quarterly*, 41 (1968), 550–566.

"Green's Journal," *Proceedings of the American Antiquarian Soc.*, XX, no. 1 (1909), 133–176.

Greer, Allan. "The Soldiers of Isle Royal, 1720–1745," *Fortress of Louisbourg Report H E 08* (1976), *RFL*.

Hammond, Isaac. *Documents Relating to Towns in New Hampshire*, XII. Concord: Parsons B. Cogswell, 1883.

Higonnet, Patrice Louis-Rene. "The Origins of the Seven Years' War," *Journal of Modern History*, no. 40 (March 1968), 57–90.

Hough, Franklin. *The Pemaquid Papers*. Albany: Weed, Parsons & Co., 1856.

Hull, John, T. *The Siege and Capture of Fort Loyal and the Destruction of Falmouth*. Portland: Owen, Strout & Co., 1885.

Hutchinson, Thomas. *The History of the Province of Massachusetts Bay*. 3 vols. London: M. Richardson, 1765–1828.

Johnston, A.J. B. "From port de peche to ville fortifiee: The Evolution of Urban Louisbourg, 1713–1758," *Proceedings of the Meeting of the French Colonial Historical Society*, 1993, vol. 17 (1993), 24–43.

Johnston, John. *A History of the Towns of Bristol and Bremen*. Albany: Joel Munsell, 1873.

Kimball, Everett. *The Public Life of Joseph Dudley*. London: Longmans, Green & Co., 1911.

Kimball, Gertrude Selwyn (ed.). *The Correspondence of William Pitt*. 2 vols. New York: The Macmillan Co., 1906.

Knox, John. *An Historical Journal of the Campaigns in North America for the Years 1757, 1758, 1759, and 1760*. 2 vols. London: 1764. Edited by Arthur G. Doughty and reprinted in 3 vols., Freeport, New York: Libraries Press, 1970.

Krause, Eric. "Construction Chronology for the Royal Battery, Actual and Proposed," *Fortress of Louisbourg Unpublished Report, H B 16* (1982), *RFL*.

Krause, Eric. "Domestic Building Construction at the Fortress of Louisbourg, 1713–1758," *Fortress Louisbourg Report H G 10* (1996), *RFL*.

Lanctot, Gustave. *A History of Canada, 1600–1763*. 3 vols. Trans. Josephine Hambleton and Margaret Cameron. Cambridge: Harvard University Press, 1963–65.

Laramie, Michael G. "Colonel Richard King: A Royal Engineer's View of the 1711 Canadian Expedition," *Fort Ticonderoga Museum Bulletin*, XVII, no. 4, 32–47.

Lee, Sydney (ed.). *The Dictionary of National Biography*, II, XVII. London: Smith, Elder, and Co., 1908–1909.

Lincoln, Charles H. (ed.). *The Correspondence of William Shirley, Governor of Massachusetts and Military Commander in America, 1731–1760*. 2 vols. New York: The Macmillan Co., 1912.

Lunn, Jean Elizabeth. "Agriculture and War in Canada, 1740–1760," *Canadian Historical Review*, 16 (1935), 123–136.

Mante, Thomas. *The History of the Late War in North America*. London: 1772. New York: Research Reprints Inc., 1970.

Mayo, Lawrence. *Jeffery Amherst: A Biography*. London: Longmans, Green, and Co., 1916.

McLennan, J.S. *Louisbourg, from its Foundation to its Fall, 1713–1758*. Toronto: Macmillan and Co., 1918.

Miles, William. *Captains and Colonies: Royal Navy Service in the North Atlantic World, 1660–1739*. PhD. Thesis, Memorial University, St. John's, Newfoundland, June 2014.

Murdoch, Beamish. *History of Nova Scotia*. 3 vols. Halifax: J. Barnes, 1865–1867.

Natstock, Joshua. *A Journal of the Proceedings in the Late Expedition to Port Royal*. Boston: Benjamin Harris, 1690.

O'Callaghan, E.B. (ed.). *Documents Relative to the Colonial History of the State of New York*. 15 vols. Albany: Weed, Parsons & Co., 1856–1877.

Palfrey, John. *History of New England*, IV. Boston: Little, Brown, and Co., 1890.

Pargellis, Stanley M. *Lord Loudoun in North America*. New Haven: Yale Historical Publications, 1933.

Pargellis, Stanley M. (ed.). *Military Affairs in North America, 1748–1765*. New York: D. Appleton-Century Co., Inc., 1936.

Penhallow, Samuel. *The History of the Wars of New England with the Eastern Indians*. Boston: T. Fleet (1726) 1924.

Pepperrell Papers: Collections of the Massachusetts Historical Society. 6th ser., vol. X (1849).

Pepperrell, William. *An accurate journal and account of the proceedings of the New-England land-forces, during the late expedition against the French settlements on Cape Breton*. London: A. and S. Brice, 1746.

Perley, Sidney. *The History of Salem, Massachusetts*. 3 vols. Salem: S. Perley, 1924–1928.

Pitcher, Daniel. *Louisbourg's Labourer-Soldiers*. Master's thesis. Dalhousie University, Halifax, Nova Scotia, 2014.

Porter, Whitworth. *The History of the Corps of Royal Engineers*, I. London: Longmans, Green, and Co., 1889.

Potter, Chandler E. *The Military History of the State of New Hampshire*. 2 vols. Concord: McFarland & Jenks, 1866.

Riker, Thad. "The Politics behind Braddock's Expedition," *American Historical Review*, vol. 13, no. 4 (July 1908), 742–752.

Roads, Samuel. *The History and Traditions of Marblehead*. Boston: Houghton, Osgood, and Co., 1880.

Sainsbury, W. Noel et al. (eds.). *Calendar of State Papers, Colonial Series, American and West Indies, Preserved in Her Majesty's Public Records Office*. 45 vols. London: His Majesty's Stationery Office, 1860–1964.

Scull, G.D. (ed.). *The Montressor Journals, Collections of the New York Historical Society for the Year 1881*. New York: The Society, 1882.

"Sewell Diary." *Collections of the Massachusetts Historical Society*, 5th series, VI. Boston: Mass. Historical Society, 1895.

Shaw, William (ed.). *Calendar of Treasury Books*, vol. 17 (1702). London: His Majesty's Stationery Office, 1939.

Shirley, William. *Memoirs of the Principal Transactions of the Last War*. London: Green and Russell, 1748.

Sylvester, Herbert. *Indian Wars of New England*. Vol III. Boston: W.B. Clarke Co., 1910.

Talcott Papers. *Collections of the Connecticut Historical Society*. IV, V. Hartford: The Society, 1892–1896.

Tapley, Harriet. *The Province Galley of Massachusetts Bay, 1694–1716*. Salem: Essex Institute, 1922.

Thornton, J. Wingate. *Ancient Pemaquid*. Portland: Brown Thurston, 1857.

Trumbull, Benjamin. *A Complete History of Connecticut*, I. Hartford: Hudson & Goodwin, 1797.

Vinton, John A. *The Giles Memorial*. Boston: Dutton and Son, 1864.

Ward, George (ed.). *Journals and Letters of the Late Samuel Curwen*. London: Wiley and Putnam, 1842.

Webster, Clarence. *The Building of Fort Lawrence in Chignecto*. St. John's: New Brunswick Museum, 1941.

Webster, Clarence (ed.). *The Diary of John Thomas & the Journal of Louis De Courville*. Sackville: Public Archives of Nova Scotia, 1937.

Webster, Clarence (ed.). *The Journal of Abijah Willard of Lancaster, Mass*. St. John's: New Brunswick Historical Society, 1930.

Webster, Clarence J. (ed.). *The Journals of Jeffery Amherst*. Toronto: The Ryerson Press, 1931.

Webster, J.C. (ed.). *Acadia at the End of the Seventeenth Century: Letters, Journals and Memoirs of Joseph Robineau de Villebon, Commandant in Acadia, 1690–1700, and Other Contemporary Documents*. St. John's: New Brunswick Museum, 1934.

Wheeler, George. "Fort Pentagoet," *Proceedings Maine Historical Society*, 2nd ser., IV (1893), 113–123.

Whitmore, William Henry (ed.). *The Andros Tracts: Being a Collection of Pamphlets and Official Papers.* 3 vols. Boston: Prince Society, 1868–1874.

Williams, Alan F. *Father Baudoin's War*. St. John's: University of Newfoundland, 1987.

Williamson, William D. *The History of the State of Maine*. 2 vols. Dallowell, Maine: Glazier, Masters and Co., 1832.

Wilson, James. "An Acadian Governor," *The International Review*, XI (1881), 462–502.

"Winthrop Papers: Part V," *Collections of the Massachusetts Historical Society*, 6th series, III. Boston: Mass. Historical Society, 1889.

Wolcott, Roger. "Journal of Roger Wolcott at the Siege of Louisbourg," *Connecticut Historical Society Collections*, I (1860), 31–160.

Wood, Arthur. *William Shirley, Governor of Massachusetts, 1741–1756*. New York: Columbia University, 1920.

Wrong, George M. *Louisbourg in 1745: The Anonymous Lettre D'un Habitant De Louisbourg*. Toronto: Warwick Bro's & Rutter, 1897.

INDEX